HOW TO OVERCOME THE CHALL
7-FIGURE BUSINESS SUCC

THE
ENTREPRENEURIAL
SCALEUP
SYSTEM

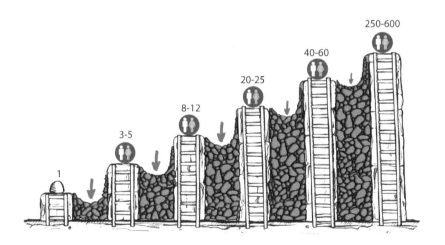

A PROVEN SYSTEM ENDORSED BY THE SCALEUP INSTITUTE

KEVIN BRENT

AND THE TEAM AT BizSmart

Cover image by: Yesna99, 99Designs
Book design by: SWATT Books Ltd

Printed in the United Kingdom
First Printing, 2022

ISBN: 978-1-7397083-0-6 (Paperback)
ISBN: 978-1-7397083-1-3 (eBook)

BizSmart Publishing
Lickey, Worcestershire

www.biz-smart.co.uk

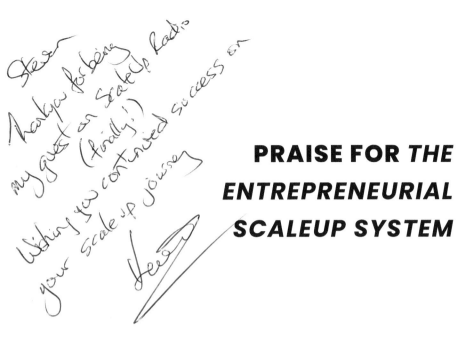

PRAISE FOR *THE ENTREPRENEURIAL SCALEUP SYSTEM*

As a founder owner of a small business I found this fascinatingly useful. I tend to work in glorious isolation so I've become an avid(ish) reader of business books – probably 4 or 5 a year, plus podcasts and audiobooks – and I've found it rare to get so many takeaways that seem to relate directly to me in one book. Every page seemed to contain a useful nugget so I will indeed be turning over page corners, making notes all over margins, highlighting sentences and referring back to it time and again.

Nigel Busby, Founder/Director, InControl Marketing

ESUS is a great guide for any business owner who is serious and committed to scaling up their business. It provides an invaluable checklist of tasks, processes and above all a change in mindset that needs to be addressed and mastered for the business to operate effectively without the business owner. For me it's a great reference point to constantly refer back to, rather like a reference manual to make sure that the right systems and processes are in place, that everybody in the organisation is going in the same direction and to make sure that everybody understands why we need to grow.

John Dillon, Managing Director, GJS Dillon Commercial Property Consultants

This is a brilliant handbook for anyone running their own business. It's full of practical wisdom, based on evidence and experience. As someone who has run an SME, I know you can learn the hard way, but this book will help you avoid many painful, costly lessons. If you want to understand what some entrepreneurs do that means they succeed where others don't, then this book is for you. Whether you are just starting out on your own, you have 1 or 2 employees, or a team of 50, this book will help you to grow a strong business that has real value and future potential.

Liz Taylor, former Managing Director, Logistix

If you are serious about scaling up, this is an essential read. I was becoming increasingly frustrated at the stop/start growth patterns and lack of momentum and it definitely wasn't down to the lack of effort.

There were a number of things we were already doing, but totally unstructured, with no real planning or end goal. We did the Inflight Checks, which were so insightful and highlighted areas for immediate attention. This book has helped me define clear goals, implement structured planning through the Smart90 process which I believe has delivered us the 'biggest bang for the buck'; we have also seen dramatic improvements in our business rhythm and to top it all, we have full accountability at every stage.

I am delighted to say since we engaged with the ESUS programme we have seen sustained growth in our B2B market, a more productive team and most importantly an improvement in profitability. I believe the ESUS book is like a 'Haynes Manual' but for your business. I think the best place to start (which I did) was to address areas that require immediate attention, then it can be dipped in and out of as and when required. As an example, we focus on one of the four pillars every quarter.

This book has given me and my team the tools to work in our 'flames and not our wax' and by doing that I know we are in a much better position than before we engaged with the programme. Thank you Kevin & the team.

Matt Busby, Founder/Director, The Name Label Company

A great book that everyone with a business should read. It has the legendary Kevin Brent attention to detail, fact-checked analysis and proven pathway to help the reader achieve significant improvement in their business – I thoroughly recommend it.

Peter Roper, The Family Business Man and Founder of the Family Business Practice

This is a brilliant book and I couldn't put it down! I read it all the way through and marked sections to go back to. I'm now working back through it and incorporating the ideas into the business – focussing on one thing at a time. This has become an invaluable 'companion' that I refer to almost daily!

[ESUS] like its author is inspiring and insightful, and drawing from Kevin's extensive experience this book illustrates the concepts of scaling up – outstanding job.

Richard Cox, Managing Director of the Langley Compass Group

The Entrepreneurial Scale-Up System is an informative and practical book that not only provides telling data and true insight into the main reasons as to why the majority of businesses fail to scale to 7 figures and beyond, but also provides valuable guidance and advice to help every business owner understand where they are going wrong and what they can do about it. Having worked with Kevin for several years, I have not only experienced first-hand the positive impact of his business experience, but have also witnessed him and his team make an incredible difference to the businesses of many others. For any entrepreneur looking to understand the true challenges in business and how they can overcome them to scale growth, this is the book for you.

Hannah Haffield, Founder/Director, Make More Noise PR

An amazing and exceptionally insightful read for anybody looking to grow or manage a truly successful business. This book should be a must on any MBA reading list – period.

Dave Perrigo, Founder/Director, Perrigo Consultants Limited

This is an excellent book for anyone starting a business or working within a long established business. Kevin has managed to create a book that gives you practical work-throughs that will drive positive change in a business of any age. At times it's a feast of information and made me constantly think about how I could apply the methods to my business. I have done and continue to apply what Kevin recommends with continuously positive outcomes. If you want a business that not only stands the test of time but continues to improve this is a must-read.

Daniel Walton, Founder, OLPRO, Queen's Award for Enterprise – International Trade

This book is an invaluable resource for those wanting to take the ScaleUp Journey with practical techniques, strategies and takeaway actions that can easily be implemented. This book can be used as a checklist and workbook and is a goldmine for business owners and business leaders. What a brilliant resource.

David Lynes, CEO and Founder of Unique IQ

As a busy mom, wife and business leader, I love to solve problems, plan and capitalise on opportunities as efficiently as possible. This book and the support of Kevin and the team are my go-to solution and this has enabled our business to grow quickly and capitalise on opportunities, attracting investment whilst retaining customers and employees.

Clare Vale FCCA, Managing Director, Sign Solutions

Kevin has taken decades of research and added up-to-the-minute business insight to produce this invaluable resource. You don't have to do everything the hard way! Save yourself a lot of pain and invest in this book.

William Copley, Founder/Managing Director, Armstrong Bell Ltd

THE
ENTREPRENEURIAL
SCALEUP
SYSTEM

OVERCOMING THE CHALLENGES OF ACHIEVING
7-FIGURE BUSINESS SUCCESS AND BEYOND

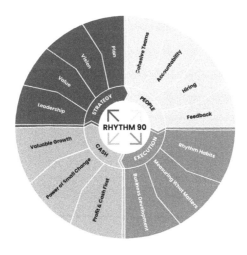

TABLE OF CONTENTS

KEVIN BRENT

ACKNOWLEDGEMENTS

Firstly I would like to dedicate this book to all business owner-managers. It is a tough gig. Only other business owners truly understand the challenges we face and it can be a lonely place. The contribution you make to our economies is immense and should never be underestimated.

I do not claim to be some 'business guru' who knows more than anyone else about business and entrepreneurship. There are far greater business minds than mine and I would be foolish to pretend otherwise.

I do believe that each of us has a unique perspective on the way we look at things, developed through our own life experiences and passions. I have a passion for business and the Entrepreneurial ScaleUp System is my unique perspective on what it takes to build a scalable business, and one that builds equity for the founders. It doesn't mean that I invented all the concepts.

ESUS combines my and the team at BizSmart's experiences in working with hundreds of business owners and our own research, with what we consider to be relevant best-in-class impactful concepts, tools and methodologies from others. The aim is to bring them all together in one 'system' that provides a practical 'handbook' for owner-managers of small and medium-sized business as they navigate their own ScaleUp Journey.

Others have shaped my thinking and I would particularly like to acknowledge the people below for their pioneering thinking and encourage you to seek out their resources and explore them further. References/sources are included at the end of the book.

We would especially like to thank Verne Harnish and his team at Gazelles, Jim Collins, the late Stephen Covey, Michael E. Gerber, John Warrillow and the team at The Value Builder System™, Patrick Lencioni, Michael Michalowicz, Bradford Smart and Greg Crabtree.

I have been fortunate to work with a number of great owner-managers who have helped to shape my thinking over the years. I'd like to thank all of our clients; we have learnt a lot from you along the way.

Finally, I'd like to thank the team at BizSmart. Without your support ESUS would still be a pipe dream! Particular thanks to Louise Blunt, Caroline Strickley, Granger Forson, Melanie Hawkett, Jack Olney, Justin Anghelescu and Liz Taylor.

FOREWORD

I have dedicated my life to the world of business and have studied great business people, business models, systems and processes in the hope of one day being one of the names on the list of greats. There is nothing I feel more passionately about than business in all of its forms. I have always been a big believer that success in business is easy if you follow the advice and blueprints of people that have been there and done it. The problem these days is that we live in a world of fake gurus and Instagram 'get rich quick' schemes which makes it hard to understand whose advice to follow, who is the real deal vs. what should be disregarded. When I first met Kevin and listened to him speak on the subject of scaling up a business, the common pitfalls scaleup businesses and entrepreneurs make and the steps to take your company to new heights, I was literally blown away. Kevin gets it! And he has developed systems, steps and explanations for any business owner to simply understand where they are on the journey and easily identify what they are doing well and not so well in order to develop the business and life of their dreams. I have spoken to thousands of business owners and mentored many entrepreneurs over the years and I have always noticed there are common trends that hold businesses and people back. In Kevin's book you will find the answers to unlock any issue that is preventing you from scaling, together with extremely valuable advice that will put you on the right track to achieving your plan and goals.

Kevin has helped me both personally and in my businesses, and I know that his book can help so many others too. The InFlight Checks is something that has really benefited my company. My senior management team and I review them regularly to ensure we continually score higher. If you are someone looking to take your business and entrepreneurial journey to the next level – you have found the right book for it!

Mark Wright, BBC's *The Apprentice* **winner, CEO of Climb Online, Forbes 30 Under 30, 2017**

INTRODUCTION

If you have been in business for more than 5 minutes, you will recognise that there are always challenges (problems, if you prefer!) in business. They normally fall into challenges around people, cash and time, and most business books and advisers will home in on these. We can spend increasing amounts of time troubleshooting these challenges but we never seem to get them to go away – and in fact as we grow we can get to the point where we cannot imagine being able to cope with our business being any bigger. We can get increasingly stressed, being pulled in many directions, to the point that it takes us away from our families and no longer seems fun to be a 'business owner'.

This is because these problems are 'symptoms' and troubleshooting symptoms will only provide a temporary fix at best, just like taking paracetamol for a migraine may provide some relief against the pain but won't cure the underlying cause and therefore won't help to reduce the frequency of reoccurrences. In fact, as we grow our business, the frequency and severity of 'migraines' will only increase.

This book is not about short-term fixes and glib tricks and promises – it is about putting a system in place that will enable you to strengthen the underlying business (and you!) so that fewer symptoms emerge, and when they do (because they inevitably will), you will have a structure for the business (note: the business, not you) to deal with them.

Equally this is not some theoretical textbook, but rather a pragmatic step-by-step guide for any ambitious owner-manager looking to develop the kind of business that gives them the freedom and control they crave – rather than being controlled by their business.

The intent of this book is to become your 'companion' as you navigate through your ScaleUp Journey – a kind of 'handbook'. We'd love it if you write notes in the margin, highlight sections and turn down the corners of pages you find particularly useful – and refer back to it regularly as your business evolves.

Why have I written this book and what makes me think I am qualified to do so? I founded BizSmart® in 2012 following an extensive business career including corporate senior management, an International Masters in Business (MBA) from INSEAD in Fontainebleau, France, strategic consultancy and building and exiting from multiple businesses – where I learned (and am still learning) how hard it can be to create a resilient, scalable and valuable business. Our mission is to create more 'scaleups' by inspiring owner-managers to have the desire and confidence to aim higher, and through providing the 'system' to enable them to do so.

What really inspired me to work with other business owners stemmed from my first experience of building a business. It was a business within another business and although I was a board director, I had limited equity in the business. With a small highly motivated and brilliantly cohesive team, we worked long hours over a two-year period building a successful business and sourcing an acquirer for £6 million – only to walk away with little to show for it other than the experience.

I vowed to learn from that experience and make sure others didn't fall into the same trap. Most of us only get one shot at building a business; it should be fun and rewarding and support our personal life. BizSmart® now helps owner-managers to create the kind of business that will ultimately give them the freedom they are looking for, whilst enjoying the journey along the way.

I don't put myself forward as some business 'guru' and neither do I propose that I have all of the answers. What you won't find in this book are overpromises and magic 'tricks' that will transform your business overnight. Whilst you may not find the answer to every challenge that you will come across on your journey, what you will find is an approach that will provide the framework for transitioning the stepping stones as you scale, enabling you to find your own answers to the challenges that you will face. The approach is based on mine and my team's experiences of working with hundreds of business owners, and our practical experiences of applying our own and others' thinking – bringing it all together in one proven 'system'.

So this is the system we have developed over those years. We call it the Entrepreneurial ScaleUp System – or ESUS for short! – and Part 2 of the book follows this structure. Starting at the centre is something we call the Rhythm90, the main heartbeat of the business. The next ring are the 4 fundamental and widely referred to Pillars of Scaling Up that we need to get right as we navigate the different stepping stones of the ScaleUp Journey – Strategy, People, Execution and Cash[1]. The outer ring are the core things within each of these pillars that we need to get right in each in order to be able to scale successfully and overcome the challenges along the way. We explore each of these and provide a 'checklist' of things to consider and to work on over time – this is something that you can come back to every 90 days as part of your Business Rhythm to identify the next focus. We call this our 'InFlight Checks'® – in flight because we have already taken off (this is not our pre-launch or pre-'take off' checks) and these are the regular checks that we need to do now that we are

 in flight as we navigate our ScaleUp Journey. You can download copies of this and other resources at www.esusgroup.co.uk. Readers of this book can trial our Smart90 software (which includes access to the InFlight Checks) for 90 days at no cost by using the code ESUS90.

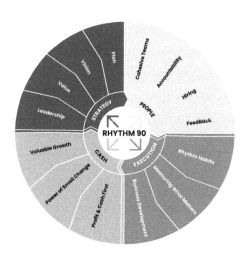

KEVIN BRENT

PART 1:
THE
FOUNDATIONS

CHAPTER 1:

THE FUNDAMENTALS

SETTING THE SCENE

Before we get into the detail of the system and the 4 Pillars, we need to set the scene regarding the ScaleUp Journey, habits and the common challenges we face as we scale up our businesses. This comes from our own research conducted with business owner-managers in 2021. The latest report can be downloaded at esusgroup.co.uk.

If you are an owner-manager of a business between 2–30 employees, and you're reading this book, then you're probably looking for some advice with scaling your business. You may even have expressed your frustration that there is no 'manual' to help you as you scale up. This aims to become that manual – or scaleup 'handbook' – to accompany you on your journey.

 You've no doubt been running a business for a few years and are enjoying a certain level of success. But maybe you're beginning to feel that things are a little out of control. You might even be feeling overwhelmed, or not sure if you're doing things right. You may have got where you are without even realising quite how you got there and are wondering how do you manage the next steps? And how do you keep control of things? You may be increasingly coming across

challenges managing time, team stress or cashflow pressures; perhaps you also have half an eye on wanting to make sure you're building a valuable business, the kind of business that someone might want to buy at some point. And you may be wondering if your business is in fact scalable.

This book sets out to identify some of the key challenges around creating and building a 7-figure (and beyond) successful business and to set out a system for entrepreneurs to implement in order to help them scale up – called the Entrepreneurial ScaleUp System or ESUS. ESUS was also a powerful Celtic deity seen as 'lord' or 'master' – which seems somewhat apt as we use it to establish mastery of scaling up!

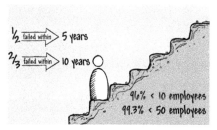

Scaling a business is not easy. And by now, you probably realise that there isn't one simple tip or magic bullet that is suddenly going to deliver phenomenal success. And the stats prove it: half of startups fail within 5 years, two thirds within 10. And of all businesses 99.3% remain with less than 50 employees, and in fact, nearly 96% remain with less than 10 employees. In our experience of working with hundreds of business owners like you over the last few years, there are two things that separate out those that successfully scale from those that do not. Firstly, they work to a proven system and with strategies to scale and build value, including an understanding of the ScaleUp Journey and the difference from linear growth. In other words, they properly plan and execute scaling up and don't just drift into growth. Secondly, they understand and harness the power of peer-to-peer working, working monthly with a small group of like-minded business owners that act as a sounding board of their peers to share their experiences, and help to overcome barriers to scaling up along the way. They also keep each other accountable to the key things that will scale their business and avoid them getting distracted. An old African proverb sums this up nicely: 'If you want to go fast, go alone. If you want to go far, go together'.

THE SCALEUP JOURNEY

Fundamental to our thinking is the concept of the ScaleUp Journey, so let's take a look at what we mean by it.

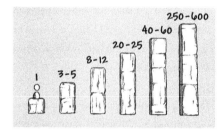

Scaling up (or scaling) is a series of stepping stones or staging posts, not a straight line, or even a wiggly line of growth. The first one of these, if you think about it, the first stepping stone, is at one employee, just us. The second is typically 3–5 employees, the third 8–12, and 20–25, 40–60, 250–600, etc, and so on. If you prefer to think about it in revenue terms, then broadly speaking, we're looking at up to around £100k, £0.5 million, £1 million, £2–2.5 million, £5 million, £25–60 million, etc.

Now, why these numbers? Well, basically, it's related to team sizes, and the number of teams. So let's look at it in a little bit more detail. The first step is just you on your own; we can build a great little business, perhaps a consulting type model, nicely profitable. And we can climb that ladder of success for the one-person business. And that is great, but it is a different kind of business from the 3–5 employee business; the success ladder for the 3–5 business is different. We've got to manage a little more complexity in terms of communication, and we've got to make sure that we have the right business model that enables us to pay decent salaries. And it's no longer okay to have good and bad months where we could cope taking less out one month because we can't ask our staff to do that. Not to mention that we've now got to face the challenge of recruiting and managing staff. So we've begun the transition from owning a job, and hopefully a well-paid one at that, to owning a real business.

The 3–5 employees staging post is a great place to be. We've now got a team that is big enough to benefit from collaborative thinking, as well as 3–5 people actively building the business rather than one person trying to do everything. But still, we're small enough for it not to be too hard to manage and control. But we can't just step from the one-person ladder to the 3–5-person ladder at the same level; we have to join at a lower rung at a lower level. And if you think about it, we're going to have to invest in the transition even if it is just in terms of paying additional staff. But we're probably also going to have to think more about making our lead generation activities more consistent.

So we're going to have a dip or a valley before we're able to start to climb up the new ladder. And these valleys are sometimes referred to as the valleys of death. Because if we get it wrong, we can either languish for ages in a valley where we're busy, but struggling to keep control and probably not earning healthy profits. We're wondering where the cash is going and we might slip back to the previous ladder; we might even kill the business altogether.

And this is why most businesses do not get to the 3–5 stage staging post. If they try many end up taking on an employee and getting it wrong, or the employee leaves and then we're back where we started.

So this is perhaps the most obvious or easy to understand transition but the same happens throughout this ScaleUp Journey. The ladder for the 8–12 employee business is different from the 3–5 ladder. Likewise, the 20–25 success ladder is different again and so on each time there is a valley of death in between, and we need to recognise this. We also need to plan the transition from one ladder to the next; we need to recognise where we are, and to plan for what the business will look like and what the business will need at the next staging post. And we need to think about what needs to happen on the way to build and climb that ladder, including how long do we expect it to take? For example is it a three-year plan? Or perhaps five year or is it shorter or longer? And how much cash will we need to get us through that valley of death? And can we manage the investment from cashflow, for example, or do we need to access additional finance?

So that introduces the concept of the ScaleUp Journey and the first step from the first to second pillar.

From 3–5 to 8–12, we then need to start thinking about systems, particularly lead generation and sales to give us a consistent stream of new business and account management. Also, to make sure that we retain and grow our existing clients, we've now got to the stage where one person probably can't really handle everything. So we typically need to think about a number two in charge or a right-hand person in the business. And we might need to think increasingly about quality and perhaps things like ISO accreditation. (International Organisation for Standardisation). At this point businesses often find they have ended up with lots of different applications and tools, running specific tasks within the business. And now's the time to look at consolidating those. But this is another great staging post; we're now big enough to really benefit from the collective and individual thinking and working and we're less vulnerable to one or even two people leaving. And we're also still not so large that communication becomes a real issue, although we do need to ensure communication is strong within the business.

From 8–12 moving to 20–25 is another big step. And often we need to think about whether to acquire or perhaps to merge to get us there quickly, or whether we feel we can do it organically. Communication and a layer of management become key, financial management becomes crucial, and this is often the time we need a financial director or a chief financial officer within the business, and so on as we go up through the stepping stones.

The reason for the stages is primarily down to effective teams. So either multiples of around 4–5 and 8–12, remembering **Amazon's Jeff Bezos's advice that a team should be no larger than can be fed by two pizzas.**[2] So recognising where we are, what is the next staging post; what does the success ladder for that staging post look like? How is it different? Planning that transition from one ladder to the next becomes paramount in successfully scaling, as well as ensuring that we have climbed the ladder to our current staging post, before we try to jump to the next ladder. If we're going to navigate the valley of death in between, we need to do so from a solid platform where the business is operating as efficiently as possible first, and by the way, it's perfectly fine to identify the staging post you want to stop at, and then run your business to be really successful on that ladder. You don't have to keep moving from one ladder to the next. But just be careful not to slip back.

Strategy:execution gap

Strategy / Execution Matrix

Good Strategy

30%   10%

Poor Execution   Good Execution

30%   30%

Poor Strategy

Fig. 01

One of the key difficulties small and large businesses face is being good at both defining and executing their strategy. We refer to it as 'bridging the strategy:execution gap'. For clarity, Strategy is about setting out our ideas, objectives and plans to achieve them, and Execution is what we actually do to deliver against those plans. From our own and others' experiences,[3] only around 10% of businesses are good at both and these businesses totally outperform their competitors both in terms of profit growth and increased value. The remaining 90% are evenly split between good at one or the other or poor at both!

One of the reasons ESUS works so well is that it not only addresses developing good strategy, it also champions good execution and bridges the gap. It does this through helping to ensure that everyone in the business understands the most important things that need to be done, and that they are aligned around achieving them.

THE 4 PILLARS

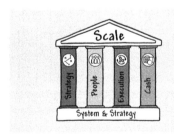

Fig. 02

In order to successfully scale, Verne Harnish and his team at the Gazelles[4] identified 4 key areas or pillars that need to be got right: Strategy, People, Execution and Cash. And this is where the system and strategies to scale come in. Any business that is not performing well on all 4 Pillars will find they get stuck. It could be early on or it could be once they have already built a significant business with several 100 employees perhaps and millions in turnover, but they will still hit a ceiling somewhere.

So let's look at those in a little bit more detail. You need to have the right truly differentiated strategy and scalable business model. You need to be able to attract, hire and retain the right people to deliver on the right strategy. You need to get the right people to execute the strategy with ruthless efficiency and focus and in the right way, and you need to manage the cash as you go. Businesses will fail to scale, or just fail altogether if they have not got all four of the above right.

The emphasis of the 4 Pillars may change depending on where you are on the ScaleUp Journey, and some of the specific aspects within, but not the pillars themselves. And we've already mentioned some of the key differences for the different ladders and we explore these further later in the book.

When planning the transition to the next ladder, we need to do so in light of the 4 Pillars. What will it mean in terms of our strategy, in terms of our people, in terms of how we execute that strategy, which by the way includes our lead generation or marketing; what are our key cash requirements and how are we going to ensure that we are on top of managing the cash?

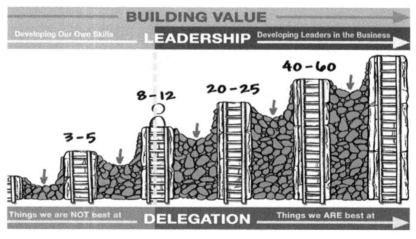

Fig. 03

Overarching everything are two further principles to be aware of: one is leadership and the other is building for value. Leadership in the early days is about developing yourself as a leader. But once we get to the 8–12 staging post, then we need to build leaders behind us.

Before the 8–12 staging post, delegation is typically about delegating the things that we are not good at and don't want to be distracted by, for example admin or bookkeeping, either by outsourcing or recruiting. As we scale beyond this point, we need to start thinking about delegating the things that we *are* good at if we want to create the kind of business that is not overly reliant on us. So for example, if we are the person that brings in all of the new business because we love it, and no-one else can do it quite like us, whilst that may work up to this point, it will cause us to stall much beyond there. So we need to find a way that we can begin to delegate the things that we are good at to others. This can be especially hard for the 'Hawk' or 'D' personality types (explained a bit later on) who tend to be super competitive and can find it difficult to find someone they consider as good or better than them!

Building for value is also essential. If we want to ensure that we create value for ourselves and potentially other investors in the business, do we understand how to create value within the business so that we build the kind of business that will give us options in the future, whether we want to sell at some point, whether we want to step back from the day-to-day running, or even pass down to a family member, because we can guarantee that we will all exit our businesses one day, willingly or not. And it will be great not to have to close the doors on the business when we do and even better, if it can fund whatever it is that we want to do next. This is super critical; many business owners we meet think their business must be worth lots of money because of the time and effort they have put in over the years. Unfortunately, if they haven't built the business in the right way then it is essentially worthless – regardless of the amount of blood, sweat and tears that have gone into it!

So there we have it. Now we have an understanding of the ScaleUp Journey, and why it is important to recognise it as a series of staging posts and valleys in between. And we also have the framework of a system for scaling up. In the rest of the book we build on these fundamentals and provide what is essentially a roadmap, or a flight plan for scaling your business.

What we are going to do next, though, is get started. You do not need to know everything to make some significant strides in the right direction. I'd encourage you to digest the section on 90-day planning and Business Rhythm and implement it straight away – you can absorb the rest of the principles and bring them in when appropriate. It does not matter if it is not 'perfect' – you will make mistakes as we all do but the important thing is getting started. A lot of what we cover in this book is about creating and fostering good habits. You know by now it is not good enough to do something brilliantly once; you have to be able to repeat it consistently over time. You can read as many books as you like but if you don't take action then nothing much will come of it – so getting started on developing good habits is where we want to take you next!

LEARNING POINTS

- There is a system you can follow to guide you through your ScaleUp Journey
- Working with and learning from your peers has been shown to increase your chances of success
- Scaling up is a series of defined stepping stones based on numbers of employees (primary unit 3–5, secondary 8–12)
- In order to navigate from one to the next, we need to make sure we are doing so from a stable platform and then plan ahead and think about the implications regarding the 4 Pillars:
  - Strategy
  - People
  - Execution
  - Cash

ACTIONS

You can do all of these before needing to read any further!

- Identify where you are on the ScaleUp Journey
- Write down where you want to get to next – and by when
- Capture what you think needs to be different about your business when it is at the next stepping stone and what you think it will take to get there successfully by when you said – Strategy, People, Execution, Cash
- Find a peer group where you can work with other business owners

HABITS

Thomas Edison is credited with saying 'Success is 1% inspiration and 99% perspiration' – and it is true for business. If you are still searching for that magic wand that will transform your business into everything you ever wanted it to be, then perhaps you are not ready for this book. Sure, there are frameworks and ways of approaching things that will help you, but it is 'executing' consistently well over time that will make the difference. Every now and then we may have a 'light bulb' moment, but mainly it is about the cumulative effect of multiple small steps in the right direction. This is essentially about creating, implementing and maintaining good 'habits'.

So we are going to start there, before needing to look at the chapter on the challenges facing business owners at different stages of the ScaleUp Journey (Chapter 2), or the chapters on Strategy, People, Execution or Cash (Chapters 4–7). First we are going to look at two fundamental habits that will enable you to get more done in 90 days than most businesses get done in a year! These are:

- Putting in place a 90-day planning cycle
- Implementing an effective business 'rhythm' (the beat of an effective company) starting with an effective weekly team meeting

It doesn't matter if you are the only employee of the business, or if you have thousands of employees, these two interlinked habits properly embedded will make an enormous difference to your business over time – providing all sorts of great things like clarity, focus, alignment and accountability to name but a few 'biggies' as well as a forum for keeping on top of the day to day and addressing any challenges that come along.

We're going to take a look at how to develop a great 90-day plan later along with ideas to help you determine and implement the best Business Rhythm for your business (or perhaps improve it if you already have something in place) – but we can get started straight away.

The first thing is to decide on your 90-day cycle and get a half-day recurring planning session in your calendar and those of your leadership team. You may not have what you would call a 'leadership team' in place but you will have people either in or linked to your business that you would value being part of that session. These need to be people that you trust and who can help with identifying priorities for the business. If you have a handful of employees then it may well be all of them but generally you want at least 3 and up to maybe 6 or 7 at the most to enable things to be kept on track.

You may like to use the calendar quarters (Jan to end March, April to end June etc) which works with many business year ends of the end of March, or you may wish to tie in with your year end if different – it doesn't really matter.

At this stage the agenda can be very simple (we will develop it further later) – for now the aims are simply to:

- Review how things have gone in the last quarter against what we wanted to achieve
- Review how we are doing against where we are headed – are we going in the right direction? – Strategy
- Check on the culture in the business. What team issues do we need to address? – People
- Review how 'operations/client delivery' are going – Execution
- Check the financials are ok – Cash
- Identify 5–7 priorities for the next 90 days (What does 'good' look like for the business in 90 days?)
- Develop 3–5 individual priorities (or rocks) for each of the leadership team (What does good look like for *me* in 90 days?)
- Identify a few key actions for each rock

Side note: If you are not familiar with Stephen Covey and the idea of 'rocks'[5], then they may need a little explanation. It comes from his example of filling a jar with rocks, pebbles and sand. They will only fit one way. If you start with the sand or the pebbles, you will find that there is not enough room for the rocks at the end – so we start with the rocks, then the pebbles (which fill some of the gaps between the rocks) and then the sand. In business, our 'rocks' are the important things (not the same as urgent) – these are the things that will help us progress to where we want to take the business. The pebbles tend to be the urgent things we need to do to keep the lights on – still important and need to be done, but are more about the day to day. The sand is all the other stuff that generally gets in the way. The idea being that we need to identify our rocks, and ensure we make time for them first, otherwise we will find that there is not enough time left in the day to do them.

Try to make sure that the 5–7 business priorities are the 'big things' you want to achieve and are in line with where we are headed and that the rocks link to the priorities, in other words that there is consistency throughout. The idea here is that if everyone delivers on their actions, that should mean they deliver on their rocks. If everyone delivers on their rocks, that should mean the business achieves its priorities for the quarter. If the business achieves its priorities for four quarters, it should achieve where it is headed for the year etc etc.

Don't worry at this stage about running the 'perfect' 90-day planning session. The most important thing is to get started – perfection can come later!

The second habit is to put in place or hone your Business Rhythm – particularly an effective weekly team meeting. This is the 'lifeblood' of your business, ensuring that you keep focused and on track with your rocks and priorities. Essentially this is about 'mastering execution' and ensuring the right stuff gets done.

Most businesses will have weekly team meetings already in place – but what we have found is that the majority are very operational based. They tend to focus on client delivery/operations and do not generally include progress against the bigger picture priorities. If you have more than 20 employees in your business, you may have a senior leadership team. Do they have their own weekly meeting separate from any operational team meetings covering the key items outlined below in the Smart7 agenda? If you are smaller and essentially one team, then this might serve as a great agenda for the weekly meeting. We will look at this in more detail later in Chapter 3 and explain concepts like 'rocks' and the 'Stop, Start, Continue' discussion.

The Smart7 meeting agenda ~ 60 minutes
1. What went well/highlight of the week? – 30 seconds each
2. What did not go so well/an area for improvement? – 30 seconds each

3.   Progress against critical numbers, rocks and important actions – 30 seconds each – on track or not for each rock, if not whether need help
4.   Learnings from the week – Feedback/intelligence from customers and employees (e.g. things we should Stop, Start, Continue doing) – 10 minutes
5.   Focused challenge – e.g. major event, opportunity or issue, or addressing off-track rocks where help needed – 30 minutes
6.   Important actions from above – What, Who, When, Measures – 5 minutes
7.   Key takeaways from each member and priorities for the week (what does a good week look like?) – 1 minute each

Typically this needs about an hour.

The idea of the progress check against the rocks is exactly that – no more than on track or not. If not on track then the question needs to be asked as to whether help is needed or not. If it is then it gets 'parked' until the 'Focused challenge' section.

The 'Focused challenge' section needs to be at least 30 minutes and is used to harness the collective brainpower in the room to work on and progress one or more challenges. This should include any rocks not on track and needing help as well as any other opportunities or issues that have surfaced in the last week. The time should be boxed, the challenges prioritised and then worked on in priority order to the point where there is a next step identified. As many as possible are worked on in the 30 minutes – any remaining are moved to next week.

Individuals should be asked for their takeaways (priorities and actions) for the week resulting from the session.

If this is run well then it becomes the backbone of an effective Business Rhythm, ensuring we don't slip on our rocks and the business priorities as well as enabling progress on issues and opportunities as they arise weekly.

So before reading any further, I encourage you to get these two things implemented in your business – get the dates in the right calendars and the agendas set! **Don't forget, 'You don't have to be amazing to start but you do have to start to be amazing!'**

LEARNING POINTS

- Sustained business success is more about embedding good habits than flashes of inspiration
- Two critical habits for long-term success are:
  - Adopting a 90-day cycle
  - Implementing a robust weekly 'rhythm'

ACTIONS

You can do all of these before needing to read any further!

- Get dates in the diary for your next four 90-day planning workshops – and invite the relevant people
- Get a weekly recurring event in the diary for the Smart7 sessions – and invite the relevant people
- Determine outline agendas for the above (we will look at example agendas later)
- Get cracking!

CHAPTER 2:

THE CHALLENGES OF 7-FIGURE BUSINESS SUCCESS AND BEYOND

QUICK OVERVIEW

This chapter reviews the key findings in our 2021 research. You can read the latest report by going to esusgroup.co.uk as well as take part by providing your own information to be included in the analysis for the next report.

Understanding and recognising these challenges is an important part of understanding the Entrepreneurial ScaleUp System (ESUS) and how it can address these. I know some of you will be tempted to skip this section and jump to the system itself, but I encourage you to take the time to familiarise yourself with the findings. Part of what you will come to realise (if you have not already) is that the challenges we face in scaling our businesses are universal. Sure there might be industry specific differences overlaid on top, but the core challenges are faced by us all.

According to the latest government statistics, there are 6 million private sector SMEs within the UK, of which 5.7 million (96%) are 'micro-businesses'[6] (by the way, I particularly dislike this term as I find it belittling of the achievement to create a business that employs more than just the owner).

Although the vast majority fall under this category, the data shows 'micro' businesses only account for 33% of UK employment and 21% of the entire turnover.

In contrast there are only 33,445 'scaleups'[7] in the UK (less than 1% of all SMEs) but they contribute 50% of the SME economy in the UK.

So why is it that just 4% of UK businesses can scale beyond 10 employees? And, more importantly, what is preventing the average business owner from continuing their ScaleUp Journey reaching 20–25 employees or 50 plus?

In early 2021, BizSmart surveyed business owners about their business, its performance in recent years, the common challenges they experience and their plans for growth. Our aim was to help business owners to understand the key challenges in scaling a business. We set out to identify the barriers to growth at each fundamental milestone, whilst providing insight into the common challenges owner-managed businesses face, including the role personality types can play in both driving and preventing success. A summary of our 2021 findings is below and the latest full report can be found at esusgroup.co.uk.

Our findings are extensive and interesting, with key takeaways as follows:

Key takeaways: challenges for owner-managers

56%	48%	42%	41%	35%
Dragged back into day-to-day operations	Generating leads of sufficient quality	The right staff in place to support growth	Getting staff to think, act and take responsibility	Keeping on track with the plan

Fig. 04

Getting dragged back into day-to-day operations (56%), generating sufficient quality leads (48%), not having the right staff in place to support growth (42%), getting staff to think and act for themselves and take responsibility in the way you would (41%) and keeping on track with the plan (35%) were highlighted as the top 5 key challenges that prevent business growth, although these differed across each turnover bracket and for each personality type.

Personality types

There is a clear correlation between business success and personality types, where those who identified as Dominance or 'Hawks' under the DISC profile were more likely to scale their business beyond 10 employees when compared to Steadiness (Doves), Conscientiousness (Owls) and Influence (Cockatoos). **DISC assessments** are behavior self-assessment tools based on the 1928 DISC emotional and behavioural theory of psychologist William Moulton Marston[8]. We explain more on personality types later.

Objectives and KPIs

73% of respondents work towards clear business objectives. Of these, the most frequently reported KPIs are finance based, with only 10% of the top 5 reported measures focused on customer satisfaction and just 4% focused on team engagement, despite a wide recognition of how important team culture is in creating a great business.

Competitive advantage

Whilst a large proportion (79%) of business owners believe they have a genuine USP (unique selling point), just 34% have either a cost or offer-based competitive advantage.[9] In addition, only a small percentage (7%) have a truly scalable business model.

Future growth rate optimism

Business owners are much more optimistic about their future growth rates in comparison to their historic financial performance. 61% of business owners expect to nearly or more than double over the next three years, whereas only 19% report that they have actually doubled or greater over the last three years.

True net profit

The true net profit figures are much lower than reported, as despite 37% of business owners reporting more than 20% in net profit, and a further 21% reporting between 11–20%, only 17% would still show these numbers if the company director(s) were paid a market rate salary. What's more, 32% of businesses would actually report either a loss or sub 5% net profit if the company director(s) was paid a market rate salary, instead of relying on dividends for income. This means many business owners are mistakenly believing they are making profit, when in fact they are not.

Fig. 05

Nearly half of businesses are over-reliant on the business owner, with 49% advising the business would 'suffer a lot' if they were incapacitated for 3 months.

COMMON CHALLENGES THAT PREVENT BUSINESS GROWTH

There are consistent challenges across all 4 key pillars of the ScaleUp Journey as identified by Verne Harnish and his team of Gazelles[10] (Strategy, Execution, Cash and People) that every business owner experiences. However, the emphasis or relative importance of these challenges differs at key employee and revenue milestones.

From our experience in working with and supporting business leaders in their own ScaleUp Journey through our peer-to-peer business support programme, we can predict that challenges around cashflow, sales and marketing are more likely to impact business leaders operating micro-businesses, whereas challenges around people, recruitment and staff management are more likely to have the most impact on those operating 7-figure businesses.

This is evidenced by our research and demonstrated by the following statistics:

Challenges Preventing Growth: Turnover Milestones

£100k – £500k turnover

75%	Dragged back into day-to-day operations
56%	Generating sufficient quality leads
30%	Financial planning – knowing how to use the numbers to make decisions
30%	Unstable cashflow
25%	Don't use monthly management accounts to inform the right financial decisions

£500k – £1m turnover

59%	Attracting and hiring enough of the right people
53%	Getting staff to think and act for themselves and take responsibility the way you would
47%	Generating sufficient quality leads
29%	Staff management – getting staff to do the right things consistently well
24%	Failing to set out a strong vision and plan to achieve it

£1m – £3m turnover

71%	Getting staff to think and act for themselves and take responsibility the way you would
50%	Not having the right staff in place to support growth
43%	Attracting and hiring enough of the right people
36%	Operations – in ensuring the work was delivered consistently well to the client
36%	Challenge of accessing funding is stunting growth

£3m – £5m turnover

80%	Getting staff to think and act for themselves and take responsibility the way you would
60%	Staff management – getting staff to do the right things consistently well
60%	Challenge of accessing funding is stunting growth
60%	Struggling to keep on track with the plan
40%	Failing to set out a strong vision and plan to achieve it

Fig. 06

KPI failures

What is most interesting about the above data is that although the severity of the challenge shifts slightly, they become progressively people focused. For example, there is far greater weight on finance and cash-based challenges for smaller businesses when compared to larger organisations, however the challenge of hiring, retaining and securing the right people who work in the right way to support growth is apparent for all businesses when they exceed a £500k turnover, regardless of where they are on the ScaleUp Journey.

Despite this, most respondents fail to create and measure themselves against people-related KPIs and only focus on financial indicators, as demonstrated by the following:

- 43% of the top 5 reported metrics were financial KPIs
- Despite accepted wisdom on the importance of people, only 4% of metrics related to staff KPIs such as team engagement and satisfaction
- In addition, only 10% related to customer engagement and satisfaction

- Just 4% of the top 5 KPIs related directly to resilience, stability and value

Generally as business owners, we don't focus enough on measuring the *behaviours* that will *lead* to the results we want. The majority (89%) of all reported indicators are 'lagging' KPIs, which means they look at the result after the 'event', as opposed to measuring 'leading' indicators that look at the actions or behaviours that should lead to the desired results.

43%	4%	4%	10%
financial KPIs in the top 5 metrics	related to resilience in the top 5 metrics	related to staff of all metrics	customer related of all metrics

Fig. 07

All business owners would benefit from introducing more people-focused KPIs. Not only would this move the needle on recurring difficulties around staff management but it would also have a direct impact on growth, enabling more business owners to buck the 96% trend and scale to seven figures.

PERSONALITY TYPES AND BUSINESS SUCCESS

DISC measures personality and behavioural style, such as how you respond to challenges, how you influence others and how you respond to rules and procedures.

In business, DISC is used to analyse leadership styles and to help business owners understand their own personality traits, their strengths, their weaknesses and the type of individuals they need within their organisation to build a cohesive and effective team.

A quick explanation of DISC follows for those that are not familiar with it. There are 4 primary DISC profiles, which we have translated into birds to represent each personality type. Whilst there are 4 primary classifications, most of us are a mix of more than one type. The explanations below relate to someone who is typical of that primary style.

The 4 primary DISC profiles

Dominance (Hawk)

Individuals with 'Hawk' profiles tend to be commanding, pioneering and resolute. They are generally motivated by authority, competition and success and tend to be self-confident, direct and forceful by nature.

In contrast to what may be seen above as positive traits, Hawks may be limited by impatience and insensitivity and can fear both loss of control and vulnerability.

Influence (Cockatoo)

Individuals with 'Cockatoo' profiles tend to be energised, pioneering and affirmative. They are often motivated by social recognition and strong relationships and are usually enthusiastic, sociable, optimistic and talkative by nature.

In contrast, Cockatoos may be limited by fears of social rejection, disapproval or being ignored and are often disorganised and may lack the diligence to follow through with actions.

Steadiness (Dove)

Individuals with 'Dove' profiles tend to be supportive, stable and collaborative. They are generally motivated by co-operation, appreciation and opportunities to help and are usually patient, calm and possess excellent listening and team skills.

In contrast, Doves may be limited by fear of change and offending others, and as a result can be indecisive and often overaccommodating.

Conscientiousness (Owl)

Individuals with 'Owl' profiles tend to be focused on accuracy, maintaining stability and challenging assumptions. They are generally motivated by an opportunity to use expertise or gain knowledge and often come across as precise, reserved and quiet.

In contrast, Owls may be limited by being overly critical and their tendency to over-analyse and usually fear criticism and being incorrect.

Correlations

The research shows a clear correlation between personality type and business success, where leaders with a Hawk DISC profile are more likely to surpass micro-business status and reach a seven-figure-plus turnover when compared to Cockatoo, Dove and Owl profiles.

Interestingly, Hawks are the rarest type of DISC profile, making up just 9% of the global population. As competitive, decisive and results-orientated individuals, could this explain why just 4% of UK businesses surpass micro status? Let's review the research in more detail:

Turnover

This is reinforced when comparing personality type to business turnover, as the proportion of Hawk profiles increases markedly compared to other personality types with larger businesses, from £500k–£1 million upwards.

In contrast, 72% of individuals with a Dove profile haven't exceeded the £500k turnover mark, with just 9% having reached £500k–£1 million turnover and just 3% at £3–£5 million.

The stats are similar for individuals with Owl or Cockatoo profiles, with 47% of Cockatoos and 50% of Owls turning over £100k–£500k and only 8% of Owls and 6% of Cockatoos reaching £3–5 million in annual revenue.

Business challenges

From a high level, it could be argued that individuals with Hawk profiles don't struggle as much with key functions of business, such as planning, strategy and sales, when compared to individuals with Dove profiles, as demonstrated by the following findings:

- Whereas 31% of individuals with a Dove profile advised they struggled to convert leads into sales, only 18% of individuals with a Hawk profile reported the same challenge.
- 50% of individuals with a Dove profile revealed that they struggled to remain on track with any plan compared to just 21% of Hawks.

- 38% of Doves struggled to set out a strong vision with a plan to achieve it, compared to just 25% of Hawks.
- 28% of Doves said they struggled with financial planning and knowing how to use the numbers to make the right decisions – a sentiment only shared by 14% of Hawks and 15% of individuals with Owl profiles.
- 66% of Doves reported that they find themselves dragged back into day-to-day operations, compared to 50% of Hawks.

However, when it comes to staff and talent management, the Hawk profile loses its edge, with 57% of Hawks advising that they struggle to attract and retain enough of the right people, compared to just 15% of Owls and 22% of Doves. 29% of Hawks reported challenges around operations and ensuring the work was delivered consistently well to the client compared to 18% of Doves.

Personality types and business success: considerations

While the research clearly indicates that an individual with a Hawk DISC profile is more likely to succeed in scaling their business beyond micro status, there is a fundamental challenge in people management that will always prevent growth.

As assertive, direct and competitive individuals, those with strict Hawk-based profiles are extremely likely to succeed by working relentlessly towards consistent business objectives (and will stick to them) but are more likely to hit a stumbling block of attracting and retaining the right staff to support business growth, when compared to the collaborative, team skills of a Dove or the enthusiastic, motivating and optimistic nature of a Cockatoo.

Therefore, taking the time to assess your own strengths and weaknesses is fundamental to the success of your business long term. Not only will it enable you to realise your own 'gaps' but will also inform hiring decisions when building a cohesive management team who can complement your own skillset. Having the right people around you – whether in senior staff or in working with like-minded peers – is key to success and is a fundamental challenge in building and sustaining a seven-figure business.

LEARNING POINTS

- Our personality type influences the likely challenges we will face
- We need to understand our own type (and those of our teams) to ensure we are best placed to overcome them

ACTIONS

In the light of the findings about personality types:

- Review/assess your own personality type and leadership style
  - There are many alternatives such as Everything DiSC® Work of Leaders – a Wiley Publishing product that we use. Visit www.esusgroup.co.uk for more information on undertaking Everything DiSC® profiling.
- Identify how your type has helped and hindered you
- Identify your leadership strengths and challenges
- Think about your team and how the different types support each other and identify potential areas of conflict
- Identify gaps – are you missing a 'Cockatoo'?!
- Identify one leadership habit you will embed over the next 90 days to improve leadership in your business

COMPETITIVE ADVANTAGE AND OTHER SCALEUP CHALLENGES

Competitive advantage

In order to create sustainable profitable growth a business needs to either compete in 'attractive' markets (where the average company makes superior profits) and/or be competitively advantaged against their competitors.

In an 'attractive' market a business may afford to be relatively average for a while and will experience growth in line with the market, but in a challenging market this is not possible.

A USP (Unique Selling Proposition) is not a true USP unless it translates into an actual competitive advantage, otherwise the USP is not important to the customer. It was our hypothesis that whilst most business owners believe they have a USP, the majority don't have a true USP that leads to a competitive advantage.

Offer and cost positions

Competitive advantage is driven by the **offer** position (how good customers perceive the **offer** to be compared with the competition) and the **cost** position (how cost efficiently the business can deliver the **offer** compared with the competition). There are many ways to create an offer advantage, for example 'ease of use', 'the overall customer experience', a 'tailored' or 'personalised' product to name but a few. Similarly with the cost position, these tend to be focused on efficiencies of operations such as superior supply chain buying capabilities/procurement enabling you to buy more efficiently/cheaper than your competitors, technology or systems that enable you to produce the product more cost effectively, maybe patents or IP that give you a productivity edge, exclusive relationships, access to scarce resources including labour, economies of scale etc etc.

Creating a competitive advantage is clearly desirable and requires creating differentiation from competitors in a way that customers value – just being 'different' does not necessarily count! The goal is to get to the point where the average customer is willing to pay a premium for your product or service.

Challenges

According to our research, 80% of businesses confirmed that they have a clearly defined USP. However, after additional analysis it is clear that just 38% of businesses have an actual competitive advantage, where 49% of these have a cost advantage and 51% have an offer advantage. This means that nearly half (42%) of businesses believe they have a USP, but it is not translating into an actual competitive advantage, therefore hindering scalability and growth.

From further analysis, we also found the following data and insights on competitive advantage:

Personality types

Hawks are more likely to build a business with a competitive offer advantage (29%) vs. other personality types (Dove 19%, Cockatoo 18%, Owls 15%).

Only 11% of Cockatoos are likely to build a business with a cost advantage vs 23% of Owls, 18% of Hawks and 25% of Doves.

Key reported challenges

Only 12% of businesses with an offer advantage cited 'Generating sufficient leads' as a key challenge, compared with 20% of businesses with a cost advantage and a massive 67% with either an 'unclear' or no competitive advantage.

Companies with an offer or cost advantage were less likely to cite 'Converting leads into sales' as a key challenge (15% vs 69% with either an unclear or no competitive advantage).

Interestingly this trend continues across other challenges and may explain why all businesses with two-plus years of trading *and* less than £100k turnover do not have a clearly defined competitive advantage.

LEARNING POINTS

- Most business USPs are weak
- We need to make sure we are 'competitively advantaged' by one or more of the following 3 strategies:
    1. Competing in 'attractive markets' – our 'participation' strategy
    2. Creating and sustaining an 'offer' advantage
    3. Creating and sustaining a 'cost' advantage

ACTIONS

To improve and build competitive offer advantage, we need to work through the following strategy questions:

- Does our current offer give us an advantage and for which types of customers or market segments?
- Which markets/customer types are most 'attractive'? Can we apply our skills in more profitable sectors?
- What improvements could we make that the customer would be willing to pay more and/or enough for?
- What do we do now that does not add value to our offer for the average customer?
- If we have created an offer advantage, should we raise our prices or should we go for volume growth?

Cont'd

ACTIONS (CONT'D)

Having an advantage from a cost perspective enables the business to make more profit than competitors at the same price. Key questions we should consider include:

- How can we minimise our overheads?
- What can we do to reduce the cost of goods/variable costs for each product or service we deliver?
- Are there things we do that are not valued by the customer and we could stop doing?
    - Are there efficiencies we could make in our operations?
- Can we renegotiate arrangements with suppliers?

CHALLENGES RELATING TO THE 4 PILLARS OF SCALING UP

Any business that is not performing well on all 4 Pillars[11] will find they get stuck – it could be early on or it could be once they have already built a significant business with several 100 employees and millions in turnover – but they will hit a ceiling somewhere. To be successful and scale beyond seven figures:

- You need to have the right 'truly differentiated' strategy and business model to scale
- You need to be able to attract, hire and retain the right people to deliver on the right strategy
- You need to get the right people to execute the strategy with ruthless efficiency and focus in the right way
- And you need to manage the cash

However, this is easier said than done, as demonstrated by the following data from our research:

Strategy: scalable business model

- 53% don't have a clear strategy that works towards scalability and growth
- Only 7% (all are Owls or Hawks) of our sample have a truly scalable business model as defined by:
    - 25% or more of sales based on recurring revenue
    - low reliance on the business owner (business would either not suffer or suffer only a little if the business owner took 3 months off)
    - would find it fairly or very easy to handle 5 times the volume, and
    - have a competitive advantage (cost or offer) as defined later.

Execution: getting the business to execute consistently well against the strategy

- 24% don't have sales and marketing resource
- 31% fail to keep on track with a growth plan
- 47% struggle to generate sufficient high-quality leads
- Overall, 64% of business owners cited 'execution' challenges as key issues

People: finding, hiring and retaining them

- 50% struggle with getting staff to think and act for themselves and take responsibility in the way that they would do as the business owner
- 46% acknowledge they don't have the right staff in place to support growth
- 41% confirmed that they struggle with attracting and hiring enough of the right people

Managing the cash

- 45% don't or only partially have the cashflow to support scalability and growth
- 20% have unstable cashflow
- Only 15% have cashflow to support 12 months of operational costs
- 41% have 3–6 months in cash reserves
- Overall, 13% of the key challenges cited by business owners related to cash

COMMON MISTAKES

There is a potential argument that one of the key reasons as to why 96% of businesses never scale beyond 9 employees is because they succumb to a number of common mistakes, which means the business doesn't have the right processes from the outset and results in over-reliance on the business owner.

Michael E. Gerber's *The E-Myth* supports this argument and explains that most businesses fail because the owner transfers their own skill (e.g. baking skills) into the business and, therefore, ends up working in the business instead of on it. This not only means the business owner doesn't have the prior experience to implement the right processes in the business from the outset but is also likely to make the wrong hiring decisions. **Or as Gerber puts it: 'If your business depends on you, you don't have a business – you have a job'.**[12] And it's the worst job in the world because you're working for a lunatic!

We can see evidence of this throughout our research, with key stats as follows:

- When questioned as to whether they would be able to fulfil 5 times the order volume or workload if customers were queuing at the door, 75% of respondents advised they would find this 'difficult' or 'not possible'.
- Just 10% of respondents advised their business would 'hardly suffer at all' if they were incapacitated for 3 months, with a further 56% of business owners confirming they get dragged back into the day-to-day operations.
- Only 33% of respondents advised they have a senior leadership team in place with clearly defined roles, with 42% advising they don't have the right staff in place to support growth.

Finances

You could also argue that one of the key reasons as to why business owners succumb to these common challenges are due to finances. When starting a business, most business owners focus on replacing their employed salary and often work with their accountant to do this in the most tax-efficient way possible. However, this creates the problem of over-reliance from the outset. In focusing on replacing their income, the business owner has no choice but to work in the business rather than on it – yet the majority stay in that position and fail to delegate the tasks they should no longer be doing even when they have the staff in place for operational delivery.

What's more, in not paying a market rate director's salary, most business owners are under the false impression that they are generating good, comfortable profits. However, as our research shows 32% of businesses would actually report either a loss or sub 5% net profit if the company director(s) was paid a market rate salary, instead of relying on dividends for income. **Although there is nothing wrong with this for directors that want to create a 'lifestyle' business, you could argue that if market rate salaries were accounted for from the outset there would be greater appetite for growth to reach profitability and more businesses would be better structured for exit.**

CHALLENGES CONCLUSIONS

Based on our findings, we would suggest that the likely key reasons and/or challenges as to why only 4% of businesses scale beyond 9 employees and 7 figures fall into 5 main areas:

1. Desire and confidence
   - Not every business owner wants to scale their business or wants to take on managing more staff.
   - Business owners become more risk averse as they grow, to the point it prevents scalability as they have more to risk and, therefore, more to lose.
   - Recognising when to scale and having the confidence to invest time and money in business growth (see points 3 and 5).

2. Personality and/or leadership
   - Understanding and recognising that we need to balance the strengths and challenges of our personality profile by building a balanced team around us as we reach different stages of the ScaleUp Journey.
   - Creating a high performing team culture – focus needs to be given to maintaining the 'common purpose' that is clear during the startup phase but is easy to lose as the team grows.

3. Understanding what it really takes to scale
   - The need and how to create a truly scalable business model that includes being competitively advantaged (not just a perceived USP) and being 'truly' profitable.
   - Recognising that scaling up is a journey consisting of a series of stepping stones and that each transition has its own set of challenges.
   - Understanding the importance of 'true' profitability in order to scale (in particular correctly accounting for market rate directors' salaries).

4. Focusing on culture and team engagement
- Placing the right emphasis on the importance of team engagement and culture – and including team metrics in Key Performance Indicators.

5. Overcoming the 'chicken and the egg'
- It takes people and cash to scale
- In the early days the business does not generate the cash required to invest in people – but without investing the business is unlikely to get to the point where it is self-financing.
- If you knew it was going to be a success you would beg, borrow and steal to get all the money you need to scale. But how do we get the confidence in our business to do that? (This brings us back to point 1.)
- Too many business owners fall into the trap of working in the business, not on it – creating an 'owner's trap' that can be difficult to break out of without cash and the right resource.

FINAL THOUGHTS ON CHALLENGES...

Scaling a business is not easy – and even by just reading this far you would have realised that there isn't one simple tip or magic bullet that is suddenly going to deliver phenomenal success.

In our experience of working with several hundred business owners like you over the last few years, there are two things that separate out those that successfully scale from those that do not:

Scaleup strategy

The first is working to a proven system and strategies to scale and build value.

Leadership

As part of understanding and driving scaleup strategies, every business owner needs to work on and establish strong leadership within their organisation. This needs to evolve from developing our own leadership (including effective delegation of appropriate tasks), to developing leadership skills in others within our team.

Regardless of whether business owners are yet to reach or have exceeded a headcount of 8–12, people-based challenges were consistently reported throughout our research. For most, getting dragged back into day-to-day operations, getting staff to act, think and take responsibility in the same way as the business owner would, and hiring enough of the right staff, are not only challenges that significantly impact growth, but all come down to leadership skills and capability.

Differing approaches

In addition, the personality types of Hawk, Owl, Dove and Cockatoo will result in different approaches to leadership and where the driven but perhaps controlling nature of a Hawk may cause challenges with delegation, the 'people-pleasing' nature of Doves may lack the capability to make decisions that benefit the business, hindering growth as a result.

Harnessing the power of your peers!

The second key thing that separates out those who successfully scale versus those whose don't is harnessing the power of peers – and one of the best ways to do this is a structured form of peer-to-peer working.

Aside from providing the opportunity to work with a balanced group of business owners, peer-to-peer working provides the opportunity for business owners to shape and advance their leadership skills by learning from the successes and mistakes of each other, spanning all 4 Pillars of scaleup.

Identifying barriers

In addition, peer-to-peer working enables business leaders to address and overcome the identified barriers to scale, such as confidence, team culture, leadership and honing your business model to create true competitive advantage.

Desire

Therefore, this brings us back to point 1 of the Conclusions – to first succeed in scaling a business, you have to have the genuine desire to do so, regardless of what it takes. Or in the words of Napoleon Hill, 'The starting point of all achievement is desire'.

- Desire to move beyond your comfort zone and work on your own leadership
- Desire to understand and work through all 4 Pillars of scale
- Desire to make the right decisions for the business – from hiring and firing, to implementing new and strategic processes
- Desire to remove yourself from the day to day and work on the business instead of in it

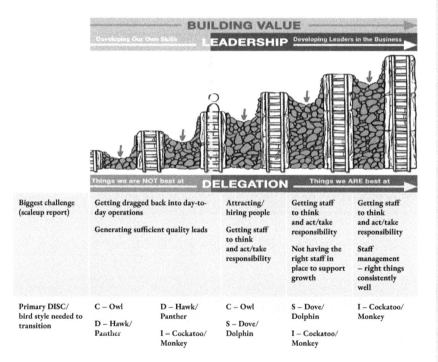

Biggest challenge (scaleup report)	Getting dragged back into day-to-day operations Generating sufficient quality leads	Attracting/ hiring people Getting staff to think and act/take responsibility	Getting staff to think and act/take responsibility Not having the right staff in place to support growth	Getting staff to think and act/take responsibility Staff management – right things consistently well
Primary DISC/ bird style needed to transition	C – Owl D – Hawk/ Panther	D – Hawk/ Panther I – Cockatoo/ Monkey	C – Owl S – Dove/ Dolphin	S – Dove/ Dolphin I – Cockatoo/ Monkey	I – Cockatoo/ Monkey

Fig. 08

ACTION

So, ask yourself this: Do you have enough desire to scale your business or are you comfortable with where you are?

If you have the desire and are serious about wanting to scale, then the rest of the book will help you implement a system that will help you to do so.

PART 2:
THE 'SYSTEM'

INTRODUCTION TO THE 'SYSTEM'!

So what we need is a system that addresses the challenges outlined in the previous chapter and combines the key thinking from business gurus such as Jim Collins, Michael E. Gerber, Verne Harnish, Stephen Covey and John Warrillow – but not in a theoretical 'business school' kind of way!

And that is what we have created. It is called the Entrepreneurial ScaleUp System – or ESUS. The system I am about to describe to you is one that we have honed over the last 9 years or so through working with hundreds of business owners. In the last 5 years alone, we have worked with hundreds of business owners and assisted them in delivering an average increase in turnover of +29% and a 36% growth in profits within the first 12 months and we aim to double the value of each business we work with within 2 years through implementing ESUS.

A further analysis of the challenges data referred to in the previous chapter shows that in the last year (during the pandemic) businesses we work with on ESUS through our peer-to-peer mastermind service SmartBoards® have increased headcount by 31.6% compared with the 'control group' average of 7.5%. 43% of SmartBoard® members report a greater than doubling of turnover since 3 years ago vs. the control of 30% with 52% vs. 34% showing growth in the last year (despite the pandemic) of more than 20%.

The most brilliant strategy ever devised won't get you anywhere if you can't execute it

As raised earlier, one of the key difficulties small and large businesses face is being good at both defining and executing their strategy. From our own and others' experiences[13], only around 10% of businesses have a good strategy and a good execution and these businesses totally outperform their competitors both in terms of profit growth and increased value. The remaining 90% are evenly split between good at one or the other or poor at both!

One of the reasons ESUS works so well is that it not only addresses good strategy, it also champions good execution and bridges the gap between the two through alignment of the team.

Strategy / Execution Matrix

Good Strategy

30%   10%

Poor Execution   Good Execution

30%   30%

Poor Strategy

Fig. 09

So what we do works and there is no question that businesses following ESUS outscale their competitors who do not use it.

It is perhaps worth taking a moment now to make the distinction between growing and scaling before we get into the detail of ESUS – because this is a mindset change that separates those that scale from those that do not.

Growth is simply increasing the size of the business in a 'linear' fashion, by which I mean if the turnover increases by 10%, so do the costs and therefore the bottom line profits. The key thing about this is that any 'headaches' you have in the business simply get magnified. It can take a lot of resources to sustain constant growth. Most business 'consultants' focus on growth and not scale and whilst this can be effective in the short term, it does not necessarily create the kind of business that gives the control and freedom that most business owners are looking for.

Scaling, on the other hand, implies that we are able to increase top line sales/revenue at a faster rate than costs.

Scaling, on the other hand, implies that we are able to increase top line sales/revenue at a faster rate than costs. This comes back to the mindset of thinking about the 'stepping stones' in our ScaleUp Journey and planning for what the business needs to look like at the next stepping stone and what needs to happen in between to get us there in terms of Strategy, People, Execution and Cash. What we call the 'business model' plays an important part in the strategy here to ensure that we do have a model that can scale effectively. Adopting a scaling mindset rather than a growth mindset will lead to a more valuable business, one that is more resilient and more fun to run, helping us to achieve that freedom and control we are looking for.

So enough background – you want to understand the system.

If we want to create an enduring business then we need to create good 'habits' in the business. Here we take a leaf out of Stephen Covey's *The 7 Habits of Highly Effective People* and apply the same thinking to a business. This frees the business up from all that distracted energy that is wasted on reinventing approaches and provides a springboard for harnessing the combined brainpower of the people in the business.

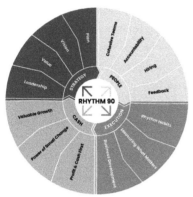

At the heart of ESUS is what we call the 'Business Rhythm' – this is the heartbeat of the business or the lifeblood and is the most fundamental 'habit' within the business. Done well, this will ensure that we bridge the 'strategy:execution gap' that often occurs, ensuring that we align the big picture with the day to day whilst harnessing the true power of our teams.

Fig. 10

The two fundamental habits to get right in the Business Rhythm are quarterly 90-day planning cycle (Smart90) backed up by a weekly strategic progress check (Smart7). Ideally we supplement these with more strategic and more tactical sessions such as our annual strategic planning and our daily and monthly rhythms – but the fundamental two are the quarterly and weekly. We cover the Smart7 in more detail later in the Execution chapter (Chapter 6), and you have already had an introduction to them in the 'Habits' section earlier. We will take a look at the 90-day rhythm next.

A good 90-day rhythm will ensure we address and refine the core pillars of scaling up identified by Verne Harnish and his team at Gazelles – namely Strategy, People, Execution and Cash. In ESUS, each of those pillars has 3 or 4 fundamental components that we need to consider and create habits for. These are the fundamentals of ESUS – a continual cycle of improvement habits driven by our Rhythm90 and addressing the key elements of scaling. Each component has a methodology and framework to enable you to implement it well, adapt to your business and hone over time – helping you to instil these great habits in your business.

The key thing of course is to get started. Think of it, if you like, as a kind of 'flywheel' – we might need to put a fair bit of effort in initially to get it turning, but over time as we give it constant nudges through our rhythm, we build up the momentum – meaning that the business has its own momentum and is not reliant on us pushing it uphill all the time. This is why we set you the challenge in the habits section to get started on your 90-day and weekly rhythm – even if you don't do it *perfectly*, you will be getting into the right habits – beginning to overcome the initial 'inertia' of getting the flywheel to turn and build momentum. The detail can always be improved and honed as we go.

The structure of the rest of this book is to take each of the 5 areas – first the Rhythm90 and then each of the 4 Pillars – one by one, looking at the concepts and tools behind each. We then pull it all together at the end by coming back to the Business Rhythm and refining the approach with this added understanding. We will also introduce something we call our 'InFlight Checks' which act as that regular check against key questions for each of the pillars.

GETTING THE MOST OUT OF THIS BOOK

The InFlight Checks® take each of the key components of the 4 Pillars and enable you to rate your business against them. We introduce the relevant 'checks' at the beginning of each key section, addressing them within the section and then summarising at the end of each 'pillar' chapter as a reminder and as action points. We include the full Inflight Checks® at the end of the book so that you can see them all together.

The way we intend you to use the book is to read the whole book in order initially to get an overall understanding of the system, and then to go back to areas that you think will have the most impact on your business if you work on them. We encourage our clients to re-do the InFlight Checks® as part of their 90-day 'rhythm', identifying the next focus area to work on over the coming quarter. This builds in a cycle of continual improvement within the business, focusing on one thing at a time rather than trying to do everything at once. You can find the full set of InFlight Checks at the end of the book. If you would like to be able to access them online with your leadership team, then you can do so via www.esusgroup.co.uk. Readers of this book can trial our Smart90 software (which includes access to the InFlight Checks) for 90 days at no cost by using the code ESUS90.

RHYTHM90

The science of achievement

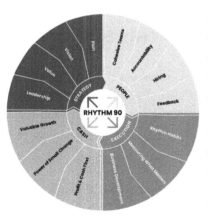

If you're like many of the owners we work with, you started your company with a goal to build a valuable business that can thrive without you doing all the work – perhaps even a business you could sell one day.

So how has the coronavirus pandemic impacted your goals? Not that this is the first crisis to impact business (though it may be the most widespread) and it probably won't be the last. Many of us that have been in business for a while will remember other crises that have impacted businesses such as the depression in 1992, the knock-on effects of 9/11, the 'jobless recovery' of 2003 when the year began with concerns over the war with Iraq, the Great Recession of 2008 and so on.

Not wanting to experience the trauma of the Covid-19 pandemic again, many of the owners we work with have become even more motivated than ever to build a valuable company. And this is the case after any crisis as we strive to rebuild our dreams.

But motivation alone is unlikely to get you the outcome you desire. In fact, motivation, on its own, is largely worthless when it comes to achieving your goals.

Before we get into thinking about setting goals for your business, let's explore goal-setting in general.

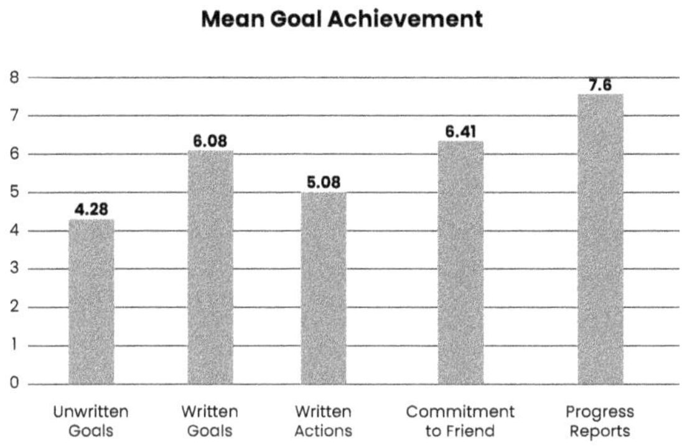

Mean Goal Achievement

Fig. 11

Dr. Gail Matthews, at the Dominican University in California, led a study on goal-setting with nearly 270 participants and showed that you are 42% more likely to achieve your goals if you write them down.[14] Not only that, if you then develop an action plan, share it and report weekly to a colleague, you can further increase the likelihood of achieving goals by 25%. Overall Dr. Matthews showed that committing goals in writing to someone else and checking in weekly increases the likelihood of achieving your goals by 77%!

So it's not enough to *want* to rebuild the value in your business, or have goals in your head. What you need is motivation combined with a specific action plan detailing 5 things:

- What needs to be done and why?
- Who is accountable for it?
- Where will you do it?
- When will you do it by?
- Regular progress reports/accountability checks

Rudyard Kipling summed it up beautifully with this extract from his poem 'I Keep Six Honest Serving Men':

I KEEP six honest serving-men
(They taught me all I knew);
Their names are What and Why and When
And How and Where and Who.

So to put it more into business-speak, you need SMART actions or objectives.

The acronym SMART[15] has been widely used and there are a few variations – we use the following:

S – Specific. This is the 'What'. Make the objective really clear and defined – too broad and you will struggle with the second letter:

M – Measurable. You need to know if you have achieved it – so what does good look like and how will you measure success? This links to the 'How'.

A – Accountable – this is the 'Who'. Who will take ownership for ensuring it gets done?

R – Realistic and Relevant – They should be challenging but not impossible – and they need to align with our long-term objectives – our 'Why'.

T – Timebound – and links to the 'When'. Give it a clear date and even time of day by when it needs to be done.

Picking up on 'Relevant', we need to ensure our actions link back to our long-term plans and objectives.

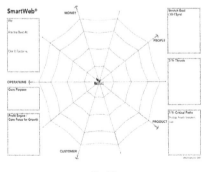

Fig. 12

We cover our SmartWeb® approach to 3-year planning in Chapter 4 on 'Strategy', helping to identify our 3-year 'thrusts' and our 1-year Critical Paths.

If we have identified our handful of Critical Paths for the next year, we can then think about breaking them down into quarterly priorities, all aligned with where we are headed. This then leads us into our 90-day planning approach.

Once we have those, then we can develop 'Relevant' Smart actions.

So we need a way of bridging the gap between the 'Why' and the day-to-day actions we need to take – encompassing the strategic long, mid- and short-term goals along the way – in a way that is simple to understand and engages as many people in the business as possible.

Sounds like a tall order, you may say, but I'm going to share with you a concept and a framework which if you adopt in your business will help you to do this.

90-DAY PLANNING AND THE SMART90®

The concept is 90-day planning.

What is so special about that?

All businesses – large and small – can benefit enormously from a solid 90-day planning process – and most businesses don't do it. We might do an annual plan (which even then many only pay lip service to), but very few have a robust 90-day planning cycle.

In our view, it is the one key thing that any business owner can implement straight away that will have the biggest impact on their chances of success – and we don't say that lightly.

We have worked with hundreds of business owners and seen how this can become the backbone for scaling the business. Without it businesses will struggle to maintain consistency and struggle to harness the power that comes from having everyone aligned around the same priorities. This is the main tool that will bridge the strategy:execution gap and put you on the path to being great at defining and executing against your strategy – putting you in the top 10% of businesses in your sector.

Why is it so great? Well for a number of reasons. It does what we said earlier that we need, which is to bridge the gap between strategy and actions, but it also enables these 5 key things to happen consistently (and that is part of the magic):

1. Clarity – it provides the ability to set goals and make decisions ensuring that we put first things first
2. Alignment – ensuring everyone is on the same page

3. Flexibility – the ability to adjust course quickly and execute accordingly
4. Great communication – especially when combined with a great Business Rhythm in the business
5. Clear responsibilities and ownership

There is one further thing that is worth mentioning here, and that is the time period of 90 days.

It turns out that 90 days is just about perfect; it is short enough that we can see things reasonably clearly and long enough that we can achieve something meaningful if we try. If I said what does good look like, or what do you want to achieve in the next 90 days, you could be pretty clear about it. If I said in the next three years it is a bit harder to envisage in any detail.

Thinking back to my flying days, it is not dissimilar to the idea that we fly by looking to the horizon on the heading we want to take – and picking a reference on the horizon. We focus on that, using the horizon to keep us straight and level and the instruments in the cockpit as a check to make sure everything else is ok. We don't fly by looking inside the cockpit as the main source of our information – if we do that we end up doing what pilots refer to as 'chasing the needles', leading to constant corrections and all our focus inside.

Without a 'guiding star', people literally do walk around in circles! Scientists from the Max Planck Institute for Biological Cybernetics in Tübingen, Germany have presented the first empirical evidence that people do end up walking in circles if lost in unfamiliar terrain.

The study, published in the journal *Current Biology*, examined the trajectories of people who walked for several hours in the Sahara desert in Tunisia and in the Bienwald forest in Germany.

Researchers Jan Souman and Marc Ernst said the scientists used the global positioning system (GPS) to record these paths.

The results showed that the walkers were only able to keep a straight line when the sun or moon was visible – thereby proving the importance of having a 'north star' to follow!

Those of you who do a lot of walking and are familiar with using a compass know that you don't navigate by watching the compass needle every step you take – you set your bearing and pick something in the distance that is on that bearing and you head towards that. When you get there, you do the same again.

So 90 days becomes our point on the horizon.

There is something implied here also, though – and that is that the point on the horizon is on the way to something further, so we need to include the longer term aims into our 90-day thinking.

So now we have the idea – the concept – of 90-day planning and why it is so critical to scaling up.

But we need to have a framework around the idea to help us to implement it consistently well.

SMART90® 90-DAY PLANNING

I'm going to share with you what we call the Smart90® which is the result of several years of development working with business owners to get it to a simple but powerful framework.

The idea of a one-page plan is not new and there are other variations. If you read *Scaling Up* by Verne Harnish and the Gazelles, they have a couple of versions, for example depending on the size of the business.[16] There is a methodology known as OKR (Objectives and Key Results)[17] which is widely used. Some, including our own, come with software to help implement it throughout the business.

What we have done is to develop something that works really well with businesses with typically between 3 and 50 employees and is illustrated below.

It is in fact two-sided (one page rather than one side!) if you use the Word document version; the first side is for the whole business, and the reverse is for the individual team member. If you are on your own in the business then there will only be yours, but if you have anyone else in the business then they should have their own – where the first side is common but the reverse is adapted to their own roles – so every member of the team can personalise it whilst being aware of the overall business priorities.

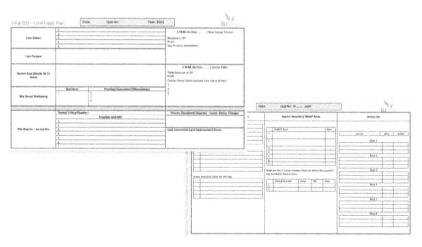

Fig. 13

This can be a very powerful way of ensuring the vision is shared with and understood by everyone in the business. And we begin to create alignment and accountability.

At the core of this are the 90-day process and cash improvement priorities for the whole business and on the reverse the individual Smart Rocks and Smart Actions to go with them. In this way we ensure that everyone is identifying their own 'rocks' and actions that align with the company priorities for the quarter.

But in order to get there we need to start further back. If we jump straight in here then we run the risk of missing something and also the chances are we will set reactive priorities.

What we want to do with any good 90-day planning process is ensure that we do combine current/immediate thinking based on what has recently happened and is currently happening, with a forward view of how we are doing against where we want to get to. To do it well, we should make use of the combined brainpower of the senior leadership team and ensure that we include some time to work on challenges that the business is facing – and in the process help to develop clarity and alignment around the priorities.

I'm going to take you through some of the key elements to consider in developing a 90-day plan. The aim each quarter would then be to review progress on each of the elements and identify any areas that might need working on – so that they can be brought into consideration when we determine our priorities for the quarter.

The business

Last quarter performance

Essentially we are reviewing how we did against our priorities for the last quarter. Firstly we brainstorm what went well and what less so from the last quarter, identifying any issues or opportunities that need addressing including internal and external risks (e.g. perhaps a key person is thinking of leaving, or we have heard that new regulations are coming into force).

These are the sort of questions we should be asking ourselves:

How did the last quarter go?

- Overall, what went well (celebrate), what less so (needs improving)?
- How did we do against priorities from last quarter/performance against KPIs? Review the Balance Scorecard (see KPIs and metrics).
- Where are we against the annual Critical Paths/goals for the year?
- What should we stop, start, continue?
- What have we learned internally and externally? – about the market, our customers, competitors, ourselves, regulations that we need to think about?
- What issues/opportunities or risk/trends need addressing?

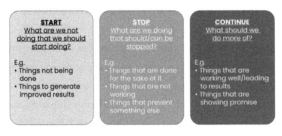

Fig. 14

As part of this, try to identify things that you are doing as a business that you should *stop* doing, things you should *start* doing and things you should *continue* doing. A great habit to get into for all senior leaders and managers is to have at least one of these conversations with an employee every week to help our thinking.

Something else to include here is a review of any emerging trends in your industry sector that might impact your business. For example technology changes (e.g. the rapid move to online working, or the potential return to face to face), or increasing lack of potential candidates due to the pandemic, for example, that might shake up our market.

You can then prioritise them according to the team's views on their likely impact and whether you need to think of strategies to capitalise on them or to mitigate the associated risks. Sometimes you might decide that the trend is outside your control and there is no action other than to keep a 'watching brief'.

So that gives us a view of last quarter internally, and it starts us thinking externally and forward with our trends. We now want to bring in our forward view and check progress against where we are headed.

How are we doing against the plan?

Are we on 'focus'? Use the hedgehog tool (see the 'Strategy' chapter)! Develop it if we haven't done it or review if we have.

What is the key product or service that will be the core focus for getting us to our Smart Stretch Goal – is it still valid and is it scaleable/does it pass the TVR test (see the 'Strategy' chapter): Teachable, Valuable, Repeatable?

What are the key elements of the value proposition? Essentially, what is your brand promise/guarantee; how do you differentiate yourself from the competition?

Make sure we can answer the following from the InFlight Checklist:

2. We have a truly differentiated strategy and scalable business model and all team members can articulate the following components:	SUBTOTAL
The team are aligned with and passionate about the Mission/Stretch Goal (SmartStretch Goal is clearly defined, understood, 'lived' and tracked)	
Our Participation (Markets/Segments) and Positioning (Offer/Cost) Strategies are clear and understood and translate to a demonstrable competitive advantage	
We know where we are on the ScaleUp stepping stones and whether we are in a period of consolidation or striking out for the next stepping stone	
Everyone can give a compelling answer to the question 'What does your company do?'	

Then review our SmartStretch and our 3-year and 1-year goals, thrusts and Critical Paths as developed with our SmartWeb®. Are they communicated to and understood by all the senior managers? Are we still on course, and if not what adjustments or changes do we need to make?

3. The Leadership Team can articulate:	SUBTOTAL
The 3-year 'Thrusts' - the focus areas for the 3-year plan - and progress is tracked	
The 4-9 'Critical Paths' for the next 12 months and progress is reviewed quarterly (the critical things that must be achieved in order to be on track for the 3-year goals)	
The 1-2 focus Value Drivers to increase the value of the business over the next 12 months	
The 'theme' and priorities/business 'rocks' for the current quarter	

Then we want to check on the culture and the Core Ideology:

- How is the team culture?
- Where are we strong?
- Where could we improve?
- Are we actively *living* our Core Values and Core Purpose?

- Which Core Value could we work on this quarter/how do we make it 'real' to everyone?
- What could we do to make sure everyone is aware of it?
- What could we do to make sure everyone understands what it means in their role?
- What could we do to make our customers aware of it?
- How could we build it into some of our core processes?

Core Purpose: define, check – is it still fit for purpose?

Core Purpose is about understanding why you do what you do – not just what you do. It is not a marketing slogan. It should be actively lived along with the values by all employees.

Things to consider from the InFlight Checklist are:

1. Leadership and Vision are strong within the business	SUBTOTAL
The Leadership team understand each other's personality and leadership styles and **all** team members identify one specific leadership/personal improvement habit each 90 days	
Core Ideology (Values and Purpose) are defined, known and made role-relevant by all employees	
Core Ideology is embedded into all aspects of the 'way we do things' (recruitment, onboarding, reviews, feedback etc.)	
A Core Ideology improvement priority is identified and implemented every 90 days	

At this point we would suggest that you review the findings from the InFlight Checklist to identify one or two Strategy, People, Execution or Cash improvement initiatives that you think will make a positive impact on the business if you work on them over the next 90 days.

Team challenge

With all the above, we are using the combined brainpower of the team to generate real insights into areas we may need to improve. The next couple of sessions on the agenda are all about furthering that use of team power to work on a team challenge. Ideally this will have been identified beforehand, or it may have come out of the work done above – but devote some time to solving a team challenge. The person who raised the challenge should lead this – they are the 'owner' of the challenge and should take 'ownership' of the discussion and resulting next steps:

- Define the challenge – in one sentence ('owner' of the challenge)
- The current situation – what is happening now?
- What does good look like/what are the desired outcomes?
- 'Walk the room'/each person gives their thoughts/opinions around the challenge description – *once only* – more than once is politics!

- What are the root causes of the current situation – not just the symptoms (keep asking why!)?
- What information are we missing to move forward?
- How can we move forward – what are some tangible next steps?
- The 'owner' defines the next steps (so they retain ownership of the challenge).

Then there is another similar exercise but this time focused on cash and profitability. Use the Cash Conversion Cycle (CCC)[18] tool and the 7 Financial Levers to identify areas to brainstorm ways to improve the cash position. Which part of the Cash Conversion Cycle and/or which of the 7 Levers is the focus? I'll cover these tools in detail in Chapter 7, Cash.

Determining our 90-day priorities

Now we should be in a good position to develop our 90-day priorities – which starts with the question 'What does good look like in 90 days' time?' or 'When we meet in 90 days, what has to have happened between now and then for us to consider the quarter to be a success?'

These will be a mix of taking a selection (not necessarily all) of the 1-year Critical Paths setting a specific target against them for the quarter, along with identifying any additional priorities, based on looking back at the previous quarter and reviewing performance and lessons learned/issues identified earlier. Ideally a priority should be captured in the form: 'The business needs to achieve x as measured by ...'

There should be no more than 7 priorities, typically around 5 because these should be the really important things. The idea is that we get these done, so we want them to be a challenge but we don't want to overwhelm ourselves into inaction by having too many 'priorities' – this is not a 'to-do list'.

Increasing sales or improving customer service are not well defined priorities; rather consider improving sales from what to what, or what particular aspect of customer service are we improving and how will it be measured. If you have a priority that you think is bigger than can be done in 90 days, then break it down and define what part of it will be done in 90 days.

Critical number for the quarter

You will now have identified a handful of priorities for the quarter. Determine which is the absolute top priority for the quarter and identify a 'critical number' that goes with your top priority and enables you to measure progress. It may be that out of the priorities, there is one that 'unlocks' the others, or when focused on makes it easier to accomplish the others. The idea of the critical number is to be able to measure progress against your top priority – failing all else, this is the one thing that must be achieved this quarter.

Theme for the quarter – make it engaging

The idea of the quarterly theme is to rally everyone around achieving your number one priority for the quarter. Think about how to make the priority and critical number into something more engaging for the team – so that everyone can rally around it. For example, you may decide that improving customer service as measured by feedback scores is the number one priority for the quarter; your critical number might then be your feedback score (perhaps Net Promoter Score). The theme might become 'Delighting our customers' and you might imagine tasking everyone to think of ways in their role to continually delight customers – and if you achieve a certain NPS score then perhaps there is a team celebration for achieving it.

Now let's make it personal!

Now we need to take some time to ensure we include our personal objectives into the thinking – so we will marry up our personal goals and priorities with the company ones.

Take some time now to think about your role – and your team if you manage one. Just like we did with the overall business, consider your annual objectives.

So, in your role as either a member of the team or perhaps a leader of others in your team:

- What are your commercial objectives for the year? What does good look like in your role for the year? You and/or your team may have additional commercial goals to the 1-year Critical Paths identified for the business. This might include a pay rise for example!
- What are your leadership and development goals – what training, perhaps? What development goals do you have for the year – or perhaps your team if you are doing this as team leader on behalf of a team? This might include technical or leadership/management training, for example.
- What are your personal goals – outside of the business? What's on your bucket list?!

You might consider using the Balance Wheel concept we introduce in Chapter 5, People, to help individuals to identify areas for focus to improve their overall engagement and happiness.

You may ask why this is important – well the simple answer is that our business and personal lives are intertwined, perhaps now more than ever. And if we want to feel we are achieving something worthwhile, we need to consider both together. For each of these we need to ask ourselves 'What is the next step towards that goal and when do I want to do it by?'

Now we should be able to pull the personal and business goals and priorities together to develop a handful (no more than 5 but typically 3) of 'rocks' for ourselves and one or two critical numbers for our role. The key question and format is very similar to the company priorities and we are answering the question:

'What does good look like for me in my role over the next 90 days?' or 'When we meet again at the end of the 90 days, what has to have happened for me to consider it a successful quarter?'

The 'rocks' should be written in the form: *I will achieve x as measured by y...*

Also don't forget to include at least one new personal habit and one new leadership habit for the quarter based on your personal goals and next steps.

I covered earlier why they are called rocks, and the difference between rocks, pebbles and sand in business terms (see Chapter 1's 'Habits' section).

If you are completing this with a team in mind, then make sure that each rock is allocated to someone. Generally you will be the one who 'owns' the rock and it will be in the 'Actions' section that you assign responsibilities. The business quarterly priorities identified in the Smart Vision need to be allocated across the leadership team so that there is a named person accountable for each priority. These become a rock for that person. Rocks should link back to the business priorities in some way.

As we did for the business priorities, we should individually identify one or two critical numbers that will define a successful quarter.

Taking action

So now we come back full circle to the importance of taking action – remember the study on this? We need to take the final step to define what we are going to do and when by.

Now we need to turn the 'what we want to do' into the 'how'.

For each rock, everyone needs to identify a few actions that will progress towards achieving that rock – in some instances it may not be you who is responsible for it so identify who is and ensure you remember to brief them!

Each action should be Smart – Specific, Measurable, Accountable, Realistic and Timebound. Remember the six honest serving men!

You don't need to develop a detailed action plan here. If more detail is required (for example a project plan) then this should be identified here and planned separately, e.g. Develop a project plan by the 15th March to launch the new service – Andy. It is then down to Andy to develop that plan with the detail required by the 15th.

The Smart90 one-page plan

As described earlier, this is a framework for capturing and sharing the outputs from the 90-day planning workshop. Described below is the template for it which can be shared electronically or printed out individually. We have developed this approach into our own Smart90® software that facilitates sharing and updating during the quarter so that it is constantly referred to, progress tracked along with any changes needed.

Remember side one is for the business, side two for the individual.

Side 1 – The business

I start top left with the Core Values and Core Purpose – sometimes referred to as the Core Ideology and covered further in the section on Vision in the chapter on 'Strategy'. Essentially this is your 'why'. I mentioned we need a framework to link the why to the actions encompassing long, medium and short-term strategy along the way and this is *why* we need to start here.

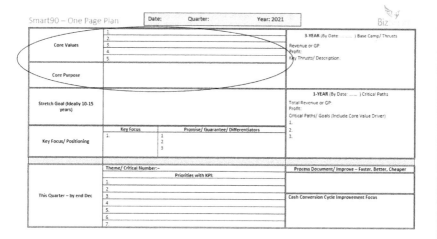

Fig. 15

In order to build a business that at some point is not reliant on you as the business owner, it is essential to define and strengthen the culture of the business so that others have a values framework against which to make decisions without constantly referring to you.

Capturing them here helps, firstly to make sure we have defined them, but then to act as a constant reminder for everyone. It also means that we may at times decide to focus on strengthening a Core Value by including it in the priorities for the quarter.

Core Ideology should not be something that changes – it should be fundamental to who and what we are as well as why we exist in business.

The Smart Stretch, however, is our long-term goal typically set for around 10–15 years' time. Sometimes it's referred to as a BHAG or Big Hairy Audacious Goal. This is our long-term destination – going back to the flying analogy, this is beyond the visible horizon but we know that is where we are headed.

Together with the Core Ideology this makes the company vision and sharing this with the team gives everyone a sense of direction and enables them to be inspired by and buy into the vision.

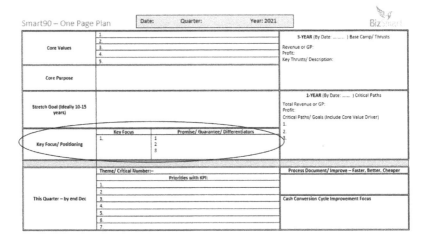

Fig. 16

If your Smart Stretch is to sell out for millions and retire on the beach, this may or may not be something you want to share with the team. So find a stretch goal that you can share!

Fig. 17

And then capture what your focus is – this is essentially your positioning and is a value or experience a company's customers can expect to receive every single time they interact with that company. The more a company can deliver on that promise, the stronger the brand value in the mind of customers and employees. You'll be able to find the detail on the 'hedgehog' exercise in Chapter 4, the Strategy Chapter, in the Plan section.

The reason we want it here is that it is essential everyone understands what that is – it should be the primary focus and driver for growth to achieve your Smart Stretch.

Next I want to move to the top right – the 3-year base camp.

We need a 3-year 'base camp' to aim for that is on the way to our Smart Stretch. These are the 'What we need to achieve' or goals for the next 3 years. At this stage it is the 'What we need to achieve', not the 'Hows'. They come later.

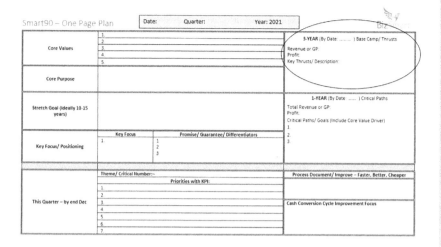

Smart90 – One Page Plan	Date:	Quarter:		Year: 2021			

Core Values	1.
	2.
	3.
	4.
	5.

3-YEAR (By Date: ....) Base Camp/ Thrusts
Revenue or GP:
Profit:
Key Thrusts/ Description:

Core Purpose	

Stretch Goal (Ideally 10-15 years)	

1-YEAR (By Date ....) Critical Paths
Total Revenue or GP:
Profit:
Critical Paths/ Goals (Include Core Value Driver)
1.
2.
3.

Key Focus/ Positioning	Key Focus	Promise/ Guarantee/ Differentiators
	1.	1
		2
		3

This Quarter – by end Dec	Theme/ Critical Number:~	Process Document/ Improve – Faster, Better, Cheaper
	Priorities with KPI:	
	1.	
	2.	Cash Conversion Cycle Improvement Focus
	3.	
	4.	
	5.	
	6.	
	7.	

Fig. 18

If you have completed a 3-year planning process using our SmartWeb® then you will have these already defined. If not then you can make a good start by describing in bullet points what the business needs to look like (at a high level) in 3 years and the key thrusts or priorities, in terms of the key financials but also for example:

- Number/types of employees
- New office locations
- New product launches on stream
- Changing blend of customer types
- Amount of turnover from overseas

By using this approach and that outlined above, we have considered all the key areas we need in order to develop our priorities and targets for the next quarter.

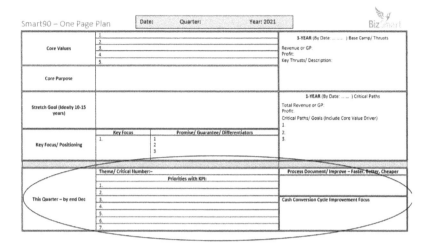

Fig. 19

These will be a mix of taking a selection (not necessarily all) of the 1-year Critical Paths forward/setting a specific target against them for the quarter, along with identifying any additional priorities based on looking back at the previous quarter and reviewing performance and lessons learned/issues identified.

Essentially we are asking ourselves the question again: 'What does good look like at the end of this next 90 days?'

So what do we want to achieve that takes us forward towards our 1-year goals, which in turn is on the way to our 3-year, which in turn is on the way to our SmartStretch?

Remember they take the form: 'The business needs to achieve x as measured by ...'

There should be no more than 7 priorities – these should be the really important things – ideally including a process or two to improve from the InFlight Checklist.

We then need to identify the critical number and the 'icing on the cake' following this is to identify an overall theme for the quarter – based on the Critical Paths and/or perhaps instilling a particular Core Value. This should be something that the whole team can get behind and celebrate when achieved.

Side 2 – The individual

The core of this side of the two-side plan is the Smart Rocks and Smart Actions to go with them – but before we look at those I just want to bring your attention to the column on the left.

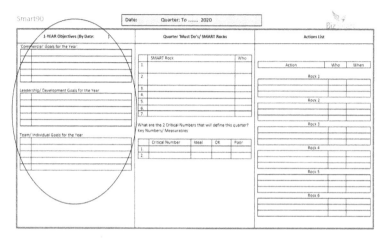

Fig. 20

This is where we capture our personal objectives into the thinking – so we will marry up our personal goals and priorities with the company ones.

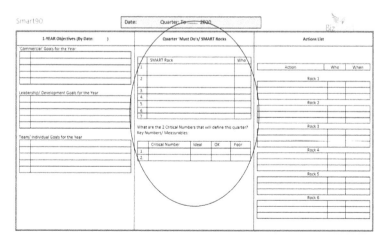

Fig. 21

Now we should be able to pull the personal and business goals and priorities together to develop one or two critical numbers for our role and a handful (no more than 5 but typically 3) rocks for ourselves.

So what does good look like for you in your role over the next 90 days? 'I will achieve x as measured by y...'

Also don't forget to include at least one new personal habit and one new leadership habit for the quarter – see above.

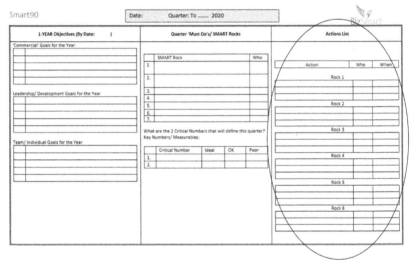

Fig. 22

And finally we capture our actions to turn the 'what we want to do' into the 'how'. For each rock, identify a few actions that will progress towards achieving that rock – in some instances it may not be you who is responsible for it so identify who is and ensure you remember to brief them!

Each action should be Smart – Specific, Measurable, Accountable, Realistic and Timebound.

So that reviews the Smart90 one-page plan and links it in with 90-day planning.

This whole approach is incredibly powerful when implemented properly – and one of the fundamental reasons is that it is the singular best approach to bridging the gap between strategy and execution.

We find some businesses that are excellent at focusing on the execution but lacking in strategy, and we find others that are forever coming up with fantastic new ideas and opportunities – but lacking on follow-through. This approach enables you to build a bridge by aligning everyone around a few key priorities for the quarter that have been developed with an eye on the long-term direction.

Fig. 23

And because it is so important, as already mentioned we have taken it one step further and developed our own Smart90 software to help with developing, capturing and implementing the Smart90 and priorities within the business.

It allows different levels of access for team members so that everyone can have visibility of the business vision and priorities, and to capture and track progress against their individual rocks.

Built into the meeting rhythm of the business, this means that not only is everyone aligned and clear on what is important, but there is a way to help keep each other on track within the 90 days.

You can find further help and guidance on implementing ESUS at www.esusgroup.co.uk. Readers of this book can trial our Smart90 software for 90 days at no cost by visiting www.esusgroup.co.uk or scanning the QR code below and using the code ESUS90.

CHAPTER 4:
STRATEGY

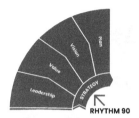

RHYTHM 90

We are now getting into the detail of the first of the 4 Pillars.

Setting the scene for Strategy

Straight away we run the risk of becoming academic – let's avoid that! The word 'strategy' itself conjures up images of spreadsheets, fancy diagrams, lengthy reports and presentations – and can often give us a headache just thinking about what it means. In this chapter we will explain some of these 'academic' terms and show how they do apply and have value in the 'real' world!

So let's cut through the chaff to what is important. Jim Collins[19] has a good view of it: 'Strategy is simply the basic methodology you intend to apply to attain your company's current mission', or in other words, 'This is how we will achieve our mission'. So that tells us that we need to define our mission (which is part of our Vision) and we need to set out how we are going to achieve it.

It does not need to be a wordy document – in fact it shouldn't be. We will show you a 'one-page' tool we call our 'SmartWeb®' that helps develop and capture the essential elements. The important part of developing a strategy is the thinking that goes into it, the buy-in of the team, and that we have captured the key elements somewhere.

In ESUS we break Strategy down into 4 fundamental areas: **Leadership, Value, Vision and Plan.**

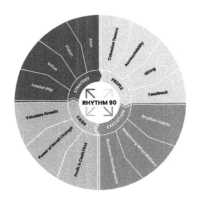

From our own research 53% of owner-managers say they 'don't have a clear strategy that works towards scalability and growth'. What is more, only 7% of our sample have what we would consider to be a truly scalable business model.[20] The reason we look at Leadership and Value first is that these are mindsets that we need to have in order for us to develop (and execute) effective strategy.

During this chapter on Strategy we will look at the key aspects behind each of these. The aim by the end of this section is to have a clear 3-year plan outlined in pictorial form with the Critical Paths for the next 12 months identified so that we can use this to guide our 90-day planning and execution. This chapter will conclude with a checklist and actions.

The key themes and habits relating to strategy that we need to think about from the InFlight Checks® are:

	SUBTOTAL
1. Leadership and Vision are strong within the business	
The Leadership team understand each other's personality and leadership styles and **all** team members identify one specific leadership/personal improvement habit each 90 days	
Core Ideology (Values and Purpose) are defined, known and made role-relevant by all employees	
Core Ideology is embedded into all aspects of the 'way we do things' (recruitment, onboarding, reviews, feedback etc.)	
A Core Ideology improvement priority is identified and implemented every 90 days	
2. We have a truly differentiated strategy and scalable business model and all team members can articulate the following components:	SUBTOTAL
The team are aligned with and passionate about the Mission/Stretch Goal (SmartStretch Goal is clearly defined, understood, 'lived' and tracked)	
Our Participation (Markets/Segments) and Positioning (Offer/Cost) Strategies are clear and understood and translate to a demonstrable competitive advantage	
We know where we are on the ScaleUp stepping stones and whether we are in a period of consolidation or striking out for the next stepping stone	
Everyone can give a compelling answer to the question 'What does your company do?'	

3. The Leadership Team can articulate:	SUBTOTAL
The 3-year 'Thrusts' – the focus areas for the 3-year plan – and progress is tracked	
The 4–9 'Critical Paths' for the next 12 months and progress is reviewed quarterly (the critical things that must be achieved in order to be on track for the 3-year goals)	
The 1–2 focus Value Drivers to increase the value of the business over the next 12 months	
The 'theme' and priorities/business 'rocks' for the current quarter	

If you didn't do it earlier, take a moment to rate yourself/your business on each of the key questions on a 5-point scale where 1=Very weak/'We don't do this', 2='We sort of do this a bit', 3='We're OK but not great at this', 4='We're quite good at this but not perfect', 5='We've got this nailed'

The maximum score would be 20 for each of the 3 key areas and 60 overall for Strategy.

In the subsequent sections of this chapter we will review the understanding behind these areas, starting with Leadership and Value, progressing to Vision and the 'Plan', covering the business model along the way.

LEADERSHIP

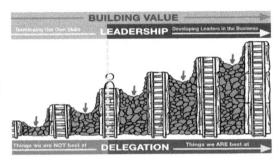

Fig. 24

I'd like to remind you about the ScaleUp Journey introduced in the first chapter. The stepping stones here are based around the number of full-time equivalent people within the business, and we know that when we scale a business, these are the key staging posts at which the business can operate really efficiently. The primary reason for this is teams operate best in units of 3–5 and 8–12 (something that the military learned a long time ago). 3–5 is the minimum size where we see the benefits of collaborative thinking/working and also we do not fall over when one person leaves or is under par. 8–12 is the maximum team size that can still harness the power of collaborative thinking and working without becoming overwhelmed by the increasing complexities of team dynamics, including communication. Remember the Jeff Bezos 'two-pizza' rule mentioned earlier.

We need to think really carefully about how we manage the transitions from one stepping stone to the next because otherwise we can get caught in what are sometimes called the valleys of death in between. The ESUS process is designed to help minimise the depth and length of these valleys, bridging the gap to help ensure that you don't get stuck in between the stepping stones.

So if you think about it, if we build a business with 3–5 employees it can work really nicely as a small team, big enough for good collaboration. But also, if one person is not quite on form we don't drop all the way back to doing everything ourselves as a business owner.

However, it is a different kind of business from if you want 8–12 and so on. We need to have different systems in place; we might need to improve our lead generation, we will have more challenges with communication, and we might need to invest in between. Then there is an even bigger jump up to 20–25 where we start to need to put in place a management team beneath us. So in between each stepping stone we need to make sure we have thought through the specific challenges, but spanning across all of these are the other principles of leadership and value.

Leadership cuts across everything. Early on, it's around developing our own skills as a leader, but around the 8–12 level we need to be developing the leaders behind us within the business. If we can't do that, then we become the roadblock.

So right from the start we need to be delegating things that we're not best at and shouldn't be doing (for most of us that means not doing our own bookkeeping, for example). Beyond the 8–12 level we need to think about delegating the things that we *are* best at, so that we don't become that roadblock.

So what is leadership?

Jim Collins defines leadership as the 'art of getting people to want to do what must be done'[21].

This is a great view of leadership. There are three really important things that will help us in the next sections:

Firstly it is an art not a science, which suggests that there is not just one way of leading that is right or wrong necessarily; we all have a different way of doing it. It is more about developing our own authentic leadership style. Art, like leadership, also develops and grows with practice – which is why it is an art not a science.

Secondly and thirdly it is about getting people to *want* to do the things that *must* be done. So it is not just about telling people what to do, it is about inspiring and aligning people such that everyone believes in where we are heading and wants to get there. We also therefore have to be able to define what must be done which brings us firmly into setting the vision, gaining alignment and then championing or mastering execution. Remember if you want your people to be pulling in the same direction, not only do they need to understand the 'why' of the business, but they need to be able to understand the 'why' of their role and the key activities of that role.

Physician, heal thyself!

If we want to lead others, we first need to be able to lead ourself. And if we want to be able to lead ourself effectively, we need to understand ourself first. You may think this obvious but you will get the kind of business you deserve. Essentially, if you want to build a better business, build a better you...!

If you have not done so already, we would highly recommend undertaking a personality profile. Start with yourself, but ideally you roll this out across your team – we will cover this more in the next chapter, People.

Fig. 25

The starting point is that we all have personality traits. Those traits lead to patterns in the way that we behave and the way that we act. Those actions in turn have consequences that then lead to the results. This is illustrated by Dr. Tom Nebel of GiANT Worldwide[22] and adapted in the diagram above as an infinity loop – because we are never done becoming the best leader we can be.

One of my traits working with business owners might be that I jump to conclusions too quickly and have a tendency to want to make a recommendation straightaway without thinking through all the options. That would be my action, making a recommendation without necessarily having thought it through properly when I am in possession of all the facts.

The consequence is that I may make poor recommendations, or suggest things that have already been tried. I may not have understood properly where the business owner was coming from, and therefore the reality or the result is that we don't actually get a very good outcome, in turn resulting in people not necessarily thinking of me as being very good at my role.

It could be similar with a salesperson. If I just tell rather than listen, then we end up with the same sort of loop.

If I then recognise that trait and understand that I might be better adapting my behaviour and action, I might take a breath and ask more questions first. This ought to mean that I uncover a few more facts and that should mean, in turn, that I make better suggestions and the results are that much better.

So this is a really important concept: to be thinking about knowing ourselves before we can get through to leading ourselves.

The Wiley DISC Work of Leaders Profile[23] (other profiling tools are available!) will provide a further analysis of your leadership strengths and weaknesses against three key tenets of an effective leader: visioning, alignment and execution. Some of us are very good at the blue sky thinking, some are better at the execution part, but bridging that gap is not so easy. Knowing and recognising that we are perhaps not so good at analysing in depth means that we can do something about it – perhaps ensuring that we have a colleague in the team who can plug that gap for us. Equally if we recognise that we have a tendency to be less open to giving praise, we might think of ways we can adapt our approach that fits with our style and remains authentic to us.

Take a look back at Chapter 2, Challenges and the section on personality types and business success and see if you identify with the challenges outlined and how they might vary as the business scales. If you are an S or 'Steady' type characterised by the Dove, then you may need to think about how you build more of a 'hunting' instinct into the business – do you need to adapt or do you need to make sure you have someone that can play that role for you? Similarly if you are that 'Hawk' or D/Dominant type, as you scale beyond a handful of people how are you going to ensure that the team remains cohesive and you are able to inspire and empower people so that they want to achieve the vision for the business?

Delegating the things we are not good at/should not be doing

I mentioned earlier that in the early stages of scaling a business we need to delegate the things we are not good at or should not be doing. We see it so many times with business owners we work with where they are doing too much and not being able to focus on the things that will ultimately make a difference. It is a big challenge, don't misunderstand me, but we need to get ourselves out of having a hand in every function of the business as soon as we can.

Assuming we don't have the luxury of deep pockets to buy in headcount (perhaps through investors) then it will take time – but it is not just about waiting to be able to employ people to take on these roles. There are things we can do in the meantime. If you don't find a way to do this, then you will hit a ceiling very quickly based on the number of hours you can put into the business – and you will burn out. It will not be fun, and you will wonder how on earth you could cope with more business because you are already tearing your hair out. **If you haven't read *The E-Myth* by Michael Gerber[24] then you should do so and think about what he is saying regarding moving from being a technician, to a manager and then to an entrepreneur – which in this context is synonymous with 'leader'.**

Jim Collins also defines five levels of leadership moving from being a Highly Capable individual, through Contributing Team Member, Competent Manager, Effective Leader and what he calls Level 5 Leadership or Executive Leadership[25]. Level 5 is about creating the kind of business that will outlive our term at the helm!

Here is a simple set of steps to help make things easier – not just for you but also as a way of thinking for your team.

1. Does the task need to be done or can we eliminate it? Is it just one of those things we have got used to doing and not thinking about whether it needs to be done at all?

2. Can it be automated? If we need to do it more than once, then spending some time automating it now (maybe with technology), or even hiring someone else to do it, will mean we save a boatload of time in the future.

3. Can it be delegated to someone else?

4. Prioritise what remains in the light of your Smart90 priorities.

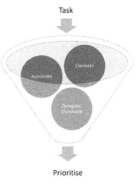

Fig. 26

Two useful frameworks to help

There are two practical things you can do – one is a simple framework, the other is a mindset that goes with the first.

The first is a Teachability/Value matrix and is a simple way of thinking about where you should be spending your time.

Think of all the things you do in your business and plot them on this matrix. If it requires a high level of skill or is difficult to teach to someone else then it goes higher, and on the other axis if it is something that is delivering real value to the business over the long term then it goes to the right. It would be the converse with things of low value and low skill level.

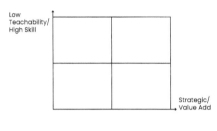

Fig. 27

So if you are doing the social media posts then arguably this is easy to teach/relatively low skill and relatively low strategic value and should go in the bottom left box.

By contrast, setting the vision and purpose of the business, for example, or strategic planning is something that pretty much only you can do and is high strategic value added.

If you do this exercise, you can then prioritise what things you should be getting off your plate and work out the best way to go about it – which could include teaching/delegating to someone else in the team, outsourcing (e.g. bookkeeping/VAT returns), automating or hiring to name a few. Clearly things in the bottom left box should represent the 'low hanging fruit' and are a great place to start.

The mindset change takes us back to habits. You should have the mindset that it is ok not to be seen to be doing everything yourself and the habit you should create is to identify something each quarter that you are going to stop doing/delegate or manage your way out of. This could be a specific task or an entire function – but over time you should be actively removing yourself from day-to-day tasks and you can use the Teachability/Value matrix to help you do that on a quarterly basis.

Over time your role as leader of the business should change as the business itself changes. Recognising this and defining the role that you want to play at the next stepping stone of the ScaleUp Journey is also part of this and will help you to decide which accountabilities you want to keep hold of, and which you don't. We will revisit this in the 'People' chapter when we look at roles and accountabilities.

Delegating the things we are good at/think we are the best at

This is where it gets interesting. To progress beyond the 8–12 employee level we need to be able to remove ourself as the bottleneck – we have to break free from the typical 'owner's trap' where we are the centre of everything and we need to develop leaders 'behind' us. In order to do this we have to find ways to delegate even the things that we think only we can do in the business – or that no-one else could do better. Otherwise we will hit a ceiling.

And this is hard – for all sorts of reasons – and harder for some personality types than others (as explained in the earlier chapter on the challenges). One of these is our fear of losing control and people not behaving and making decisions in the way that we would. From our scaleup research cited earlier, 'Getting staff to think and act for themselves and take responsibility the way you would' was cited as the number one challenge for businesses beyond £500k turnover – cited as a top 5 challenge by 53% of owner-managers with turnover between £500k and £1m, 71% between £1m and £3m, and 82% between £3m and £5m!

The typical advice is to 'systemise' everything – make a process for all the key business processes. This is often referred to as a 'turnkey' or 'franchise' approach. Don't get me wrong, this is a really good thing to do (and you should aim to do it) but it is not the whole answer. And the reason it is not comes down to a fundamental problem described by L. David Marquet[26] in the way that we have been led to believe leaders should behave – that we should be seen to 'take control and attract followers' and that the leader should make the decisions and issue instructions. Whereas what we really need to do is 'give control and create leaders'. By the way, I thoroughly recommend you watch an animated video put together by him. Many of the owner-managers we have worked with have not only found it extremely useful for themselves, but have shared it with their senior teams with great reaction. Just search for 'Submarine Captain David Marquet video' or equivalent!

So how do we create leaders? First of all we need to accept that we have to trust that others want to do a good job and that we need to empower others in the business. But we can't just 'abdicate' everything and expect it to work – we need to provide the environment and framework for people to be empowered effectively.

Culture plays a huge role here and we will look at this further in the section on Vision. David Marquet has a great approach. As a new captain of a new class of nuclear submarine and with an inspection looming, he recognised that the engrained approach of him giving instructions for people to follow simply would not work. So he vowed never to give an order again (with one exception – he kept control of the order to launch missiles!).

He replaced instructions with 'intent'. This starts with knowing the answer to 'What are we trying to accomplish?' This is the intent. Then others say what they intend to do rather than the captain giving orders. 'Captain, I intend to submerge the ship and set course 255 to reach a destination three miles off the coast of Dover', for example.

He set out a three-step approach which, over time, transformed the way the ship ran, leading to the officers thinking like him and in his words creating a team of '135 Thinking, Active, Passionate, Creative, Proactive, and Taking Initiative' personnel instead of one captain and 134 people following instructions.

- Step 1 – Stop giving orders, give intent. This is akin to asking 'What would you do in my shoes?' This can lead to an almost immediate shift.
- Step 2 – Ask 'What do you think I am thinking right now?' – this starts to get others to think in the way you would. For example, 'You want to know if it is safe to dive – yes, the hatches are closed, the submerge alarm is sounded etc etc'.
- Step 3 – Ask 'Is it the right thing to do?' – this is the final longer term step and encourages an understanding of the bigger picture.[27]

In his model of giving control, he is ensuring 'competence' (this is the equivalent of 'Is it safe?') and providing organisational clarity – which is around intent. This is a fundamental component of ESUS in that we need to be able to provide real clarity around long and short-term goals.

You can see the parallels between this approach and the definition of leadership by Jim Collins – the 'art of getting people to want to do what must be done'[28]. There is no easy answer but it starts with self-awareness, understanding what makes an effective leader and then instilling good habits to ensure we constantly improve. If you combine the thinking and approaches outlined in this section, over time you will stand a good chance of building the kind of business that is not reliant on you and your team really are your biggest asset – where they think and behave in the best interests of the business.

The changing role as a leader

Our leadership focus needs to change and evolve as our business scales. Initially it is all about rolling our sleeves up and getting stuck in. There is no real alternative in the early days. But then we need to focus on where we can add the most value. Very quickly we will find ourselves consumed by the business if we don't, so we need to go through some of the steps above to free us up to focus – essentially we specialise within the business and eliminate, automate or delegate the things we decide we should not be doing, or that others can do better.

As we scale even further, we need to change our focus to developing a 'turnkey' business that is not so reliant on us or other key individuals within the business. This is essentially around habits and systems – automated where possible.

As we get beyond the 8–12 stepping stone, we need to be able to delegate even the things we are good at – we need to develop leaders behind us and our role changes to supporting them to do their roles effectively. So we take on a more supportive style of leadership.

Beyond the 40–60 employee level then our leadership focus evolves again to becoming an 'ambassador' for the business – our focus shifts outwards so that we can represent the business on a wider stage.

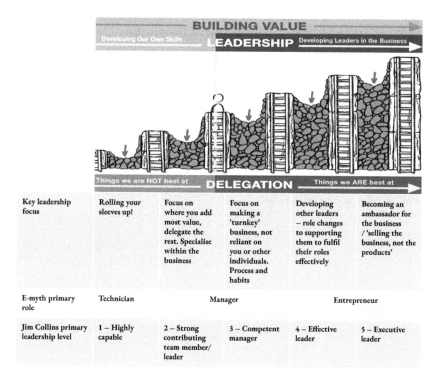

Key leadership focus	Rolling your sleeves up!	Focus on where you add most value, delegate the rest. Specialise within the business	Focus on making a 'turnkey' business, not reliant on you or other individuals. Process and habits	Developing other leaders – role changes to supporting them to fulfil their roles effectively	Becoming an ambassador for the business / 'selling the business, not the products'
E-myth primary role	Technician	Manager		Entrepreneur	
Jim Collins primary leadership level	1 – Highly capable	2 – Strong contributing team member/ leader	3 – Competent manager	4 – Effective leader	5 – Executive leader

Fig. 28

Highly effective people

Before we wrap up on leadership, I want to remind you of Stephen Covey's *The 7 Habits of Highly Successful People*[29]. His thinking has been the basis of many business books and approaches and is well worth a read (or a listen if you prefer audio books). If we are looking for habits we can adopt and embed to be an effective leader, we can do a lot worse than remind ourselves of his 7 habits[30]:

1. Be proactive – the habit of 'Choice' – take responsibility
2. Begin with the end in mind – the habit of 'Vision'
3. Put first things first – the habit of 'Integrity and Execution'
4. Think Win Win – the habit of 'Mutual Benefit'
5. Seek first to understand and then to be understood – the habit of 'Mutual Understanding'

6.   Synergise (uck!) – the habit of 'Creative Co-operation'
7.   Sharpen the saw – the habit of 'Renewal'

I first came across these habits early in my corporate career working for a large pharmaceutical company; it was required reading for managers. It is fair to say that I didn't appreciate the power of these 7 simple habits at the time. It was only much later that I really took the time to think about them and apply them. You may read them and think 'Yep – I get those', kind of 'Well yeah – pretty obvious', but take the time to think about them. If you lead your life according to these habits, and encourage your employees to do likewise, you set yourself on the path to becoming a great leader.

LEARNING POINTS

- Leadership is the 'art of getting people to want to do what must be done'
- It starts with self-awareness before we can 'lead ourself'
- In the early stages we need to delegate the things we are *not* good at/should not be doing – see the Teachability/Value matrix
- To scale we also need to be able to delegate the things we *are* good at/consider ourselves to be the best at and create other leaders in the business
- Creating the right culture for empowerment is what will free you from being the rate limiting step
- Give *Intent* not *Instructions* – review the 3 steps by L. David Marquet
- Stephen Covey's *7 Habits* are a great basis for becoming a better leader (and individual)

ACTIONS

- Undertake a personality and leadership benchmarking exercise to help you to identify your traits, leadership strengths and areas for improvement
- Identify one leadership 'habit' that you are going to embed over the next 90 days in yourself and/or your business to improve leadership

VALUE

A quick reminder that we are in the 'Strategy' section of the ESUS model which is made up of 4 key elements – Leadership, Value, Vision and Plan. The challenge we left you with was 'What new habit are you going to start and embed this quarter to improve either your own leadership or to develop the leadership potentially within others within your business?'

Now we move on to Value.

As a quick recap remember Jim Collins's view of leadership as 'the *art* of getting people to *want* to do what must be *done*'.

Why Value?

Jim Collins also defined 5 levels of leadership[31].

Level 5 leaders create enduring valuable businesses that will last beyond the term of that leader in the business. They are thinking consistently about developing the business to be the best that it can be, for its long-term future, not just about short-term profitability, short-term goals and aims, or how they can benefit most from the business.

These are not egotistical leaders; they often underplay or downplay the part that they play. It is not 'all about me'.

So this is where building for value starts to come in. It is a mindset change – starting to think beyond just simply the day to day and creating profits within the business to creating enduring value. Value and Leadership should frame the way we think and therefore influence our strategic decisions. This is a fundamentally different way of thinking about our business from simply focusing on growth and short-term profits. If you want to scale and build a great business beyond 10 employees then you need to start thinking this way. It will lead to different decisions and sometimes that will mean sacrificing profitability in the short term (and yes, potentially what you can take out of the business) for longer term success and potentially a much bigger pay cheque.

I'm sure you can think of many examples where there might be tension between short and long term and we have seen many ourselves; often it is in businesses under 10 employees that are thinking about making the transition to the next step.

For example, the owners are doing most of the selling and the way they take money out of the business is through dividends – i.e. based on the profits of the business. They know that to scale the business beyond the reach of the two of them they need to take on one or more driven salespeople – but *good* salespeople are expensive (as well as difficult to find) which means that profits will be reduced and likely their dividends. This comes back to the concept of the 'ScaleUp Journey' we introduced at the beginning being a series of stepping stones with 'valleys' in between where profitability is reduced. If we are risk averse (which naturally we become more so when we have more to lose) we may opt for continuing as we are and not building a sales team to take us to the next level.

We've also seen this become a conflict between two owners of different life stages. One was looking to retire in the next couple of years, the other looking to continue to scale the business. The shareholder agreement structured the approach for a leaving director based on a weighted multiple of the last two years' profits. So clearly it was not in the interests of the retiring director to agree to any investments in the business that, although they might be best in the long term for the business, would reduce his payout when he retired. Not surprisingly this led to some difficult conversations!

I was introduced to the importance of building for value when I worked at management consulting company Marakon. Marakon clients were high profile publicly quoted corporations and the core idea was that the best measure of business performance was the total share value (or market capitalisation/company value essentially) growth compared to their competitors. If the company value outgrew the competition then that was the market giving their approval to the strategies adopted by the company.

Now that's all very well with a publicly quoted company – you have a publicly available measure of the value of the business. With small and medium-sized businesses you don't – but there are core principles that do apply and we cover some of these in this section. The thinking behind this has been inspired initially by my time at Marakon and the principles of Value Based Management (VBM) but honed by the excellent work carried by John Warrillow and his team at The Value Builder System™ to make 'value' relevant to owner-managers of small and medium-sized businesses. John has authored three books which are all highly recommended – starting with *Built to Sell*.[32]

The owner's trap

By the way, building a business for value doesn't mean you have to be thinking about selling your business. It is about creating an enduring business, one that is resilient, scalable and one that gives you the freedom and control you are after – and is hopefully enjoyable to run. Yes this will ultimately mean your business is valuable and this will give you options in the future to decide if, when and how you might want to exit your business. (As an aside – we will all exit our businesses one day, whether by choice or not!) Not only that, but if you build your business this way then it will be more 'investable' – one of the top challenges cited in our research by 45% business owners scaling up was that they 'don't or only partially have the cashflow to support scalability and growth'. You may find building your business to the principles outlined below will reduce the need for external cash, but if you still need it then you will be a more attractive investment opportunity, whether it be for debt or equity financing.

Many business owners we work with started their business because they were good at something and they wanted freedom and control – they wanted freedom from having a boss telling them what they should do. They wanted freedom and control to choose the kind of work they did, the people they did it with and ultimately the money they earned. Ideally also a little bit more control over their life, whether it be work–life balance or simply financial freedom.

A lot of reasons for starting a business come down to freedom. But what actually tends to happen is that most of us get caught in something referred to by The Value Builder System™ as the 'owner's trap' because we've created the kind of business that is over-reliant on us as the business owner.

When we start a business, it's generally just us (we may be on our own or perhaps have a co-owner). And we're the ones that do everything including the selling – and we have the most industry knowledge/expertise. We start to work with a couple of clients, and because we are probably good at what we do (maybe making widgets) they come to us even if we have a team. Because we want to please our customers (and pride ourselves on our customer service) when they ask us if we can do other things as well (perhaps tuits – generally round[33])

Fig. 29

we tend to say yes. So we start to extend the range of things we do and we start offering more/too many things. When we start to do that, even if we do actually end up getting other people on board, it's quite possible that we're the only ones that can really deliver all of those things well, so we're the ones that end up delivering and dealing with the customers because our employees do not have the depth and breadth of knowledge that we do. So the customer keeps coming to us, and we keep getting dragged into the delivery.

We probably deliver a great product or service, which means the customer is happy and comes back to us to buy more – so we start the cycle again.

So we're caught in that trap where all of the business or decisions come through us as the owner, and it's very difficult to scale a business like this. There will be a ceiling to how far you can take your business.

How do you know if you are in the trap? Typical signs, even if you've got a few people working for you, are:

- Business slows down when you go on holiday or take time off
- Customers come to you with their problems
- Business growth has plateaued

Businesses that have fallen into this trap create stress for the owner and they also lack inherent value – no-one will buy a business that is overly dependent on the owner.

Now that might sound a bit blunt, but if all the business is reliant on us, why would someone else take the risk of paying you to go and sit on a beach whilst they watch all of the business disappear?

So how do we break this cycle? Well the first thing is to be aware that it exists – which you now are! Then we need to assess ourselves on some key measures that drive value and scalability – and then work on improving them.

We'll outline the key drivers below to give an understanding of the big picture, but it is not in the remit of this book to explore this in depth – rather to understand the principles so that we can include them in our strategic thinking. Further reading should definitely include John Warrillow's books.

With our clients we include the benchmarking exercise[34] developed by John and his team based on more than 40,000 data points from companies around the world and you can do this directly using the link in the endnote or through us[35].

The 8 Drivers of Value

Through their research, John and his team have identified 8 key drivers of value that correlate closely with the value of a business as seen through the lens of an acquirer or potential investor. They are explained individually in this section and are:

1. Monopoly control – what gives you an advantage?
2. Recurring revenue – how much of your income is 'guaranteed'?
3. Customer satisfaction/loyalty – how likely are your customers to recommend you?
4. Hub and spoke – how much is the business dependent on you?
5. The Switzerland structure – how reliant is the business on a key employee, customer or supplier?
6. Valuation seesaw – how long is cash 'tied up' in your business?
7. Financial performance – how robust is your historic financial performance?
8. Growth potential – how much potential is there and can you capitalise on it?

1. Monopoly control

So let's get into it. I always like to start with the monopoly control driver.

Monopoly control concerns how differentiated your business is from the competition – but it's more than just how different you are, it is a measure of the extent to which you have a competitive advantage.

So, do you have something about your business that makes you different? Warren Buffett is famed for only investing in businesses where he says there is a 'wide and deep moat' around them. In other words something about what you do gives you an element of control over pricing and/or profits, because if we're in a business where there is no differentiation, then the only option really left to you is to compete on price. In a situation like this, the chances are you will find that your prices and profits are driven down to the lowest common denominator so the more we can carve out a niche, or a strong positioning for ourselves, that is differentiated, then the better.

In a true monopoly, of course, we are the only ones able to deliver a service or product that people want – so we can dictate our terms. It is unlikely that you will be able to create a true monopoly, but you can work to create elements of 'monopoly control' by careful thinking on your positioning.

Fig. 30

A positioning strategy fundamentally only has two key components that will influence our ability to create sustainable and profitable growth: our participation strategy and our competitive advantage within it.

So if we focus on markets or sectors that are highly profitable we can make strong profits by being 'good' (we hitch our wagon to the right train and enjoy the ride, essentially) – this is our participation strategy – we choose where to compete.

In addition to this (and absolutely vital if the markets we participate in are not so 'attractive'), we need to think about our competitive advantage – which again is made up of two factors – our 'offer' position and our 'cost' position. The first is about how differentiated we are in the eyes of the customer (so that they perceive our offer to be 'better'), and the second is about the way we operate that enables us to deliver the same quality but at a lower internal cost – so we can make higher profits at the same price, or we can afford to undercut our competitors but still make good profits.

It could be that we are in a market where it is hard to differentiate from the offer perspective, for example double glazing windows. It is possible to differentiate to an extent but we know it's a very cut-throat market, so it might be that there's something about the way you do business that allows you to make higher profits at the same price for double glazing units – maybe you are the market leader in volume and you can use your 'might' to buy in bulk and get preferential discounts on your supply, for example. It could be that there's something clever about the way that you operate your production or service company, the way you deliver, that means you can make higher profits. Maybe you're very lean in the way you do things or you have automated key processes enabling you to have higher efficiencies.

The reason that we start with monopoly control is that, frankly, if you haven't got that, it's going to be difficult to get some of the other things to come into place. If we see a 'challenged' business, more often than not, the symptoms can be traced to a poor positioning strategy as the root cause – so it's always worth starting here, really thinking about what can we do that would strengthen our differentiation and really give us a competitive advantage.

And it's not enough just to be different. We can be different in a way that our customers really don't care about – or don't care enough about. In many instances owner-managers think they have a unique selling proposition (USP), but when it comes down to it, they don't have something that translates to a competitive advantage. 79% of business owners in our research believed they have a USP but this has not translated to a competitive advantage in more than half of this number.

If you think about a USP, if it is a real USP that customers care about, then given a choice between your offer and your competitors' the customer will either choose you even if your price is higher, or will buy more of yours relatively if at the same price. So you should either be able to maintain or grow volume market share if you charge premium prices, or you should be able to gain market share (outgrow the market) if you charge comparable prices.

So it's always worth revisiting our positioning and making sure we are confident we have the right participation and positioning strategies – are we:

- Participating in the right markets/segments/niches?
- Truly creating a competitive advantage and is it through our 'offer' and/or our 'cost' position?

If we can develop a strong 'monopoly' control then that will help in many ways, including developing recurring revenue.

2. Recurring revenue

If we want a scalable business that has built-in resilience then the more the proportion of recurring revenue that we have, the better. And before you dismiss this with a 'no s#it Sherlock' there is a big difference between knowing this and really prioritising it.

Firstly let's clear up a common misunderstanding – there *is* a big difference between repeat revenue and recurring revenue. Repeat is income that may re-occur at some point, sometimes predictably, sometimes not. Whereas recurring revenue is income that can be relied upon with almost certainty – strictly speaking a model whereby the customer is signed up to regular payments for a product or service that will continue automatically unless they actively decide to stop it.

A subscription service would be a good basic example – it could be monthly or less frequent payments (e.g. annual), but the point is that it will automatically roll over and continue unless a conscious decision to cancel is made by the customer, as opposed to a decision to purchase again (repeat revenue).

There are different 'hierarchies' of recurring revenue, and the best form is a long-term contract where the payments are essentially guaranteed over a lengthy period of time. You can intuitively see why this has an impact on value and scalability. If I'm looking to acquire your business and you tell me that all of your income is completely ad hoc, there's no guarantee that that will continue when you leave. Even if you tell me that you've grown 20% year on year for the last three years and you genuinely predict it to continue, I would be sceptical. When I've paid you your money and you retire to a beach somewhere, how do I know that the income won't completely stop? On the other hand, if you tell me that 75% of the business is on a recurring revenue basis and the clients are locked in for two or three years on contracts, and also we've got a very high retention rate on renewal, then I've got a lot more confidence that that business is going to continue.

What is more, from a stability and scalability point of view, you will have a high degree of predictability of future income as a 'platform' from which you can think about growth. You can begin to be more confident investing the company's money back into the business or even your own money in terms of growing that business, let alone somebody else's money, because you have created that predictability.

Another common misconception is that recurring revenue models only work in some industries, and therefore by inference not in all. It is true that some lend themselves more naturally and recurring revenue models are more common than in others, such as IT managed services, or HR retainers, but we have yet to come across an industry where it is not possible to create one. Yes it may be harder, and yes it may be that no-one else has done it in your industry, but that only makes it all the more worthwhile focusing on it. If you sell products that don't lend themselves to recurring purchases, it may be that building in a service 'wrapper' around the product will enable you to create a recurring revenue stream, for example.

Going back to the previous section on monopoly control, in order to create a recurring revenue model it really helps if there is something about the way you do business that is different from your competitors and that customers want. In other words, you have a degree of leverage in the buying decision – you have something in short supply that someone wants. Without this it is much harder to persuade people to sign up to some kind of retainer, whatever it might be.

So monopoly control and recurring revenue go hand in hand typically. If you identify what you have 'control' over or can create 'control', then you can think about how that might become a recurring revenue model. So do you have specific expertise/content that is in demand and in short supply, for example? Can you increase control over the repurchase of a 'consumable' by tying the customer in somehow? Can you create demand and control through some kind of exclusivity where clients have to reach a certain 'bar' to get in? Do you have your customers on contracts that provide a degree of lock-in over time?

Even if you are in an industry where subscription services are more common, there may be additional levels you can build on top. Generally around 20% of customers are prepared to pay a premium for 'special' service or features. Figure out what these are and you may be able to develop a whole extra stream of recurring revenue.

Do not gloss over this. It is worth focusing your attention on where you might be able to develop recurring revenue. It will pay you back in so many ways.

3. Customer satisfaction or customer 'delight'

The next driver we'll review is customer service, or more accurately the degree to which your customers rave about what you do. Increasingly customer satisfaction is not good enough; we need to develop raving fans. This is all about delighting our customers.

This might be another one that is easy to dismiss as obvious, so why does this rate as one of the 8 key drivers? In a nutshell, there is a strong correlation between customer delight and future growth rate – so in other words, customer delight is a good predictor of the likelihood of growth.

Intuitively this makes sense; if we have a really high customer loyalty score, the chances are they will come back for more and are also more likely to refer us to somebody else.

So do you really know what your customers think of you? In our experience most of us do not have a process or habit within the business to regularly track customer experience – we tend to base our views on the occasional testimonial or review. This is backed up by our recent research which highlighted that 'customer service' measures only made up 10% of the top reported Key Performance Indicators. Think of it in a way as your customer 'balance sheet'!

So what do you do, or what can you do, in your business to make customer delight measurement a habit? You might carry out customer satisfaction surveys already, but often these are not getting to the crucial question outlined below.

The increasingly accepted measure by businesses large and small all over the world is something called Net Promoter® Score or NPS[36] developed by Frederick Reichheld of Bain Consulting. This has been shown not only to be a really good measure in and of itself, but also a good predictor of future buying patterns. In most industries, Net Promoter® Scores have been shown to explain 20% to 60% of the variation in organic growth rates among competitors. On average, an industry's Net Promoter® leader outgrew its competitors by a factor greater than 2 times. Reichheld also showed that standard measures of 'customer satisfaction' do not have the same correlation and do not explain growth rates. NPS is also a 'harsher' measure than standard customer satisfaction measures, meaning that we are less likely to convince ourselves we are doing better than we really are!

Essentially NPS is really simple – it asks the single question, on a scale of 1 to 10 typically, 'How likely would you be to recommend our ... (company, product or service) to friends and colleagues?' This enables us to separate out three groups, those that are raving fans (promoters scoring 9 or 10), those that are essentially neutral (passives scoring 7 or 8), and those that are detractors (6 or lower). The 'net' bit of Net Promoter Score comes from subtracting the number of detractors from the number of promoters (ignoring the passives). So if out of 100 responses we have 20 promoters and 5 detractors (75 passives), we have an NPS of 15 – whereas our customer satisfaction might well be high 70s or 80 percent calculated as an average. Thinking you are at 15 rather than at 80 tends to focus the mind somewhat!

So we can track this number over time and work on constant improvement – but there is another angle to it: because we now have three groups this enables us to have three different strategies or approaches. We can challenge ourself with how we can make the most of our promoters – how can we use the fact that they love us to our benefit? They should be the ones that are happy to shout about us from the rooftops – so how do we encourage that? For passives we might challenge ourself with how to move them up to being a promoter and for our detractors we might challenge ourself with how to limit the 'damage' as quickly as possible before thinking about potentially moving them up.

How you implement NPS in your business will depend on your specific business. If you have lots of customers transacting frequently online, for example, you may automate it for every purchase. If you are a boutique consultancy it may be more appropriate to do it in person at key stages of the relationship (e.g. end of a project) as part of an account review process.

However you decide to do it, doing it is the thing! Consider it as your customer 'balance sheet' and treat it with the same importance if you want to scale and build value.

4. Hub and spoke

Hub and spoke is a measure of how reliant the business is on you as the business owner. To what degree are you at the centre of the hub? Does everything come through you? If you were to step away from the business, what would happen? Would the business not miss a beat, or would it come to a grinding halt?

We see this a lot in a lot of businesses that we work with – not surprisingly at the earlier stages in particular. For businesses under £500k turnover, 'Getting dragged back into day-to-day operations' was cited as the top challenge, cited by 75% of owner-managers. As the business scales, this is still apparent, demonstrated by the increasing appearance of the challenge 'Getting staff to think and act for themselves and take responsibility in the way that you would'.

This refers back to the 'owner's trap' outlined at the beginning of this section. If there is a high dependency of the business on you, then you become the roadblock to scaling and there will be a ceiling to how far your business can scale. Equally from a potential investor's point of view, if you were to get run over by a bus or were to leave the business, then that's going to leave a really big hole in the business.

Within smaller businesses it is perfectly natural that this happens. As the owner, generally we start off doing everything, but what we need to try and do is to make sure that we gradually take ourselves out of the day-to-day operations. I refer you back to the ScaleUp Journey diagram and the need in the early stages to delegate the things we are not so good at and that distract us from where we can add most value to the business, and then later we need to find a way to delegate even the things we are really good at so that we do not become that roadblock. This was covered in the previous section, Leadership, so take a look back.

You should be actively and regularly looking for ways to delegate things off your 'plate'. If you don't, not only will you not be able to scale, you will also run the risk of burnout and not enjoying running your business. It will become a chore rather than a vocation.

5. The Switzerland structure

So that's the hub and spoke and that's the reliance of the business on you, the business owner. Next is something called the Switzerland structure.

The reason it's called the Switzerland structure is due to Switzerland's famed neutrality. It is viewed as being independent and the relevance is that what we want to try and do is to create a business that is not overly dependent on any one of three key areas, namely on any one customer, supplier or employee. You can imagine why; essentially it is about power and control and where it lies – trying to ensure that the business cannot be put in a position of weakness.

Employees

So let's start with reliance on key employees because we've just considered hub and spoke and the degree of dependence on you. Now we are considering the degree of dependence on any key employees that you have. How much would the business be affected if they were to leave the business? What impact would that have on the business? We need to identify key employees and then how to mitigate the dependence, typically by considering three things: how can we make it so that they would never *want* to leave, how can we make it so that they would have something to *lose* if they did, and finally what is our *contingency* plan for if they did? However good we are at the first two, there will always be times when we need the third – perhaps illness or just life circumstances get in the way.

Customers

Secondly within the Switzerland structure is the degree to which we are over-dependent on one or more customers. The golden rule here is that if you've got any customer that represents 15% or more of your turnover and/or profits then that's a little bit too high and reduces our resilience or increases our risk. Ideally, of course, what we want are thousands of relatively small customers meaning we really are not reliant on any individual customer – so if we lose one customer it doesn't make any impact really on the business. Clearly the opposite is true if we have the kind of business where we have a small number of large customers. So what's the situation in your business? If you do have that over-reliance, what sort of things can you do around reducing it? We generally don't want to reduce the turnover from that customer (unless we are providing non-core products and services to them), so how can you focus your efforts to maybe bring up levels within other customers? We see this often where a business landed a big customer and has then grown within that customer (for example other divisions), or the customer itself has grown rapidly and taken the business along with them. This is great of course for a while and can be the way that many businesses get started and grow – but we need to be aware of the increasingly precarious position we are creating for ourselves if we don't look to balance out our revenues. It is almost guaranteed that we will lose our biggest customer at some point – it could be next week, it could be in ten years' time, but it will almost certainly happen.

Suppliers

The final element of the Switzerland structure is any over-reliance on any one key supplier. You might have some strategic suppliers (ones that you need to be able to deliver your product or service) where, if they were to decide either to stop supplying you or to hike up their prices, you would be 'over a barrel'. It might be a particular piece of software, for example, that is integral to your business, or it might be a key component of something you make. What would be the impact on your business if there was an issue with the supply? The business world changes at a pace and there could be many reasons why your supplier may want to change terms, or have a problem themselves. Brexit has caused many such issues, as has Covid, but it could also be things like getting acquired and the new owner taking the opportunity to change terms. So it is good practice to review your supplier relationships at least annually and to look for alternatives in advance (not when you are desperate).

So those three elements make up the Switzerland structure. You can see they are all about mitigating risks – essentially making your business more resilient and helping you to keep moving forward from a stable platform.

6. The valuation seesaw

So far we have managed to have a discussion around value and scale without discussing money! The valuation seesaw is where we start to bring the cash discussion in. This is around cashflow and Cash Conversion Cycle in the business. We look at this in more detail in the chapter on 'Cash' but essentially this is about when the money comes in and goes out in the business. This leads to the idea of cash being tied up in the business – often called working capital. If the working capital requirements of a business are high, then a potential investor is going to factor this into how much they think the business is worth, because essentially they will be making two transfers, one to the owners and one to the business to keep it running – hence the seesaw.

Cash gets tied up in a business if there is a significant lag between when we start investing time and money into a client vs. when we get paid. This is easy to imagine in a manufacturing business where we might have to pay upfront for raw materials and wait for them to be shipped before we can turn the materials into our finished product, and before we can even think about selling and invoicing let alone collecting the cash into our account. But it also affects service businesses – the moment we start our sales cycle with a client we are investing time and money. We then have to provide whatever service it is we offer (committing people's time) typically before we can invoice. And then we may have to wait 30, 60 or even 90 days before we receive the money.

This is what is called a 'negative' cash cycle, where we do the work upfront before we get paid. This means that the more sales we make, the more we have to fund that gap – or the bigger the 'hole' gets in our finances. From a scalability perspective this acts as a brake on growth and there are many examples of businesses that go out of business even though their Profit and Loss statement looks good. You may have heard of the term 'overtrading'.

So if we have that kind of cycle, what can we do to 'balance' the seesaw? It may not be possible to completely reverse the cycle and get paid fully upfront, but there will be a number of things you could do to move towards balance. If we go back to the idea of recurring revenue, if you have a recurring revenue model then essentially you know you're getting regular payments, and often they are in advance – another reason why the hierarchy of recurring revenue is so important.

7. Financial performance

If we're looking at value in a business, then clearly our financial performance is really key. And this particular aspect is around our historical financial performance. Similarly if we are looking to scale, then we have to have a business model that generates cash in a way that we can scale. Taking a poorly performing business and expecting growth to make it wonderful is unrealistic unless we really understand our numbers and why increased volume will lead to improved financials. Growth is generally not the saviour for a rocky business any more than having a child is the answer to a rocky marriage!

Understanding our numbers is key. We do look at this in much more detail in the 'Cash' chapter and being able to understand your numbers and being able use your financials to make good decisions is paramount to being able to scale. It is one of the key weaknesses of owner-managers; if you want to scale then make sure you understand your numbers.

Think back to the ScaleUp Journey and the stepping stones. Imagine a ladder up against each stepping stone – we should aim to climb each ladder to the top before starting the journey to the next one. If you can't make your business work at the 3–5 employee level, what makes you think it will work at the 8–12? So focus on making the business as profitable as possible, get the model right, and understand how the numbers will change as you move to the next stepping stone, *before* you make the move.

From a potential investor's perspective, they are going to want to see a good financial 'story' for at least the last three years – preferably strong year-on-year growth in turnover and profits. This gives a certain degree of confidence that the future growth will be strong also, as opposed to what is often referred to as a 'hockey stick' projection where historically performance has been poor, but we 'forecast' things to magically get better next year!

This expectation will depend somewhat on your stage in the business cycle – so if you are in a rapid growth phase investing in capturing market share, there will be an understanding that your profitability may be lower, but equally if your growth rate is dropping off then you would expect your profitability to be increasing. As you transition the valley from one stepping stone to the next, your profitability will likely dip, but then as you climb the next ladder the profitability needs to increase. This introduces the idea of phases as you scale: after each milestone journey between stepping stones, there should be a period of *consolidation* where you focus on profitability through productivity, before you embark on the next *investment* phase to take you to the next stepping stone.

We build on this idea in the 'Cash' chapter. For now, take away the need to understand the numbers behind how your business works – where and how you make profits – and the need to ensure you have got things working as well as possible before you strike out for the next stepping stone.

8. Growth potential

And that brings us then to the final consideration around value, which is the future growth potential – what are the key opportunities for growth and how well placed are you to be able to capitalise on them? To scale we need to understand and prioritise those opportunities, and we need to find a way that we can capture them as quickly as possible, overcoming key constraints. To scale properly we need to be able to take on additional customers at a faster rate than we take on cost – e.g. employees.

So ideally we have a huge untapped market that needs our product or service, and we don't have to do much extra work for each new customer we acquire! The opposite of that would be that we have dominated our market niche and there is hardly anybody left to sell to (and for the sake of argument there are not any other niches we could enter) or that the untapped market is huge but we are held back by something limiting our ability to scale – such as a severely restricted supply of materials, or specialist labour. Unless we can find a way to overcome these then our ability to scale is severely restricted.

A potential investor will look at it in the same way; they want to see the future potential of the business because they want to be able to see how they make a return on their investment. So lack of demonstrated growth potential will significantly impact the value of a business.

So that's a quick whizz through the 8 Drivers of company value identified by The Value Builder System™, but as I said right at the very beginning, it's not just about value or selling your business, it's about creating a scalable and resilient business. Many of the drivers are around mitigating risks within the business, creating stability and confidence from which we can scale – a little like the foundations of a building or the story of the three little pigs.

If we manage this then we will have created a business that is more predictable, easier and more fun to run and more likely to be able to scale, and ultimately, we will have created a business that somebody else might want. That is what gives us the value within the business and gives us the options for when we decide to exit.

All of these drivers are important to have in mind as we scale. The relative importance will change according to the business and stage, but as a rough guide the diagram below illustrates how the key value driver focus changes as we scale. Financial performance and the valuation seesaw, along with the customer score, are priorities at all times!

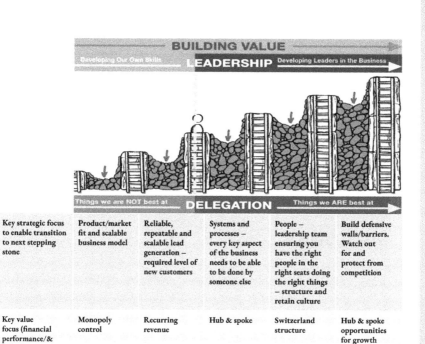

Key strategic focus to enable transition to next stepping stone	Product/market fit and scalable business model	Reliable, repeatable and scalable lead generation – required level of new customers	Systems and processes – every key aspect of the business needs to be able to be done by someone else	People – leadership team ensuring you have the right people in the right seats doing the right things – structure and retain culture	Build defensive walls/barriers. Watch out for and protect from competition
Key value focus (financial performance/& valuation seesaw & customer score all through)	Monopoly control	Recurring revenue	Hub & spoke	Switzerland structure	Hub & spoke opportunities for growth

Fig. 31

LEARNING POINTS

- Adopting a 'value' mindset will enable you to make superior strategic decisions and escape the 'owner's trap'
- There are 8 fundamental principles to building a scalable, resilient and ultimately, valuable business

ACTIONS

- Review your business against the 8 Drivers (if you would like to benchmark your business against your peers then contact us at admin@biz-smart. co.uk, or visit esusgroup.co.uk)
- Identify one driver that you think would make the most impact on your business if you worked on it – include it in your next 90-day plan
  - Brainstorm/identify key actions

VISION

It is easy to get confused with terminology around vision and mission statements if you read around the subject. We will keep it simple and recommend the Jim Collins approach where Vision is made up of three components: Core Ideology (Core Values and Beliefs), Core Purpose and Mission[37].

Core Values and Core Purpose together make up our core 'ideology' and define what kind of business we are and how we behave – essentially our culture – and what drives us[38].

Together they give the business a set of guiding principles and the fundamental reason for the business's existence. They are the 'essence' of the business and act as our 'North Star' – they should last 'forever' and not be subject to change, whereas our Mission is the next big strategic objective (typically a 10–15 year horizon) or what we **envision** our desired future to look like (our Envisioned Future).

Fig. 32

Together these make up our Vision for how we want our business to be and where we want to get to.

If you are going to work on your strategic plan, you need to have a strong Core Ideology to frame your decision making.

Core Ideology

You may be tempted to skip this step in the mistaken belief that you need to get to something more tangible – don't.

If someone had come to me in my early days of business and said, 'Kevin, let's go and do an exercise on Core Values', I would have told them, politely of course, that 'I was too busy with getting the work done to talk about that kind of stuff'.

However, the longer I've been in business and the more businesses we have worked with, it is clear that those with a strong sense of Core Values and Core Purpose are the ones that succeed over time and go further than the others. It is not that surprising when you think about it – think of people you know (not necessarily in business) and I am sure that there are a few that come to mind that you would say are driven – that have strong values/ standards and have a real sense of direction. Equally you will know some that aren't and don't. Which ones achieve success or seem to make things happen?

The single most common challenge cited by owner-managers scaling businesses beyond £500k was: 'Getting staff to think and act for themselves and take responsibility in the way you would'. Processes may help but if you really want to empower people (and you should) then you need them to have a set of guiding principles. When faced with a difficult decision, rather than running to you, you want them to be able to think what you would do – and a great set of Core Values should do exactly that.

In the Leadership section we discussed giving *intent* rather than *instructions*. Your value framework is the organisational clarity David Marquet was referring to that enables this to happen without chaos!

However, it is no good paying lip service to Core Values – we have to do them properly in the first place and then we have to make sure that the business lives these Core Values.

You will have heard of and seen businesses that have mission statements and value statements on the walls in reception. This is ok, and part of making Core Values work is communicating them and making sure everyone is aware of them. But it is more than that – we need everyone to buy into the Core Values and to incorporate them in how they work day to day.

Realistically you are not going to jump overnight from a blank piece of paper to an organisation where everyone lives and breathes a core set of values – but you can make a start and you can work on honing and embedding over time.

In a young business, our Core Ideology may evolve over the first few years as the business 'grows up' – but then we are looking to set them in stone.

We build this into ESUS in the 90-day planning, looking to identify an improvement initiative each 90 days.

We want to rate ourselves on how well Core Values and Core Purpose are lived by the business and the relevant questions from our InFlight Checklist are:

- Core Ideology (Values and Purpose) are defined, known and made role-relevant by all employees
- Core Ideology is embedded into all aspects of the 'way we do things' (recruitment, onboarding, reviews, feedback etc.)
- A Core Ideology improvement priority is identified and implemented every 90 days

So if we don't have our Core Values defined, then that would become a priority for the next quarter. If they are defined but not known very well by the team, then we might focus on communicating them that quarter and ensuring everyone understands what they mean in their role.

What makes a good set of Core Values?

What you are looking for is a behaviour or something you think as a business that you stand for or that is fundamental to the way you do business and the kind of relationship that you have with your clients. What are you known for or think you should be known for? You are looking for a handful of Core Values (typically 3–5) that define the business's culture and personality – and help everyone in the business to test 'should/shouldn't' for all behaviours.

Ideally it should be an 'intent' statement rather than just a noun – so if you have a noun ('thing'), add a verb ('doing word') to make it more of an action statement.

So it could be that you 'Treat all customers and staff with respect/as you would wish to be treated yourself' rather than simply 'Respect'.

Core Values are not necessarily about differentiation but if there are things that you do that are different from your competitors then they should come out here. Some of these behaviours will be to do with how you treat customers (external), some with how you treat staff (internal) – many with both.

The following questions may help:

- What does your organisation stand for?
- What do you want to be known for?
- What do clients say about you/what do you want them to say about you?
- What are you passionate about?
- What kind of behaviours do you hate?!

The values can be a short phrase – ideally not one-worders and ideally describing behaviours. The important thing is to define what each means to give it a level of richness.

Here are some examples from two well-known global companies (they have more than 3–5 but no-one's perfect!) and one medium sized:

Google has a list of 10 company values called 'Ten things we know to be true':[39]

1. Focus on the user and all else will follow.
2. It's best to do one thing really, really well.
3. Fast is better than slow.
4. Democracy on the web works.
5. You don't need to be at your desk to need an answer.
6. You can make money without doing evil.
7. There's always more information out there.
8. The need for information crosses all borders.
9. You can be serious without a suit.
10. Great just isn't good enough.

Uber's company values are listed below. Note the short 'descriptor' on their website which is also backed up by a descriptive paragraph:[40]

1. Go get it – Bring the mindset of a champion
2. Trip obsessed – Make magic in the marketplace
3. Build with the heart – We care
4. Stand for safety – Safety never stops
5. See the forest and the trees – Know the details that matter
6. One Uber – Bet on something bigger
7. Great minds don't think alike – Diversity makes us stronger
8. Do the right thing – Period

There's a great blog by the CEO of Hotjar[41] on company values and their journey along with how they applied them in the business. He describes how they evolved to the five they have today and how defining them helped them with their recruitment and quarterly evaluations. We'll return to this in the 'People' chapter and look at including Core Values in recruitment and evaluation.

Hotjar's refined 5 Core Values are:

1. Obsess over our users
2. Be bold and move fast
3. Work with respect
4. Build trust with transparency
5. Learn by doing

With these examples from Google, Uber and Hotjar it is easy to get an instant feel for the culture of the business. You can also see how the values act as a guide as to how to behave, respond and act in all sorts of situations. Not only that, you should be able to see how interview questions could be crafted to identify 'right fit' candidates and how they could form part of an evaluation process.

Defining Core Values should be a team exercise – although it needs to be led by you/the founders as they should represent an extension of your personal values. There are many ways to go about it but it need be no more complicated than a simple Post-it exercise where team members are asked to think individually first, then share and work together to group them and refine the meanings. They can then be 'tested' by the group to determine whether they really are *Core Values* (not just nice sounding phrases) that you believe will stand the test of time. Jim Collins has a great set of questions to test your Core Values.[42]

In order to ensure that your business lives these values and that they really become and remain your culture, you as the leader must go beyond posting them on the wall in reception. You have to make sure that they are embedded into the habits of your business. Think particularly in recruitment and onboarding, appraisals and recognition, internal (and external) communications (e.g. newsletters) and in quarterly themes and feedback.

What makes a good Core Purpose?

Core Purpose is about understanding why you do what you do, not just what you do. Simon Sinek also refers to it as 'start with why' and you can find his TED talk online.[43]

A strong Core Ideology is absolutely fundamental to long-term success. You need to have identified and be able to articulate why you do what you do. It should derive from your Core Values – which is why we started there. There should be something in your Core Values that leads you to your Core Purpose.

A good Core Purpose will help you to rekindle the passion you have in what you do and help with focus – it should be something that you are passionate about and the reason you get out of bed each morning to do what you do – but it will also do two other things:

- It will help you to think outside the box and identify other things you can do that support your Core Purpose – so it will help you to think expansively about things you could do
- It will also help you to focus and reject ideas that do not fit with your Core Purpose

A number of years ago I was a director of a medium-sized business (£35m) that provided home care delivery services to chronically ill people under hospital care but living at home. Fundamentally we were a logistics company delivering high value critical medicines to patients at home.

Our revenues were based on contracts with hospital trusts and margins were under increasing pressure. In the early years we were able to charge a percentage of the value of the medications but the model was changing to a fixed fee per delivery.

We took time out to do the exercises on Core Values and Core Purpose. We looked at what we did but asked ourselves why we did it – and we came to the conclusion that what we were passionate about/the reason we were in business was to *help avoid unplanned or unnecessary admissions to hospital'*. After all, the patients we delivered to had serious long-term conditions that if not managed well would mean that they would end up back in hospital – something that the patients and families didn't want but also something that the hospitals were keen to avoid because unplanned admissions are very expensive.

Once we started thinking this way it led us down the path of asking the reasons for unplanned admissions and what we could do to help avoid them. Many of the reasons came down to not taking the medications correctly – which of course could be down to not having them delivered on time but also forgetting, not understanding how and why there was a need to take them and a number of other things. So we developed a range of reminder and adherence or compliance programmes to help patients and their carers to make sure that the medications were correctly administered at the recommended time and frequency. Of course we needed to consider who would pay and we found that hospitals and the pharmaceutical companies were keen to support these kinds of services.

So we expanded our range of services to higher margin services where margins were not being constantly squeezed – and it started with asking 'why' we do what we do.

If you think through defining your Core Purpose properly and give it the thought it deserves, you may well have some real 'light bulb' moments. It will also give your team – both current and future – a real sense of purpose in what they do rather than just turning up and working their hours. When things get tough and we come up against obstacles in our path – which happens at times for all of us – it helps provide motivation to find a way through or around.

We did this exercise for a telephone call minding service and agreed on their Core Purpose of *'Making the right first impression for our customers'* – simple but powerful. Everything they do is about that – so they can develop processes and procedures to make sure this is what they do – and they could measure it also. They could include it in their staff evaluations and they also then built it into their recruitment process – holding the first interview over the telephone and deciding very quickly if the candidate was able to make a good first impression, before progressing to a longer second step. It also helped them to think about areas that they might not want to pursue, such as admin services, unless directly linked to creating an impression with the clients' customers.

The simplest exercise to get the root of your Core Purpose is the well-known '5 whys' exercise that can be applied to all sorts of challenges. Essentially it involves asking what it is we do and then asking 'why?' or 'so what?' Once we have that answer, we ask 'why?' again and continue until we get to the heart of your Core Purpose – usually 5 times is sufficient!

For example with the home care delivery service outlined earlier it might go something like this:

What do we do? We deliver critical medications (meds) to patients at home under the care of their hospital consultant/secondary care team.

Why is that important? They need to have received their meds otherwise they can't take them.

So what/what happens if they don't take their meds? They are likely to relapse and become worse.

So what/what happens if they relapse? They might need to be rushed into hospital because these are generally serious conditions.

Why is it bad if they have to go to hospital? It could have serious consequences for the health of the patient – death at the extreme!

Why else is it bad? Unplanned admissions are really expensive for the NHS to manage – and it also isn't great for the manufacturer of the medication as it reflects poorly on the evidence as to whether the treatment works.

And this is essentially getting us to the point where what we are about is 'avoiding unplanned admissions into hospital'.

It is important to think long term with your Core Purpose. This is something that should remain true pretty much forever, so don't limit it to a particular technology or similar.

So a good Core Purpose should help you think 'outside the box' about things you could do, but at the same time help you to know what you don't do – Steve Jobs was quoted as saying 'Deciding what not to do is as important as deciding what to do'!

So both the examples given above help us think about all sorts of possibilities, but they also provide guide rails so that we can easily reject ideas that fall outside.

One of my favourite examples of a Core Purpose is 3M's 'To solve unsolved problems innovatively'[44]. I love it for all sorts of reasons:

- It links back to their values – innovation clearly being one of them ('collaboration, innovation, perseverance, passion for change, integrity, and honesty')
- It is 'expansive' in that it does not limit 3M to a particular industry or sector
- At the same time, it tells us that they are only interested in 'unsolved problems' – so they are only going to enter a market if there is an unmet need (they are not going to be a 'me too' product)
- When they look to provide a solution, it will be innovative
- It gives a strong indication of the likely culture within 3M – and indeed they provide opportunities for and reward innovative thinking

So in the same way that we tested our Core Values, we should do the same for our Core Purpose. It needs to be authentic and inspiring as well as something that can stand the test of time. As before, Jim Collins has some great questions to test your Core Purpose.[45]

Within ESUS and the 90-day planning, we want to make reference back to our Core Purpose and remind ourselves of it, check it is still 'fit for purpose' and use it to guide our priority setting.

Mission/Envisioned Future

The final piece of the Vision is our Mission. We refer to this as our 'Smart Stretch'; Jim Collins refers to it as the BHAG or Big Hairy Audacious Goal. It takes the Core Purpose (our 'North Star') and picks a point we are aiming for and by when – typically 10–15 years but it does not have to be. The important point is that it is a specific 'destination' with an 'ETA' rather than just a direction. It is the bridge between our Core Ideology and our Plan – it becomes the guide for our mid and short-term plans.

Mission is one of those words that is used in different ways in the business world. You will find various definitions and examples of Mission Statements that have some mix of Core

Purpose, Values and Smart Stretch, and often these can be 'grand statements' but with little substance. Looking at it in the way we have described will link them all together and form part of your 'narrative' in a way that makes logical sense, that starts with the 'forever stuff', what defines and guides us as a business and makes us who we are, what drives us in what we do and where we are aiming for as our next big milestone. This in turn then enables us to put a Plan together to get us there – with everything aligned in the same direction – providing a cohesive narrative throughout.

The relevant check from the InFlight Checklist is:

The team are aligned with and passionate about the Mission/Stretch Goal (SmartStretch Goal is clearly defined, understood, 'lived' and tracked)	

So it needs to be clearly defined but also something that we can all get passionate about – something that everyone can feel they would love to play a part in helping to achieve.

And it needs to be a 'stretch' but not so much so that no-one really believes it is achievable.

As a reminder of what we are doing here, we are starting out with the long term and step by step bringing it back to the day to day – each time with a little more detail. In this way we can ensure that everything we do, every tactic that we implement, will be taking us a step closer to where we want to be in the long term. We can also turn our vision into a plan as opposed to just having a dream.

So we are working backwards from our Core Ideology, through our 10–15 Smart Stretch, and then in our 3-year plan and then to the next 12 months.

So – where do you want to be in 10–15 years?

Actually it is not so important whether it is 10 years, 20 years or even 7 or 8 – what is important is that we can see it as a point in time that is important to us and that it is far enough ahead that we can consider things without what is happening today in the business constraining our thinking.

So if you know that in 12 years' time you will be 60 and you want to retire on a beach in the sun – or on your 90ft yacht – then that is the moment you should pick. If you know that you are aiming for a business sale in 8 years then let's pick that horizon. If you do this exercise with your senior management team, you may not say why you have picked 12 years if you are thinking of selling (although arguably you may) but you can still pick the time horizon.

It can be a little tricky to define a good Smart Stretch immediately, so a better place to start is to describe what we want the business to look like at that point in time. Just bullet points – we don't need to write an essay.

Try this exercise proposed by Collins and Porras.[46] Ideally do it with your senior team if you have one – or with your business or life partner or someone else that's important to you.

Individually to start with, imagine a journalist has written an article about your business. Who do they work for; is it a local, regional, national or international publication or other media – either specific to your sector or to business or to general news? What is the publication called? This is great because it helps to establish the scale of the ambition.

Next, imagine what they have written and start to make notes of the key points – bullet points are fine. Are they writing about a specific event, for example a business sale or acquisition or merger, perhaps a relocation or the opening of the hundredth site, or recruitment of the hundredth franchisee? Could it be that the business has won some highly prestigious award in your sector or for something like customer service or is simply that you have reached a milestone in turnover or customer numbers/market share or similar?

What are the key things they are saying in the article?

- What are you known for?
- What milestones have you reached?
- What awards have you won?
- What do your employees think of working there?
- How big are you (turnover, staff)?
- What kind of customers have you got and how many?
- What kind of products and services are you providing?
- Where are your offices/premises; are they owned or leased...?

And any other relevant things you can think of that might be specific to your business and market.

The next step is to pool each other's thoughts and agree a set of 'descriptors'. Agree as a group the top few ideas (it may be five or so) and add a little more information so that they become real and you can really imagine how they look – and then these become your vivid descriptions.

So now you should have a great image of the future business – one that you can picture in your minds and one ideally that the team has shared in, are passionate about and are committed to.

Now we reach the last part of the Vision – we need to set ourselves a Smart Stretch – or BHAG. This is not some small easy to achieve goal like increasing sales by 10% – nor is it some ridiculous unachievable goal. It needs to be something that at a stretch, with effort, focus and perhaps a fair wind, we think we stand a 50 to 70% chance of achieving in the time frame of our vivid description.

Now this shouldn't be too hard. We've done the thinking and the likelihood is that it will be one of our snippets we have already written down in our vivid description. We may need to tighten it up and make it a bit more specific – but it should be there. If you come up with something else entirely then perhaps your vivid description thinking wasn't complete enough.

Your Smart Stretch should also link back in some way to your Core Purpose – so you can start to see how these all work together and they should be aligned.

There are many types of Smart Stretch; it does not have to be based around turnover for example. The key thing is that it needs to be something all of the team can get passionate about and that you can know when you get there – remember it needs to be a destination so it needs to be specific.

A Smart Stretch can be numbers based or more qualitative; it can be competitive or aspirational – so a target-based, competitive or role model example could be:

- Become a £xm turnover business with y% net profits by end of year z
- Build a business that could be sold for £5m by x
- Take 10% market share from our leading competitor by ...

- Become number 1 or number 2 in our key market sectors ...
- Become seen as the 'Rolls Royce' of the catering equipment industry in the UK

Any of these types of Smart Stretch are good – what is important is that you and the team are absolutely behind it and that there is a way to know if you have got there or not!

What we normally do at this stage is document the Vision in a simple table like this one below – showing the Core Ideology on the left hand side and the Envisioned Future on the right. This can then be something that is built into our planning and execution and referred back to and progress is tracked against it on an ongoing basis.

Business X	
CORE IDEOLOGY	**MISSION**
Core Purpose	SmartStretch/Long-term aim/10 years
Helping customers be distinctive and enhance their image with timeless products that stand out from the crowd through their beauty and individuality	To be seen as a market leader in Aluminium Caravan production and distribution
Core Values	Vivid Description
Excellence/Quality • Right from early beginnings • Premium product • Customer service to match – from start to finish **Loyalty/Commitment** • Internally of workforce to values/growth plans and of leadership to workforce • Externally – providing good product and service, generating customer confidence/enthusiasm **Profitability/Growth** • Sufficient profitability to fund growth from within • Sustainable growth – new markets and products • Constant evaluation of profitability **Creativity/Innovation** • Ahead of the game • Spotting needs/creating market trends • New ways of doing things • Involving team in 'ideas' creation	**We will ...** • Be known internationally amongst target groups for creating timeless products that stand out through their beauty and individuality • Be market leaders in building aluminium caravans • Be known for our superior products and excellent customer service • Be operating globally through dealer/distributor networks with production/finishing centres in key continents • Operate from custom individual premises in Worcestershire combining production and showroom facilities • Be highly profitable and attractive to external investors

Fig. 33

So now we have a really powerful vision. We understand our core culture (our ideology), we know our values and our purpose, and we have envisioned where we want to be in 10–15 years' time and described how our business will look at that point.

Now we have to make a plan to make it happen – and this will require focusing on the right things and setting ourselves a 3-year 'base camp' with an action plan to get there that will enable us to continue onwards and upwards to our Smart Stretch. We'll start on that next!

LEARNING POINTS

- Vision is made up of three components: Core Ideology (Core Values and Beliefs), Core Purpose and Mission.[47]
- These are not 'optional' to your business!

ACTIONS

- Use the InFlight Checks to identify a focus around Vision and develop appropriate actions
  - Spend time reviewing and undertaking the exercises suggested
  - Establish how you are going to make them 'alive' within your business

PLAN

RHYTHM 90

By the end of this section the aim is to have a clear 3-year plan outlined in pictorial form with the Critical Paths for the next 12 months identified so that we can develop 90-day priorities and actions.

The relevant checks from the InFlight Checklist are:

2. We have a truly differentiated strategy and scalable business model and all team members can articulate the following components:	SUBTOTAL
The team are aligned with and passionate about the Mission/Stretch Goal (SmartStretch Goal is clearly defined, understood, 'lived' and tracked)	
Our Participation (Markets/Segments) and Positioning (Offer/Cost) Strategies are clear and understood and translate to a demonstrable competitive advantage	
We know where we are on the ScaleUp stepping stones and whether we are in a period of consolidation or striking out for the next stepping stone	
Everyone can give a compelling answer to the question 'What does your company do?'	
3. The Leadership Team can articulate:	SUBTOTAL
The 3-year 'Thrusts' – the focus areas for the 3-year plan – and progress is tracked	
The 4–9 'Critical Paths' for the next 12 months and progress is reviewed quarterly (the critical things that must be achieved in order to be on track for the 3-year goals)	
The 1–2 focus Value Drivers to increase the value of the business over the next 12 months	
The 'theme' and priorities/business 'rocks' for the current quarter	

In order to be able to develop a meaningful plan, we are going to need to introduce a few concepts along with our SmartWeb® visual planning tool. The concepts will help to frame our thinking to be able to use the SmartWeb® effectively. We have developed it over a few years of testing and found it to be very effective in developing the key components of a 3-year plan along with serving as a visual and 'tactile' reminder – we'll come back to it once we have reviewed a couple of concepts.

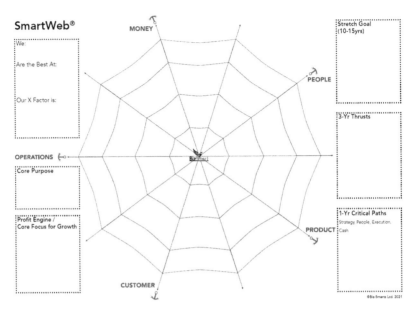

Fig. 34

We've already introduced the concept of building for value which should frame our decision making. To help our thinking further we need to introduce/consider the following:

- Participation and positioning strategies
- Competitive advantage/X-factor
- The hedgehog concept
- The potential to scale (TVR)
- Identifying and prioritising opportunities for growth

All of these taken together will help to make sure that we focus on the right things when we come to develop our plan – that we focus on things that will strengthen our competitive advantage/enable us to make superior profits over the long term, that we focus on things that combine what we are passionate about with what we are good at and can make money from, that our chosen focus areas are scalable and that we have identified and prioritised where future growth is going to come from! The thinking behind each concept will link into the next, and sometimes will cause us to think differently about an earlier conclusion. And that is as it should be; our decisions get better the more information we have and the more we develop our thinking.

And the really good news is that this does not need to be complicated and we are not proposing that you invest huge amounts of time and money into researching and writing reports. We are entrepreneurs after all and want to make things happen – so this approach will get us quickly to the point where we can be confident we are taking action based on sound strategic thinking. After all, however much we try to make the 'perfect' plan, we all recognise there is no such thing and that we will need to test and adapt as we go. You might enjoy this quote from 'Murphy's Laws of Combat':[48]

- The important things are simple.
- The simple things are very hard.
- No plan survives the first contact intact.
- Perfect plans aren't (perfect).

Participation and positioning strategies – competitive advantage and our 'X-factor'

Competitive advantage

We introduced the concept of competitive advantage when we discussed monopoly control in the section about Value.

In order to create sustainable profitable growth a business needs to either compete in 'attractive' markets (where the average company makes superior profits) and/or be competitively advantaged against their competitors.

In an 'attractive' market a business may afford to be relatively average for a while and will experience growth in line with the market, but in a challenging market this is not possible.

Fig. 35

A USP (Unique Selling Proposition) is not a true USP unless it translates into an actual competitive advantage, otherwise the USP is not as important to the customer as you may think. According to our research, 80% of businesses confirmed that they have a clearly defined USP. However, after additional analysis it is clear that just 38% of businesses have an actual competitive advantage, where 49% of these have a cost advantage and 51% have an offer advantage. This means that nearly half (42%) of businesses believe they have a USP, but it is not translating into an actual competitive advantage, therefore hindering scalability and growth.

Positioning strategy – offer and cost positions

Competitive advantage is driven by the **offer position** (how good customers perceive the offer to be compared with the competition) and the **cost position** (how cost efficiently the business can deliver the offer compared with the competition).

Creating a competitive advantage is clearly desirable and requires creating differentiation from competitors in a way that customers value – just being 'different' does not necessarily count! The goal is to get to the point where the average customer is willing to pay a premium for your product or service.

As a reminder, we mentioned earlier that if we focus on markets or sectors that are highly profitable we can make strong profits by being 'good' (we hitch our wagon to the right train and enjoy the ride, essentially) – this is our participation strategy – we choose where to compete. This helps us to define our target customers and create ideal customer 'avatars'.

In addition to this (and absolutely vital if the markets we participate in are not so 'attractive'), we need to think about our competitive advantage – which again is made up of two factors – our 'offer' position and our 'cost' position. The first is about how differentiated we are in the eyes of the customer (so that they perceive our offer to be 'better'), the second is about the way we operate that enables us to deliver the same quality but at a lower internal cost – so we can make higher profits at the same price, or we can afford to undercut our competitors but still make good profits.

So we need to understand our participation and positioning strategies in order to be able to understand where we have a competitive advantage (if at all) and where we are going to focus our efforts to strengthen it. It could be, for example, that we have developed a clever

Does your business have a competitive advantage?

"We can charge **higher prices** and maintain market share/grow at market rate."

"At average prices we grow faster than the market/grow market share."

→ Advantaged from an offer perspective

"We charge average market prices and we are able to make higher profits than average."

"We charge lower prices and are able to make profits at the same as the market or greater."

→ Advantaged from a cost perspective

"At average or lower prices we don't grow faster than the market/can't grow market share (same or lower than market)."

→ Not advantaged

Fig. 36

approach that we are using to great effect addressing a need in schools – but are struggling to get them to pay a sufficient amount for it because of their budget constraints. The question here (amongst others) may be whether there are other sectors with a similar need but that might have greater budgets.

Participation strategy

The thinking behind participation strategy is that we should choose the markets we want to play in to maximise the potential that we will make money. I am making the assumption that if you are reading this book, you are interested in making a profit potentially even if you have a mission in life – so you are trying to build a business and are not totally altruistic. Therefore it makes sense to choose markets and clients that are willing and able to pay – and that we stand a chance of succeeding in. We come back to this a little more in the hedgehog concept and this is where the textbooks would normally suggest you dig out the market data reports and crunch the numbers, identifying the market value etc. Well yes, we need some idea, but we don't need to know everything to 10 decimal places.

What we need is a way to choose 'attractive' markets that we can compete in. Generally if you have worked in a market for a few years, between you and your leadership team you will have everything you need to make a subjective assessment. You can always look for the data afterwards to confirm your reasoning rather than waste hours and money on expensive research first.

We call this the 'bubble chart' – I'm sure there's a better name for it but you'll see why in a moment. It is another 2-by-2 matrix with 'Segment Attractiveness' on the vertical axis and 'Relative Capability to Exploit' (this can also be thought of as our 'Ability to win' vs. competitors) on the horizontal. We then plot different segments with a circle (or bubble) representing the 'size' of the segment.

The idea is that a large circle to the top right should represent a large and 'attractive' segment where we reckon we have a chance of beating the competition. The opposite would be true of a small circle in the bottom left.

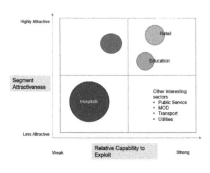

Fig. 37

In this way we can make all sorts of decisions. Top right should be our 'low hanging fruit' and may be all we ever need, but a large circle in the top left might suggest a later opportunity that we could work towards by strengthening our capability to compete.

What makes a segment 'attractive'? This is where we can use a combination of good 'theory' and guided 'gut feel'! If we understand the theory, we can then apply the expertise in the room to get us 90% of the way there – which may be all we need. If we are still in doubt then we can do some additional research and analysis afterwards.

The theory is guided by Michael Porter's 5 Forces[49] which provide a framework for thinking about the competitive environment and attractiveness of the industry or segment – and have since been extended to 6!

They are:

1. **The intensity of competition**
2. **The 'power' of customers**
3. Intensity of indirect competition – or the threat of substitutes
4. Threat of entry of new competitors
5. The power of suppliers
6. Regulatory pressures

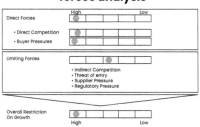

Fig. 38

The two most important forces are the intensity of *competition* and the power of *customers* – these will directly impact on the attractiveness and profitability of an industry or segment. The other forces will have a secondary limiting effect – which means we can focus on the first two to give us the main feel and then use the others for the fine adjustment!

So if there are lots of competitors and choices of products and services, then we are likely to see price undercutting and high rivalry between competitors. Typical indicators of high intensity of direct competition are:

- Many competitors – highly fragmented
- Similar/standardised products and services
- Low growth rate
- Spare capacity

The more of these that apply, the more that industry or segment is likely to see competitors attacking each other as they fight for market share resulting in declining prices and profits.

Similarly, if customers hold a lot of power then we will also see a greater likelihood of price discounting or adding in free 'value added' products and services. This will be seen by high customer sensitivity to price and the customer having high negotiating leverage.

So if you are looking at a sector and you see lots of fragmented competitors, not much differentiation and customers are able to shop around, then it should be in one of your 'less attractive' boxes/below the line. If, on the other hand, you see a fast growing segment with few competitors with differing products and services, then it should go above the line – with a caveat! This caveat is that things may not stay that way and this is where the other forces come into play – particularly perhaps the threat of new entrants. If barriers to entry are low, then we will see new competitors coming into the market when they catch up with the opportunity, which will have a limiting effect on the long-term profitability of the segment.

A quick definition of the remaining 'limiting' forces:

Intensity of indirect competition: This is about the availability of alternatives or 'substitutes' to the product or service. For example, ferry companies across the English Channel would consider other ferry companies as direct competitors, but they also need to consider the Channel Tunnel train and even flying as indirect competitors. So if I want to take the ferry, I will start by comparing the ferry services – but at some point I may move to considering the tunnel. Thus there will be a limiting effect because whilst I may prefer the ferry, there will be a trigger point at which I will look for an alternative – it could be a price or availability or something else.

Threat of entry: This is covered above but essentially if barriers are low, there will be a ceiling on pricing and profitability before new entrants are attracted in. If barriers are high (perhaps training, knowledge, investment) then there is a higher ceiling.

Power of suppliers: If supply of a key element of your product or service is in limited 'supply', perhaps only available from one or two sources, then your suppliers will have power over you. This was referred to in the Switzerland structure driver of value earlier in terms of our dependence on one or two key suppliers. This will limit the attractiveness of a segment – unless you can find a solution.

Regulatory pressures: This is the 6th force in the 5 Forces model! It can work both ways – if you are already in a segment and have invested in meeting imposed regulations, then this acts as a barrier to entry for new competitors and works in your favour. It could be, though, that the regulators can impose pricing or profit limits on a product or service, or differing tax levels across substitutes.

So that is the theory. We should be able to rate a segment with these forces in mind (focusing on the intensity of direct competition and the power of customers/buyers) and considering the others as limiting forces.

There may also be some specific criteria you wish to apply that are pertinent to the way you do business. For example:

- Budgets in place
- Understand quality/not just about price
- Buying process fits with our approach
- Technically aware – or not!
- All year round need or seasonal
- Etc.

Be careful not to 'override' the two main forces with your own assessments – and it may be that some of these are better considered in the 'capability to exploit' rather than the overall attractiveness.

In terms of our capability to exploit, we want to consider our capabilities against the 'average' competitor. Do we have particular capabilities that might mean we have a better than average offer or ability to open doors, perhaps? For example strong sector experience with good sector-specific testimonials, industry membership/access to sector-specific information, a tailored offering for that sector etc.

Finally the size of the bubble is our estimate of the size of the opportunity. Typically this is in 'volume' terms or number of potential customers as the 'value' is normally included in the attractiveness criteria, and therefore represented by how high up the chart the bubble is.

If you have the right people in the room when you do this, you can get a really good idea of what the key segments are and where they fit without needing to carry out lots of desk research in advance. You may raise questions as a result of this exercise which can be followed up, for example if you are a bit shaky on a particular sector. You can then decide if it warrants the time and possibly money to access the data.

X-factor

You can survive in business for a while in an attractive market without a competitive edge. But if you want to survive let alone thrive in a challenging market then you will need a competitive edge – or X-factor.

What is exactly is an X-factor? The X-factor is an age-old idea. It is using your company's unique skills and resources to implement strategies that competitors cannot implement as effectively. It's also known as a competitive edge or competitive advantage.

It could be in your offer position, it could be in your cost position or it could be a combination of the two.

Tony Robbins describes it as '...the ability to add intangible value to your product or service. It's finding a way to do more for your clients than any of your competitors and consistently maintaining that standard'.[50] Verne Harnish describes it as the '10–100x competitive advantage that organizations gain by solving an industry bottleneck or revolutionizing the marketplace with a new way to create customer value or conduct business'.[51]

It's your secret sauce, your secret ingredient – something you know how to do that others don't. In Apple's case it is mainly their ability to innovate, in McDonald's (going right back to the days of Ray Kroc and the McDonald brothers), it was their innovation to bring the average customer waiting time down from 30 minutes to 30 seconds. This is a great example because they challenged the accepted 'norm' and did something about it. They answered the question 'What bugs us about our industry?' and focused on making it better.

Apple is a good example of how you can look to your Core Values and Core Purpose to find inspiration. At the end of the day, the combination of values and purpose that defines 'the way you do business' and your culture, could be your X-factor.

It doesn't always have to be something that will disrupt your industry; clearly all the well-known examples do, but it could be something that just gives you that 'edge' over your competitors. Ideally whatever it is should be something that you can defend, that isn't too easy for your competitors to copy (they will eventually if it is good enough, so be prepared to evolve it) and it should be a source of power or 'leverage' for you.

So how do you go about finding yours? Start with all the good stuff we have discussed before – around Core Purpose, Core Values and your 'hedgehog' (which we will look at shortly) – which gets you the answers to:

- What are we really passionate about?
- What can we be the best at, or if not the best then really really good at?
- What does the market/customer really want and is prepared to pay for/what is the pain?

So this partly addresses the focus element – getting us to focus on a niche or a segment that we can 'own' and which is aligned with our Core Purpose.

It might give us some clues about what we can do differently but try asking yourself and your team these three questions:

- What is the one thing that I hate most about my industry?
- What is driving me nuts?!
- What is the bottleneck constraining the business? It could be a massive time or cost factor, for example.

So if finding good people and recruiting them to join your business is the bottleneck that is holding you back, don't carry on doing what everyone else is doing and expect it to get better. Think around it; ask yourself how you could turn the constraint into a competitive advantage. In hospitality this may be around staff turnover, for example, so how could you reduce it? In homecare it might be around hiring carers – well how could you get access to more or different sources of carers? It might be that in your industry quoting for new work is the rate limiting step – perhaps it is accepted that you have to send a salesperson to visit and measure up – well do you? Is there a technology solution perhaps that would enable you to quote without visiting?

You are biased!

If you have worked in your industry for any length of time, you will have become biased or 'blinkered'. You will undoubtedly have come to accept certain 'truths' about the way your industry works. But are they 'truths'? As well as looking internally into what you see as the bottlenecks, think about looking externally into other industries for potential ideas. This is one of the real powers of peer groups, or mastermind groups, or bringing in non-executive directors from other industries; they will be free of your biases and will challenge those 'truths'!

What are you afraid of?

Is there something that you fear might happen in your industry that might spell the end for the way you do things, or at least make it more challenging? Well if there is (maybe 'making tax digital' if you are an accountant) then what could you do to accelerate it? I know, you thought I was going to say 'mitigate it' but if you are truly looking to create an X-factor then this could be a way to do it – identify the biggest fear that your industry has and then instead of hoping it will go away, 'become it'!

If you find your X-factor then keep it secret and act on it. Keep it close to your chest until you can fully exploit it!

Of course, even huge advantages don't last forever. If you are able to make profits well above industry norms then someone is going to notice and find a way to copy you or find a different way. We come back to this in the 'Cash' chapter. If you are able to make *true*[52] net profits of more than 20%, then you should enjoy it while you can *and* look for new ways to keep one step ahead – because over time the true or 'economic' profits within an industry tend to zero as new entrants come in and competitors wise up.

So you should never stop looking for ways to keep competitors in your wake. You don't want to be caught unprepared. Fortunately, there are unlimited ways to find a competitive edge. The key is to pull yourself away from day-to-day operations long enough to think more broadly about your business from an outsider's perspective. Brainstorm with your team, bring in people from outside your business/sector – perhaps other business owners. But there is an X-factor inside you and your business!

I mentioned the 'hedgehog' concept earlier in this section, and we now need to see how this relates to the above.

Find your hedgehog!

The hedgehog is all around focus which is an essential component of a scalable business model.

Most of the business owners that we work with are not short of ideas – in fact quite the opposite. So what we want to do is to focus on products and services that we can become known for doing brilliantly and that are also ones that we can scale. If we want to build the kind of business that doesn't require us being involved in every single decision and every single step then we need to focus on products and services that are scalable.

This is simple in concept but not necessarily so easy in practice – to quote Steve Jobs, 'That's been one of my mantras – focus and simplicity. Simple can be harder than complex; you have to work hard to get your thinking clean to make it simple.'

Two key concepts to working out the right focus are the 'hedgehog' and the 'potential to scale' to assess whether our focus really is scalable. First the hedgehog!

It is called the hedgehog principle. The hedgehog concept is based on an ancient Greek parable that states, 'The fox knows many things, but the hedgehog knows one big thing.'

Philosopher Isaiah Berlin took this parable and brought it into 'modern times' in his essay, 'The Hedgehog and the Fox' which he published in 1953[53] and Jim Collins developed the idea for businesses in his book *Good to Great*.[54]

Berlin classified people into two groups, foxes and hedgehogs, and the basic idea he put forward is that the foxes pursue many goals and interests at the same time. As a result, their thinking is scattered and unfocused, and ultimately they achieve very little. Hedgehogs, however, simplify the world and focus on a single, overarching vision, which they then achieve. The hedgehog has one big idea – one big thing it does whenever the fox comes close is it rolls up into a ball so that its prickly spines form an impenetrable barrier to the fox.

It does this every time and it does it very well.

It doesn't try something new; it doesn't think one day, 'I wonder if I can outrun the fox today?' It sticks to the thing that it knows it is great at and it has perfected it. It knows the fox will eventually get bored and then when it does, the hedgehog can go about its business.

So what has this got to do with business and our planning? Well we need to find our 'hedgehog'. Businesses that do this stand the greatest chance of achieving long-term success and becoming great businesses.

Jim Collins proposed a simple model for businesses to articulate their hedgehog. It's based on three things: what we are passionate about, what we can be the best at (or best in class at) and the economic or profit engine (what drives our profits/how do we make money?).

Put even more simply, what we focus on in business should be the crossover between:

1. What we love doing
2. What we are really good at
3. What makes good money

Fig. 39

Any two of these without the third mean that it won't work in the long term – 1 & 2 without 3 mean we will be happy but broke (we love doing it and are great at it, but no-one will pay well for it); 2 & 3 without 1 mean we will be wealthy but unfulfilled (we are good at it and people will pay for it, but we are not really passionate about it), and 1 & 3 without 2 is just a pipe dream (we love it and people will pay, but we don't have the capability to do it well enough to succeed).

The sweet spot is where these three circles interlock and if we've done it well this should directly link with our Core Purpose and our Smart Stretch. What we love doing or what we are passionate about should essentially be our Core Purpose and it is pointless having a focus that does not lead to us being able to achieve our Smart Stretch!

Imagine we are a nationwide pharmacy chain, dispensing medications and health and wellness products and services.

What we might be passionate about – or our Core Purpose – could be 'To help people live happier and longer lives through helping them get well, stay well and live well'.

Where we think we can build differentiation from our competition – or what we think we can be the best at – might be 'The best on the "high street" and most convenient provider of "wellness" support and advice'.

And our profit engine might be 'Profit per customer visit'.

This gives us real clarity and focus because if we've agreed this then everything we do needs to be about increasing customer numbers through driving customers into our stores and then ensuring that we make the most profit from each customer through upselling etc. In this example the pharmacy has been able to identify a specific profit measure that will drive their success and ideally this is what we need to do – find the single overarching measure that we can use to drive and monitor success.

To do this exercise well, not only do we need to have defined our Core Purpose well but we also need to understand what we are good at – sometimes referred to as the 'core competencies' of the business. Ideally your business is the best in the world at something, but being really good may be good enough. You could be the best in a specific aspect, or perhaps in a geographic region, or within a specific sector. So it links back to the concepts of monopoly control, competitive advantage and X-factor that we looked at earlier. Being really honest with yourself and working out where you already have an advantage is the start, and then focusing on strengthening that advantage over time.

It is also worth noting for later that the hedgehog is not set in stone forever – it needs to be reviewed in the Plan. What we are passionate about should be 'forever', what we are 'best at' might evolve but typically remains true for the duration of the 'Mission' or Smart Stretch time frame, and the 'profit engine' may change within that but typically is 'set' for the next 3-year plan.

When a business has 'found its hedgehog', its leaders should devote all of their energy and resources to pursuing it. Collins argues that when the going gets tough, it's the organisations that focus on what they're good at that survive and thrive.[55]

We have seen this through the Covid-19 pandemic; the temptation for many business owners when faced with their usual business being disrupted was to behave like the fox and grab the nearest opportunity, which may or may not be a good idea for the longer term. Those that understood their hedgehog realised that whilst they could not deliver in the same way, their Core Purpose had not gone away or changed – so they focused their energy on finding different ways of delivering on their Core Purpose. Businesses that did this will have put themselves in a much stronger position for once the pandemic eased. In some ways this may seem counterintuitive, to even narrow your focus further in a crisis rather than broaden it, but this is the better long-term route. It may have meant that profits in the short term were hit, but it is the better 'value-based' decision.

Before we close on the idea of focus and the hedgehog, we need to make sure that whatever we have chosen as our focus is scalable – so we want to test it against the 'potential to scale' proposed by John Warrillow and the team at The Value Builder System™ in *Built to Sell*.[56]

The potential to scale

For a product or service to be scalable (as opposed to just being able to grow), it needs to meet the following three criteria (TVR):

- It needs to be **T**eachable – in other words, it cannot be something that can only be done by you
- It needs to be **V**aluable to your customers – something that they want and which is not just a commodity that they can get anywhere (is it differentiated?)
- It needs to have an element of **R**epeatability – ideally something that your customers need on a recurring basis or that might lead to additional service or product sales – rather than being just a one-off purchase.

Before you finalise your hedgehog, rate your key products and services against these three criteria. A simple exercise scoring out of 10 for each criteria will help you to work out which are more scalable than others, and therefore where your focus should lie. A common challenge in the early days is that the business owner may do some consulting work related to the business. They may have a particular area of expertise that clients are prepared to pay well for as a 1:1 service. This would score a 10 probably for 'Value' but very low for 'Teachable' and possibly low for 'Repeatable' even though it may be a relatively high source of profits right now.

This is not scalable unless we find a way to address these constraints. It may be that we could find a way to take that expertise and develop a 'system' that could be taught to employees who in turn can teach it to clients or it may not. Either way, doing this exercise will highlight this clearly, either where we already have scalable offerings or where we might look to be able to create them.

There is a natural tension, you will see, between valuable and teachable. More often than not, something that is highly valuable and differentiated will be harder to teach, and similarly something that is very teachable may not be that differentiated. So we may need to do a bit more thinking along the lines above (can we find a way to make a valuable service more teachable?) or potentially could we create something differentiated from a combination of lower value but teachable 'components' by packaging them together in one 'bundle'?

So now we have identified a focus that fits with our Core Purpose, we know we are good at it, we know it makes us money and it is scalable. The final piece in the jigsaw before we put our 3-year plan together is to identify our key opportunities for growth.

Identifying and prioritising opportunities for growth

Part of our thinking needs to include where growth is going to come from, in the short and longer term. It may be that we just want to do 'more of the same' or it may be that we plan additional products or services, or new markets to enter into. We need to be clear from our short and medium-term planning, but also refer back to the Value Drivers, of which you may recall that one was growth opportunities. Identifying opportunities, even if we do not plan to exploit them ourselves, will help our strategic thinking (perhaps looking at partnerships) and also enable us to demonstrate additional opportunities to a potential investor that they may be able to help us exploit.

To help your thinking on this we are going to look at a framework to facilitate brainstorming how you can look for opportunities to grow your business with the highest opportunity and the lowest risk. It is the Ansoff Matrix,[57] invented by the mathematician Igor Ansoff and published in the *Harvard Business Review* in 1957, so it's not new but is extremely useful and simple to understand.

It looks at your business from the standpoint of what markets/customer groups you are in today – existing markets. It also looks at what potential markets you might enter – new markets – on the vertical axis.

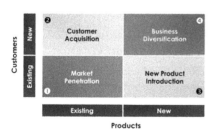

Fig. 40

On the horizontal axis it looks at product and service lines – that you currently offer – existing products/services, and ones you might think about offering in the future – or new products and services.

This enables us to bring risk into our thinking because what the Ansoff Matrix tells us is that the markets we are in today with our existing products and services represent the lowest risk of failure.

So essentially re-doubling your efforts with your existing customer groups and product mix is the lowest risk option for growth – and therefore where we should start looking.

Next we can look at entering new markets and acquiring customer groups with our existing products and services – but know that this is going to be more risky than the first option.

Not surprisingly, we don't know new markets as well so there will be things we might not be aware of and it will probably be harder to succeed.

To illustrate this let's look at a really simple business, one I did with my brother when we were growing up, and think about it in the context of the Ansoff Matrix. It was selling apples that grew on our trees at home.

How could we increase sales of apples to passers-by if we focus on it?

- Can we increase the average order value?
- Can we increase the frequency of purchase?
- Can we encourage more people down the road?
- Can we encourage more people to stop and take notice?
- Do we need more apples? If so what can we do about that?
- Etc.

Next we might think about taking apples to different customers – in this case perhaps at a fete or maybe to the local high street and putting up a stall there where we think there might be more people.

A bit more unknown and more things to think about – so more risky. Do we need a licence, will we be asked to move on, how do we make sure we have enough apples with us, etc etc?

In this case the different market is geographical – a new location. But in your business it might be a different demographic, for example by age or sex. Or it could be a different psychographic segment – such as personality traits, values, interests or lifestyles – for example people who play tennis.

Similarly we could think about selling our passers-by a new product to complement our apples – such as vegetables, cider or apple juice, jam – it doesn't have to be apple related necessarily.

Clearly this is different from selling apples – especially if we now have to process them in some way and work out how to produce, package and sell these new products – so more unknowns than sticking with apples.

And lastly we may even think about taking these new products into the high street or other locations – perhaps with a shop unit – the most unknown and therefore the most risky of growth options.

So that's what you can do, look at your business through the lens of what the highest opportunities for growth are with the lowest risk of failure so that you can include this (along with the earlier concepts thinking) when it comes to developing your Plan.

From the Ansoff Matrix, that has been around for over 50 years, to something that is absolutely brand new which we have been working on and developing. We like to have tools that are simple to use and that really have impact. Our DREAM© tool is one such tool that is getting great feedback. DREAM is about building on the Ansoff Matrix and identifying specifically where growth is going to come from, typically over the next year. Most business owners are focused on acquiring brand new customers and they can easily forget that it is much more cost effective to acquire additional business from people we have already worked with. DREAM ensures we don't forget this in our thinking. It also helps us to be much more confident and accurate in predicting our turnover for the next planning period.

DREAM©

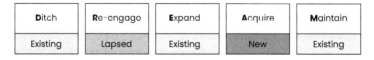

Fig. 41

We start by segmenting our existing customers so that we can develop specific tactics, then identify where new customers are going to come from, and finally take it a step further by turning it into a really good forecasting tool. We've included DREAM in this chapter as it ties in with the Ansoff Matrix thinking, but it also links in with the Chapter 6 on Execution and specifically where we look at business development and our lead generation activities.

DREAM stands for Ditch, Re-engage, Expand, Acquire and Maintain. We start with ditch, which may seem odd given this is about helping to identify where growth will come from! The point is that not all customers are good customers and some may be holding us back from being able to find and support customers that could be great for us. We have seen many examples where ditching a customer (sometimes even a customer that represents a significant amount of a client's turnover) has enabled the business to increase profits markedly. It is a natural consequence of a growing and evolving business that we will 'outgrow' some of our customers. In the early stages we are focused on generating new business and will naturally be keen to take any customers we can get. As we become more established and more confident in where we can and want to add the most value, we generally find that we have some 'legacy' clients that we perhaps would not have chosen now. These customers are costing us more than we realise in terms of time and lower profit margins and it is important to take a hard look at them. So the D in DREAM is about going through our existing customer base and thinking about who we want to ditch, who should we no longer be doing business with?

Keeping with existing customers, next we jump to the M of DREAM and look at Maintain. So again, going through our existing customer list, who do we want to keep and maintain at current levels? By this we mean customers with whom we already have as much business as we want, or that we can realistically expect. These are customers that we don't particularly want to grow and develop, but we want to retain. So we need a simple set of tactics that address how we maintain and look after these customers. From a forecasting perspective, we can simply forecast existing business levels.

Now we come to the E for Expand. So again, we're looking at our existing customers but this time we are identifying customers we want to grow/expand. What additional business can we do with them? For example upselling or cross selling services or products that they don't currently buy. Again, we list our existing customers that we want to expand and we can develop another simple set of tactics by customer, addressing how we are going to expand what they do with us, and by how much.

Next we move on to R for Re-engage. This is about lapsed customers, people we have worked with previously, but are not currently doing so. Who do we want to re-engage with?

Again, we identify specific customers and develop a simple approach addressing how we are going to go about re-engaging with them, along with what level of business we might be able to do with them.

Finally we come to the A for Acquire. What new customers do we want to be doing business with? You can approach this by sector or business type but the real power of this tool is to be even more specific and name names. Really think about who you want to be doing business with, and put them on that list. We then need to develop our tactics for finding and acquiring these customers, and this is where it links in with the section on lead generation activities and our seeds, nets and spears (see Chapter 6 on Execution and the section on Business Development)!

So that's the first part of it. We look at our customers, we look at who we want to be working with and we stratify them, identifying specific tactics and potential levels of business. So how do we take this from a targeting tool into a forecasting tool? Well as you've probably realised, if as well as identifying customers and tactics we are also identifying the potential value of each of the tactics, all we need to do is to pull it together into a spreadsheet. Not forgetting of course that we need to deduct any business from clients we decide to ditch!

We can now use these numbers as our targets for the coming 12 months, split by each of the 5 areas of DREAM knowing that we have tactics behind each of them. Ideally you will be ensuring that someone is accountable for each of the areas and delivering on the targets.

So we now have our forecast for what we want our turnover to be in the next 12 months we can extend it out further, although we will lose some of the specificity and therefore accuracy.

Now we can compare with our longer term plan and identify whether this keeps us on track or whether we have a shortfall. Maybe we had originally planned a million turnover in the next 12 months and through this exercise we can clearly see three quarters of a million. We can then focus on how to bridge the shortfall, or even adjust our plan downwards if we need to be more realistic. On the other hand, maybe we can clearly identify more than the million, in which case perhaps we should raise our sights.

LEARNING POINTS

- Understanding and creating competitive advantage is key to successful scaling
- It is more than just differentiation – it is made up of our participation and positioning strategies
- True competitive advantage will give us more control over pricing and margins and will translate to customer buying habits
- We need to focus our efforts onto our 'hedgehog' sweet spot and ensure our focus offerings meet the 'potential to scale' criteria!
- Using the Ansoff Matrix and the DREAM tool will help us identify and prioritise opportunities for growth

ACTIONS

- Review the above in light of the InFlight Checks (and the key strategic focus according to the ScaleUp Journey below) and identify a focus for the next 90 days

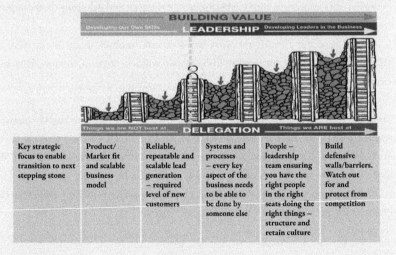

Key strategic focus to enable transition to next stepping stone	Product/Market fit and scalable business model	Reliable, repeatable and scalable lead generation – required level of new customers	Systems and processes – every key aspect of the business needs to be able to be done by someone else	People – leadership team ensuring you have the right people in the right seats doing the right things – structure and retain culture	Build defensive walls/barriers. Watch out for and protect from competition

Fig. 42

Smart Plan/SmartWeb®

So now we have everything we need to enable us to put together our 3-year plan.

The remaining Strategy questions from the InFlight Checklist are:

3. The Leadership Team can articulate:	SUBTOTAL
The 3-year 'Thrusts' – the focus areas for the 3-year plan – and progress is tracked	
The 4–9 'Critical Paths' for the next 12 months and progress is reviewed quarterly (the critical things that must be achieved in order to be on track for the 3-year goals)	
The 1–2 focus Value Drivers to increase the value of the business over the next 12 months	
The 'theme' and priorities/business 'rocks' for the current quarter	

As a quick reminder, we've been through the thinking of our Core Ideology, our long-term horizon planning or Envisioned Future, we've thought about and understood the hedgehog concept, learned about value, participation and positioning strategies, competitive advantage, the potential to scale (TVR) and identified our growth opportunities. So next up is our base camp for achieving our Envisioned Future – the 3-year point and the steps in between.

So we are going to work backwards from our Core Ideology, through our 10–15 year aim, our 3-year plan and then to the next 12 months.

We will use our SmartWeb® planning tool to help create the pictorial 3-year plan – so you will end up with a 3-year plan pretty much on one page.

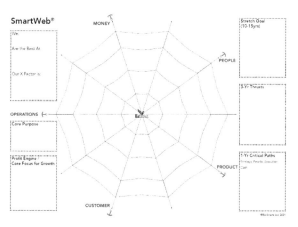

Fig. 43

The SmartWeb® allows us to consider the key drivers or aspects of our business and map them out over the next 3 years and then to tease out the things that are critical over the next year.

This will give us the 'whats' that we need to achieve in the next 3 years in order to be on track and the 'whats' we need to achieve in the next 12 months to be on track for the 3-year plan – not necessarily the 'hows'. These come when we link it with our 90-day planning where we then develop Smart Action Plans for our 90-day priorities. This is covered in Chapter 6, Execution.

The SmartWeb® is an incredibly powerful tool to harness and align the collective brainpower in the room and to capture it in a visual way rather than in a dry Word document or equivalent. We have clients that have kept their original scribbled version on a wall for years and come back to it regularly to keep check and to update – ideally of course you would do a fresh one each year as things progress!

It is straightforward once you get your head around it. Before we begin your planning let me take you through the SmartWeb® itself and then how you can use it.

The first thing to note is that much of our thinking from earlier is captured here in the boxes around the web itself – things like our Core Purpose, the elements of the hedgehog (what we are the best at, our 'profit engine'), our X-factor or competitive advantage and our Smart Stretch. The reason for this is two-fold – firstly it means that we have them front and centre and refer back to them as we complete the web, secondly it means that when finished we have all the key elements of our 3-year plan on one page. You should be able to show it to someone for the first time and they can instantly understand the essence of your strategy around the outside/in the boxes, and they can see the detail within the web if they wish. You will complete the 3-year thrusts and the 1-year Critical Paths as a result of completing the web.

The next thing to understand is that the 'rings' in the web represent years – from now in the middle ring to 3 years for the outer ring.

Then notice the 'anchor' points around the outside – any business can be described using these 5 fundamental anchor points – so our web is just like a spider's web in that it is anchored at key points:

- The way the money works in the business
- The numbers and type of people
- The key products and services
- The types and numbers of customers
- The operations of the business

These 5 key anchor points will be the same across all businesses – we could model any business with these axes – but the sub-segments or axes in between will differ by business.

So one of the first steps in using the SmartWeb® is to decide on what we are going to include as our axes – the key things we want to model.

Our description of our 'Smart Stretch' will help us to do that – because we will have picked out some key points that describe where we want the business to be at that point – so we need to plan or model those. It might be, for example, that we have talked about a particular service or product line, that we want to have won certain awards, or that we will have made some key acquisitions or entered certain countries – these are all things that should be included on the SmartWeb if they are relevant to your plans.

Here are some more examples of potential axes for the SmartWeb®:

- Sales turnover
- Profit = Gross and Net – actual and/or percentage
- Number/types of employees
- New office locations
- New product launches on stream
- Changing blend of customer types
- Amount of turnover from overseas
- Amount of turnover from adjacent markets
- Key strategic appointments to the team
- Raising finance
- Alliances/Strategic partners
- Acquisitions
- Quality standards/Accreditation
- Average sales value

What you might like to do is to start off writing your axes on Post-it notes so that you can change things a little more easily as you go.

Have in mind as you do this that one of the things you will want to do afterwards is to develop some financial forecasts to ensure your thinking makes financial sense – so try to include what you might need, either to do it yourself or be able to brief someone else on the key assumptions. For example you might need to include costs, perhaps for different types of employees that you plan on recruiting.

The SmartWeb® approach caters for very simple businesses through to complex; you might have a very simple business with few axes and little detail or you might have a much more complex business.

But one of the tricks is to keep it simple using the hedgehog idea to focus on what will make the most difference rather than getting bogged down in the things that are less important. Remember, what we are trying to get to are the few 3-Year thrusts and the 1-year Critical Paths.

Now we have the axes that link back to our vivid description and Smart Stretch – and we have in mind that we are going to model this in a spreadsheet so need to tease out all the relevant revenue and cost drivers as we do it.

The key to making this work, along with keeping it simple, is to start at the outside (where we want to be in 3 years) working our way around the outside of the web, before then coming back to the centre and capturing the current or last year numbers before working out the steps in between.

In this way we have established a base camp at the 3-year point that is a sensible stage towards our Smart Stretch and then worked out what we need to do to get there – rather than start where we are now and simply add a bit each year. It also means that we consider things 'in the round' rather than in isolation. So if we want to hit a certain revenue target in 3 years, we might then ask how that might break down in terms of key customers which in turn might lead us to ask what products and services and how many they will be buying, which might bring us back to the financials to break that down in sales by product line. We might then ask what the implications of having that many customers and delivering those products and services will be on the number and types of people we need, maybe any new equipment we may need to buy, and how much it will cost. This might bring us back to modelling the personnel and capital investment and overhead costs. If we need to attract that many customers what might that mean from our marketing activities – exhibitions perhaps, new website, awards entered and won? If we take on new staff, do we need to think about new offices etc etc.

Depending on the Smart Stretch, the starting point on the SmartWeb® may differ. In the example above I started with the sales, but that won't always be the case. If our Smart Stretch is around numbers of customers, or market share, or reputation, then we might start with these axes rather than going straight to the sales.

The trick is to find a starting point that matches or supports your Smart Stretch and your profit engine from your hedgehog – this will not only help you get started but will also make the logic flow more easily.

Once you have the outer ring completed to the point where you think you have covered all of your axes and are happy it makes sense ('sanity check' it by making sure you keep challenging it and asking questions to make sure you aren't coming up with impossible numbers), then we move back to the centre of the circle, and capture the current situation for each of the key metrics/axes. This identifies the size of the gap (in practice we may have noted some of these down along the way as part of our 'sanity checks') and enables us to break down the intervening two years – so for that particular metric we want to get to x, we are now at y so where do we need to be at the end of the next year, and the second year to be on track? Do we 'straight line it' or are we ramping up, for example?

So now we have a completed inner SmartWeb®!

If you've involved your senior team or partners in this, then you should all be in agreement and aligned in your thinking – which is a huge outcome in itself. If a question comes up that you are not able to answer in the session, then make sure you capture it for following up later; maybe you aren't sure on the market salary of a particular role, for example.

If by working through the SmartWeb® process you have realised that your Smart Stretch is either unachievable or not challenging enough, then revisit the Smart Stretch and set it to something that is. This is an iterative process and you should not be afraid to revisit it in the light of better information and/or thinking.

So this should allow us to pick out the key 'thrusts' for the next 3 years, the key things that will describe our journey between now and then. It could be something like:

Developing international markets through distributor agreements and creating a profitable and sustainable business that might attract investment for the future

The next step is to tease out the 1-year or 12-month Critical Paths – these are things that we need to achieve in the next 12 months if we are to stand any chance of getting to our 3-year base camp.

You'll find these in the first ring out from the middle. Pick out the key things here, not necessarily everything in the ring.

Ensure these are as specific as you can be; avoid things like 'increase sales'. Remember these are the 'whats' so it's OK to have 'Increase sales turnover with existing customers from £1m to £1.5m by November 20xx' because we will develop Smart Actions to achieve them in our 90-day planning.

These should be captured in the appropriate box on the outside of the SmartWeb®. Good examples of Critical Paths might include:

- Increase sales turnover with existing customers from £1m to £1.5m by November 20xx
- Achieve £0.5 m turnover from new export strategy by July 20xx
- Generate £400k from the launch of new product X by year end
- Win a £600k contract from public sector before December 20xx
- Reduce cost of goods by 10% by June 20xx
- Acquire/switch a £500k customer from a competitor by September 20xx
- Develop a lead generation plan to deliver 5 new leads per month from August 20xx
- Develop a sales conversion plan to convert 1 new customer per month from August 20xx
- Develop a hiring process to deliver 3 new technical members of staff by …

Note that they are all specific, measurable and timebound (they have a target date). If you have ensured that they are realistic and not just wild fantasy, then all you need to do to make them SMART Critical Paths is identify someone who is accountable for each one – that has primary ownership of achieving it.

A good sanity check on the Critical Paths is to think whether you have something for Strategy/Leadership, People, Execution and Cash – coming back to our 4 Pillars of scalability. If you haven't then you should probably have a further think. The chances are for example that if you are growing rapidly you are going to need to attract, hire and retain key people – so do you need a retention plan and a hiring plan? Will you need to strengthen your management processes to make sure the plan is executed in the way you need? Will you need to improve your cash and key performance indicator (KPI) monitoring; will you need to set KPIs if you haven't got them? Ideally you would also identify one or two Value Drivers that will be worked on over the next year.

Don't go mad though; we only want 5–10 Critical Paths really, otherwise we are just listing loads of semi-important things.

Now you've got an outline business plan on a page.

Whilst it is definitely the thinking behind it that is the most important part of it, it is a good idea to check any key assumptions you have made (you may not have had all of the answers in the room) and to put together at least a simple financial model. You will have estimated sales and costs, probably gross and net margins, and you do need to plug all the assumptions into a model so that you can make sure that your thinking is robust. It will also help you to identify which assumptions may be more critical than others, enabling you to pick out some Key Performance Indicators that you will want to keep a close eye on. You might for example have made an assumption of the 'utilisation rate' of a particular machine (what proportion of the day the machine is running/how many hours a day), or of your staff (what percentage of their time is spent on client delivery). It is good to know what a change in this number means to your overall profitability – and you will find that some things are much more sensitive than others. This may also cause you to revisit part of the plan – again this is good. Each time we iterate because of improved information and/or thinking, we are making it more likely that we will achieve it.

Even though you have the Plan on a page, it may still be worth capturing it into a short report. We find the simplest way is to use PowerPoint and create a series of slides based on the outputs including the earlier thinking prior to completing the

SmartWeb®. Generally it can be done in 10 or fewer slides and an added benefit of this is that if you need to raise funding, most routes will require you to have a business or growth plan. We've used this format successfully to help several 100 businesses gain grant funding, for example.

That now completes the main elements of 'Strategy' around scaling up. You should now be able to see how you can work towards being strong at the habits and questions from the InFlight Checks.

Now that you understand a little more behind each of these, take a moment to re-rate yourself/your business on each of the key questions on a 5-point scale where 1=Very weak/'We don't do this', 2='We sort of do this a bit', 3='We're OK but not great at this', 4='We're quite good at this but not perfect', 5='We've got this nailed'

Now take a look at where you think you are weak and prioritise one or two of them that you think would make the most impact on your business if you were to improve them.

This brings us to the end of the Strategy 'Pillar'. Review the elements of the InFlight Checks relating to strategy below and think about what would make an impact on your business if you were to make it a focus for improvement.

1=Very weak/'We don't do this', 2='We sort of do this a bit', 3='We're OK but not great at this', 4='We're quite good at this but not perfect', 5='We've got this nailed'	Score 1-5
1. Leadership and Vision are strong within the business	SUBTOTAL
The Leadership team understand each other's personality and leadership styles and **all** team members identify one specific leadership/personal improvement habit each 90 days	
Core Ideology (Values and Purpose) are defined, known and made role-relevant by all employees	
Core Ideology is embedded into all aspects of the 'way we do things' (recruitment, onboarding, reviews, feedback etc.)	
A Core Ideology improvement priority is identified and implemented every 90 days	
2. We have a truly differentiated strategy and scalable business model and all team members can articulate the following components:	SUBTOTAL
The team are aligned with and passionate about the Mission/Stretch Goal (SmartStretch Goal is clearly defined, understood, 'lived' and tracked)	
Our Participation (Markets/Segments) and Positioning (Offer/Cost) Strategies are clear and understood and translate to a demonstrable competitive advantage	
We know where we are on the ScaleUp stepping stones and whether we are in a period of consolidation or striking out for the next stepping stone	
Everyone can give a compelling answer to the question 'What does your company do?'	
3. The Leadership Team can articulate:	SUBTOTAL
The 3-year 'Thrusts' – the focus areas for the 3-year plan – and progress is tracked	
The 4–9 'Critical Paths' for the next 12 months and progress is reviewed quarterly (the critical things that must be achieved in order to be on track for the 3-year goals)	
The 1–2 focus Value Drivers to increase the value of the business over the next 12 months	
The 'theme' and priorities/business 'rocks' for the current quarter	
Strategy Pillar – add all the blue subtotals above	SECTION TOTAL

STRATEGY

CHAPTER 5:
PEOPLE

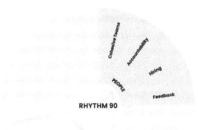

RHYTHM 90

Setting the scene for People

'Culture eats strategy for breakfast' – Peter Drucker[58]

However good your strategy is, you won't get far without a team. People can be the magic ingredient that makes a company great – but people can equally be the biggest headache. Get a good set of people and the culture right, and they will rescue even a bad strategy – the opposite is also true. A quick internet search will reveal a host of leaders that have been quoted as saying something similar.

Our research clearly showed the increasing number of people-based challenges as businesses scaled and took on more staff. In businesses turning over between £500k and £5m, the top challenges cited were:

- Getting staff to think and act for themselves and take responsibility the way you would

- Attracting and hiring enough of the right people
- Not having the right staff in place to support growth and
- Staff management – getting staff to do the right things consistently well.

Getting your staff to work as a truly cohesive team and retaining good people also featured in the top 15, albeit a little further down. So altogether, 5 of the top 15 challenges relate directly to people, with a few more indirectly (such as developing a strong value-based culture, and getting buy-in from your team to the plan). Clearly people challenges cut across Strategy, People, Execution and Cash, and we will expand on aspects such as 'getting staff to do the right things consistently well' in the 'Execution' chapter.

An interesting finding of our research was that despite these challenges, when we asked owner-managers for their top 5 Key Performance Indicators, people or team-based KPIs represented a mere 4% of the total measures. Given the adage, 'What gets measured gets managed', perhaps it is not so surprising that we see a large proportion of people-based challenges as we scale.

We began the idea of culture in the 'Strategy' chapter looking at Core Ideology. The four primary components around People in ESUS are: **Cohesive Teams, Accountability, Hiring and Feedback**. We will take a closer look at each of these in turn and the relevant habits and questions from the InFlight Checklist that we need to consider are:

	SUBTOTAL
8. All teams function Cohesively	
Team members understand each other's styles, differences and priorities	
Team members trust each other enough to admit mistakes	
Team members feel able to challenge each other and engage in constructive debate	
Team members are motivated to and work well to achieve the team goals	
9. We have a culture of Individual Accountability and Joint Responsibility	SUBTOTAL
We have the right people in the right roles with clear roles and accountabilities	
Individuals are empowered to make decisions for their area of responsibility	
Teams are focused on achieving collective results and we celebrate team success	
Everyone has visibility of and religiously track progress against 'Rocks' and Critical Numbers	
10. Our ability to retain and hire good people is a strength of the business	SUBTOTAL
We have a retention, development and succession/contingency plan for every key employee (score 1 if just you in the business) and hold regular (quarterly) 'retention discussions' with key employees	
We have a clear view of organisational needs/structure over the next 3 years and whether we are hiring in or developing internally for each role	
We are clear on our Employee Value Proposition and are able to attract sufficient good candidates (we are able to 'punch above our weight' in recruitment)	
We have a robust hiring process in place that minimizes the chances of making a bad hire	
11. We actively listen to our staff and track engagement	SUBTOTAL
Managers actively seek ongoing feedback from team members – e.g. all managers have a 'Stop, Start, Continue' discussion with at least one employee each week and feedback is shared at weekly leadership meetings (score 1 if just you)	
A 'Balance Wheel' or equivalent personal and professional 'happiness' discussion is held monthly with all team members (or you if you are on your own)	
We have a working process for informing staff on actions taken following feedback	
We track and work to improve employee engagement levels (e.g. NPS, Gallup12, TPS)	
12. We actively listen to our Customers	SUBTOTAL
Net Promoter Score or equivalent is tracked as a KPI	
All managers have a meaningful discussion with a customer each week (How are things going, What's the latest in your industry, What do you hear about our competitors, How are we doing?)	
Insights from these discussions are shared at the weekly leadership meeting	
One of the leadership team is accountable for actioning and reporting on customer feedback – positive and negative	
People Pillar – add all the yellow subtotals above	SECTION TOTAL

PEOPLE

COHESIVE TEAMS

RHYTHM 90

According to Ed Catmul, president of Pixar, 'Getting the right people and the right chemistry is more important than the right idea'[59] – an idea echoed by many.

At BizSmart we have seen many examples of the power of effective teams, and with some of our clients the effectiveness of the team becomes a distinct competitive advantage – indeed with small and medium-sized businesses competing against larger ones this is sometimes a real opportunity to differentiate.

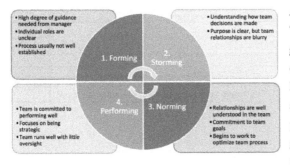

Fig. 44

According to Bruce Tuckman[60], all teams go through four stages of development which he defined as forming, storming, norming and performing. Before they can get to the last stage where they can focus on achieving team goals and success, they have to go through a forming stage (essentially where they are getting comfortable with working together), a storming stage (where they begin to gain each other's trust but often where disagreements start and need to be resolved) and a norming stage where a spirit of co-operation emerges. Teams can get stuck in the first two stages and never progress further.

I'm sure you can all think of examples where you have led or been in a team that has worked really well – and equally ones that haven't. In fact, a very simple but powerful exercise you can do with your team is to brainstorm what characteristics make a great team and what characteristics hinder one. Don't do it as a theoretical exercise; ask people to think back to when they were part of a great team and reflect on what made it great. Equally get them to think of when they were in a dysfunctional team and why it was. It doesn't need to be to do with business – it could be a sports team, a club – anything where a group of people worked together in a small team. If you capture all these great things then you will effectively have developed a team 'charter'. This is how we behave in our organisation, these are behaviours we expect and these are ones that we don't.

Before we get into the detail of cohesive teams, it is worth reminding you of the 'two-pizza rule' in relation to team size.

There are plenty of examples in the military – the RAF being organised around 'flights' and the army around 'sections' – both typically around this size.

It is a great rule if you think about it, large enough to benefit from collaborative thinking but small enough to care and keep clear communication. It is essentially what is behind the concept of the ScaleUp Journey we presented at the start: businesses will be at their most productive when we have the right number and sizes of individual teams or 'units' within the business.

So what is the right size? Researchers have conducted numerous studies to determine the ideal team size at which we balance the benefits of putting more heads together with the challenges in terms of coordination and motivation loss leading to a loss of cohesiveness. The exact answer varies depending on the exact task, but the modal answer is 3–5 people. Ivan Steiner arrives at about 5–6 people[61], with the answer varying slightly depending on the exact task. When we put peer groups together we aim for six people based on the research and advice from INSEAD Professor Anil Gaba[62] who is Professor of Decision Sciences. Professor Gaba has found that six is the ideal size for optimal decision making.

So that brings us back to the stages on the ScaleUp Journey – or the stepping stones. Remember the first stepping stone on the ScaleUp Journey (after the one-person business) is at the 3–5 level where we are just large enough to benefit from some collaborative thinking as well as support, then 8–12 where we reach the maximum effective size of an individual team (and really this is a stretch requiring probably at least a 'number 2' to take some of the weight) – so we then need to structure the business into sub units with leaders – so we need a layer. Realistically this is likely to be 3–5 units of around 5–6 on average – leading to the 20–25 step depending on your particular needs in the business.

As we scale, this idea of team sizes continues, ideally keeping units of 3–5. We will come back to this when we look at accountabilities and a way of structuring your business to make sure you facilitate clear roles and accountabilities.

The Five Behaviours model

As Patrick Lencioni says in his book, *The Five Dysfunctions of a Team*:

'Not finance. Not strategy. Not technology. It is teamwork that remains the ultimate competitive advantage, both because it is so powerful and so rare.'[63]

There are many models describing effective or cohesive teams including the Tuckman model discussed earlier. As with most things to do with business, it is easy to overcomplicate it and get lost in the weeds. There are similarities in most and we have found one particular model to work well, based on the book *The Five Dysfunctions of a Team* by Patrick Lencioni[64] – and it spells out five behaviours required by any team to function cohesively. More than that, it gives us a kind of mini 'roadmap' for us to develop our teams.

The Five Behaviours of a Cohesive Team™ is the result of a partnership between Wiley Workplace Learning Solutions and best-selling author Patrick Lencioni.[65] The short version is that a cohesive team: Establishes **TRUST** between team members, Engages in **CONFLICT** around ideas, Commits to **DECISIONS**, Holds team members **ACCOUNTABLE** and Focuses on achieving collective **RESULTS.**

Adapted from https://www.fivebehaviors.com/Home.aspx

Fig. 45

Each behaviour builds on the previous one – so it is a journey and you should not treat each one in isolation.

To really make it work, team members need to have a sound understanding of themselves as well as their peers – and the starting point for this is often behavioural profiling, for which we use DISC. We have already talked about the benefits in the Leadership section and how we need to start from a good understanding of ourselves and each other, our motivations and our fears. The Five Behaviours model has DISC built into it but regardless of whether you undertake a profiling exercise, the model itself is a simple but powerful way to think about your teams.

Trust

Looking at the Five Behaviours, the first is around establishing trust between team members. This is more than trusting someone not to steal your sandwich from the fridge, or even that they will do a reasonable job – this is about trusting each other enough to admit our own mistakes, without the fear that this will be used against us somehow.

If this is strong within the team it implies that there is confidence among team members that we all have good intentions and that there is no reason to build protective barriers. This means that we are willing to be open and honest.

Trust is the single most important behaviour in not only Lencioni's model but almost every other team model, including recent work undertaken by Google where they referred to it as 'psychological safety'[66]. How comfortable do you feel taking risks in this team without feeling insecure or embarrassed?

Trust is the foundation of any effective team. If this is lacking then whatever else you try to do with the team it will be the equivalent of building on sand. So if you suspect that trust is lacking in your team then you need to do something about it.

Indicators that the level of trust is not all that it could be include team members holding grudges, avoiding meetings and spending time together, covering up weaknesses and mistakes, people reacting badly if they are challenged and being unwilling to ask for help or offer constructive feedback.

So how can we build trust or overcome the lack of trust?

Well you're not going to change it overnight but there are some simple things you can try. I reminded you of the 'Physician heal thyself' comment when we discussed leadership. It starts with you again – you must create an environment that does not punish vulnerability. We may think that we have to show strength by being right all the time but a stronger show of strength would be to admit our own mistakes and show our own vulnerability every now and then (caveat: don't take it too far!). You must also follow through on what you say you will do – remember 'actions speak louder than words!'

Consider getting everyone in the team to undertake **personality and behavioural profiling** – this is a great starting point to get the team to understand themselves and each other as individuals and as a team. You can combine this with asking the team to share examples of where their 'style' has helped them and hindered them in the past. There are many simple exercises you can find with a quick internet search to encourage people to share something about themselves, so consider trying a couple. I took part in something recently where the facilitator asked us to share any nicknames we might have had at school and how they came about – it was fascinating!

And you can also think about trying that team exercise I mentioned earlier in this section on what makes a cohesive team – and what does not.

Conflict

So now you've worked on trust, they should all get along without any conflict shouldn't they?

You may think that the goal is to avoid conflict – well I'm afraid not! All great relationships require productive conflict, and if you want a team to produce the best possible solution you need to be able to engage in productive conflict. Note the word 'productive' – it is all around engaging in 'constructive' debate and you can see how this is almost impossible if you haven't first established trust.

Lencioni suggests we think about it terms of a conflict spectrum: at the one end we have 'Artificial Harmony' where everyone keeps their real thoughts hidden and simply 'follows' what the leader says, and at the other where we have 'Mean-Spirited Personal Attacks' with manipulation and back- stabbing.[67] We want somewhere in between where we can engage in constructive conflict around issues and ideas. If we have a team of 'followers' we go back to the submarine captain David Marquet issuing orders that others follow.

Conflict isn't personal; it is around ideas and issues and it is not mean! But it can be uncomfortable, which is why the trust/vulnerability is so important first, otherwise we descend into politics.

Some personality types are more or less at home with conflict than others – which is another reason to understand each other's styles. If you have 'owls' in your team (DISC profile C), they will naturally fear speaking up if they have not had the chance to think things through first and be sure of their facts. This often means their ideas are not heard, or are drowned out by some of the other styles. So recognising this, perhaps give a chance for people to think before being put on the spot and maybe hold back some team members and encourage the owls to speak.

So how else do we overcome a natural fear of conflict? Firstly the team has to acknowledge that it is a good thing and that we need to encourage open debate around ideas in a way that is not 'personal'. Secondly we have to recognise that we may need to probe further to get the real thoughts – a bit like not accepting 'fine' as the answer when you ask someone how they are. We know we say fine when we are not; sometimes it is best to let it be but occasionally we need to probe further to uncover the real feeling. It is the same in teams; sometimes we need to probe a little to uncover true thoughts and get them out on the table and the team should acknowledge that this is acceptable and good if we want the best outcome.

The Challenge section of the Smart7 (and Smart30) team meeting outlined in the next chapter, Execution, provides a great way to begin to encourage constructive debate around specific 'challenges'.

Here is our challenge solver approach:

- Define the challenge – in one sentence ('owner' of the challenge)
- The current situation – what is happening now?
- What does good look like/what are the desired outcomes?
- 'Walk the room'/each person gives their thoughts/opinions around the challenge description – **once only** – more than once is politics!
- What are the root causes of the current situation – not just the symptoms (keep asking why!)?
- What information are we missing to move forward?
- How can we move forward – what are some tangible next steps?
- The 'owner' defines the next steps (so they retain ownership of the challenge)

This provides a structure for constructive challenge, focusing on the challenge itself (not people/it is not personal), builds in co-operation, commitment to resolution, respect for others (through listening to each other and all having an equal say), open and honest communication. It also facilitates ownership of the problem, requiring the person affected by it to define the challenge but also to wrap it up by defining the next steps at the end.

Commitment

Conflict is important for the next behaviour – achieving commitment.

If you or I as the leader impose our decision then what do you think the levels of buy-in and commitment will be like? If, however, we allow constructive conflict and everyone in the team has their say, how much stronger will the buy-in and commitment be? But this is not the same as consensus – or leading by committee. We are not making decisions by putting everything to a vote!

We want to avoid team members being unclear of expectations; we need them to have clear direction and priorities. As entrepreneurs, we tend to be more comfortable than most with uncertainty (otherwise we probably would not have started our own business) but most people are stressed by ambiguity and uncertainty. Teams without commitment tend to avoid making decisions and have a high fear of making a mistake. This is one of the reasons why a good 90-day planning 'habit' is such a great thing to instil in a business.

Going back to 'conflict' and ensuring everyone's ideas are out on the table is the best way to start addressing commitment. Once everyone has had their say, this is when you need to show some leadership and explain why you are going with a particular decision – and why not others. The goal is not that everyone gets their way, simply that they have been heard and listened to and then can understand why a particular decision was made. So communicate that decision and formulate a simple action plan using Rudyard Kipling's Six Honest Serving Men (What, Why, When, How, Where and Who!).[68]

You can help to mitigate the fear of making a wrong decision by thinking of milestones and a contingency plan in the event of things not working out as we hoped.

As you go through the rest of the book and in particular the Rhythm section in the 'Execution' chapter, you should note how the suggested approach supports the Five Behaviours, including commitment to actions. As a reminder, they are:

establishing **TRUST** between team members, engaging in **CONFLICT** around ideas, **COMMITTING** to decisions, holding team members **ACCOUNTABLE** and focusing on achieving collective **RESULTS.**

Note also that this is not about 'managing by committee'. Everyone needs to have their say and feel understood. That is not the same as taking a vote! This is about seeking first to understand, and then to be understood. Depending on the topic, it may be down to you to bring it to a close and define the next steps/actions, or it may be down to the individual who has brought the challenge (as in the challenge solver approach above). Either way, the group is brought to a defined way forward once all the views are aired.

Accountability

Accountability is overused as a term and is about 'owning and tracking' and is different from responsibility – it is about tracking progress not about authority. Lencioni in this model defines it as: 'The willingness of team members to remind one another when they are not living up to the performance standards of the group.'[69]

So again it is about tracking and also about bringing to the attention of the team. In this context of cohesive teams, it is not just about the numbers, it is also about raising concerns over behaviour of other team members. So you will again see the importance of the trust within the team – that acceptance that you can raise concerns without fear of repercussions.

Accountability is an interesting one. Some of us fear the idea of it, and perhaps feel that it might lead to conflicts and awkward conversations for us as the business owner. That should not be the case. Firstly, there is no more guaranteed way of losing good people from your business than having a culture where there is no accountability. Good people want to feel rewarded for their contribution and seeing others consistently underperform without consequence is a huge turn-off. Secondly, it should not fall on your shoulders to enforce accountability. In a well-functioning team, the team members understand what should be happening and will 'self-police' out of line behaviours. If you have instilled a strong values-based culture (see Core ideology section in the 'Strategy' chapter) then everyone knows the intent and the guidelines within which everyone operates – it shouldn't fall to you to enforce them.

Of course, if the trust is not there then this won't happen or won't happen in the right way.

If you get it right then you will establish respect among the team who are held to the same standards and poor performers will feel the pressure to improve. You will also avoid the need for excessive performance management and corrective action.

Again, instilling a robust 90-day planning habit and Business Rhythm are excellent places to start in instilling accountability through sharing and communication of **goals and standards;** no-one can ignore them and everyone knows who is responsible for what and with simple and regular **progress reviews,** team members should comment on their peer performance against objectives and standards.

Again the Business Rhythm structure we define in the next chapter ensures accountability is clear – including in the challenge solver approach above.

Results

If we get everything else right, the ultimate goal of creating a cohesive team is to achieve results.

In the context of a cohesive team, results are not limited to financial measures, but are also related to expectations, behaviours and outcome-based performance. We also want to encourage a focus on collective goals of the team rather than individuals – so the best outcomes and key results are ones that the team achieve together rather than creating a 'prima donna' culture.

When a team is focused on results in the right way the team members value collective success more than individual achievement and will look to help colleagues for the good of the team. So we all feel a joint responsibility to ensure the team achieves the goals set – which means we don't just do our bit and leave everyone else to sink or swim. You will notice team members actively pointing out the contributions made by others.

A great example of beginning to transform the culture of an organisation can be found with Alan Mulally[70] who was brought in as CEO to a struggling Ford in 2006. He found a leadership board that was afraid to give bad news. In his initial sessions, all the board members were reporting performance priorities in the green on their traffic light system, even though they were heading towards losing $17 billion.

Alan responded: 'We are about to lose $17 billion this year, and you are saying that everything is OK? Did we plan last year to lose $17 billion this year? If the answer to that question is yes, then we are in the green. Otherwise, we are not!'[71]

After a significant period of silence (under the previous CEO it was career suicide to admit to failure!) one leader eventually admitted that he was in red.

Alan Mulally thanked the leader for his honesty, stood up, and applauded him. He said 'Thank you for having the courage, telling the truth, and admitting that you have a problem and don't have all the answers, and are unsure how to get things back on track.'

Alan went a step further, which was to admit that he didn't have the answers – that he knew very little about making and selling cars. Definitely less than the others in the room. But he went on to say, 'We just need to act on reality. Then we'll be back making the best cars in the world. I know nothing about building cars. It is ok to admit that. We have to be completely honest, accept reality, and then decide a further course of action.'

Going back to the first level of Lenzioni's model, Alan Mulally had the humility to be vulnerable and admit he didn't have all the answers. He made it clear that it was ok to bring bad news and that the way forward was to face it head on and work together to make things better.

LEARNING POINTS

Key learning points around Cohesive Teams are:

- We start with building **trust** so that we can master conflict to achieve commitment to embracing accountability and focusing on results. Are you like Alan Mulally or are you like the previous Ford CEO?
- Trust, remember, is about vulnerability or feeling you can be open with the team without fear of judgement or repercussions – so we don't hide things.
- We want constructive debate not personal **conflict** – challenging ideas not personalities.
- **Commitment** is about clarification and buy-in and **accountability** is about behaviours and not letting our own or others' slide.
- And **results** are about that focus on collective results.

The relevant points from the InFlight Checks are reproduced below.

8. All teams function Cohesively	SUBTOTAL
Team members understand each other's styles, differences and priorities	
Team members trust each other enough to admit mistakes	
Team members feel able to challenge each other and engage in constructive debate	
Team members are motivated to and work well to achieve the team goals	

ACCOUNTABILITY

RHYTHM 90

'Accountability is the glue that ties the commitment to the result' – Bob Proctor

We introduced the topic of accountability in the previous section on cohesive teams and we will look into it further here.

Let's start with Charles Osgood's story about four people named Anybody, Everybody, Somebody, and Nobody.[72] There was an important job to be done and Everybody was sure that Somebody would do it. Anybody could have done it, but Nobody did it. Somebody got angry about that, because it was Everybody's job. Everybody thought Anybody could do it, but Nobody realised that Everybody wouldn't do it. It ended up that Everybody blamed Somebody when Nobody did what Anybody could have done!!

A fun little story but the takeaway is that if we want our team to be truly productive, we must ensure that we are clear on roles and accountabilities. Just to illustrate the point, as mentioned previously when we asked 80 owner-managers of businesses with more than £100k turnover to list their top 5 challenges in running their businesses, by far the greatest was getting their staff to do the right things consistently well. It is hard to get your staff working in the way that you would like them to. So we need to work at it.

The key things we want to ensure are that we have a culture of individual accountability and joint responsibility. The relevant points from the InFlight Checks are:

9. We have a culture of Individual Accountability and Joint Responsibility	SUBTOTAL
We have the right people in the right roles with clear roles and accountabilities	
Individuals are empowered to make decisions for their area of responsibility	
Teams are focused on achieving collective results and we celebrate team success	
Everyone has visibility of and religiously track progress against 'Rocks' and Critical Numbers	

The right people in the right roles

Jim Collins proposed this concept in *Good to Great* where he posed the killer question: 'Do you have the right people on your bus and would you enthusiastically rehire them all?'[73]

Most of us know that we are better off with people that have the right attitude even if they don't have all the skills; we should 'hire for will and train for skill'.

Working in your flame

Dr Ivan Misner (Founder and Chief Visionary Officer of BNI,[74] the world's largest business networking organisation) proposes the concept of 'working in your flame'[75]. As a business person you are either working in your flame or you are working in your wax. When you're in your flame you're on fire, you're excited, you're energised. But when you're working in your wax, you are drained and fatigued.

As our business grows, it is easy to get caught up doing more and more in our wax. We raised the idea in the Leadership section on delegation, how in the early stages we need to delegate the things we are not good at or shouldn't be doing – well this is essentially the idea of working in your flame. So find out what your flame is and work to understand it, and then do your best to work more in that flame. Everybody is different, and if we understand the motivations and priorities of our team we can find people whose flame is 'our wax' and put them in the roles we no longer love doing. This will free us up to work in our flame – but equally it will mean that we have our people working in their flames.

So the right people in the right roles is about making sure we have good people and that we help them to find their flame with the right role – not just about forcing someone into a role. Even the right person's flame will wither and die out if they are in the wrong role for any length of time.

But how do we know if we have the right people in the right roles?

Essentially the answer is whether they display the right values and attitude through their **B**ehaviours (do they live the Core Values?), do they have the **A**ptitude to do the role (the competence – the knowledge, experience and skills required), do they truly **U**nderstand the role and how it contributes to the vision, and do they have the **D**esire – do they want to be 'on the bus'? This is our **BAUD**© rate and a simple way of giving a little bit of structure to answering the fundamental question: 'Would we enthusiastically rehire this person in this role knowing what we now know?'

So would you?! Have you thought about it beyond a subjective feeling about your team members? Rating each key team member on a quarterly basis is another great habit to get into. Combined with the 'Job Scorecard' from Topgrading[76] which we will review in the following section on hiring, this gives you a way of ensuring accountability.

Of course we need to try to make sure we hire the right people in the first place – and we will look at that more in the 'Hiring' section on making hiring a strength of the business, so that we are punching above our weight in this area. As already mentioned, though, we should be hiring on attitude first – so making sure we include a way to assess on the company values, for example, should be a key component of any recruitment process.

Clarity – are roles and accountabilities clear?

Is it absolutely clear who is doing what? Individuals need to be accountable and hold each other to account but the only way this can happen is if everyone understands their own role and areas of accountability. Each component of activity should have people assigned as accountable.

The magic phrase here is 'individual accountability and joint responsibility'. Going back to Osgood's poem, someone needs to take ownership – otherwise we are in trouble. That is the individual accountability. But equally we need to pull together to maintain the values and the culture and to achieve the Vision of the business – so whilst someone owns a particular task for example, we are all responsible for helping to make sure they can complete it. If we spot they are having difficulties, we don't turn our back saying 'not my problem'; we look to see if we can help.

Words like **accountability, responsibility and authority** are bandied around and used interchangeably sometimes. Although it might seem a bit like semantics, we need to be clear on the differences if we are going to improve clarity in our teams.

Accountability – This is about tracking progress and 'owning' it – not about authority. If more than one person is accountable, then no-one is accountable, as described by Osgood. Accountability is not something that can be shared. Accountability is literally about the 'ability to count'.

This doesn't mean he/she does everything, or needs to be the smartest or most senior. It doesn't even mean they need to make the decisions. He or she is the person to give the activity a voice – to care that something is happening relative to the specific deliverable.

Responsibility – This is about proactively supporting the team. This falls to anyone with the 'ability to respond'. It includes everyone involved in a particular process or issue. For example, it is the responsibility of all staff to uphold the reputation of the company. So responsibility can be shared.

Authority – This is about the final decision-making power. This lies with the person or team who has the final decision-making power or the 'right to author the decision' and, like responsibility, this can be shared.

For example, think of a leadership exercise where the leader might delegate accountability for monitoring the time to Fred, the group is jointly responsible for keeping to time/to support the team in getting the task done in the time, and Fred is accountable for making everyone aware of the time but the leader is the one with the authority to make the decisions as to what to do about it.

Getting accountabilities clear throughout your business is crucial – right from the start. The golden rule to bear in mind is that if you have more than one person that thinks they are accountable for something, then actually no-one is!

I'm going to take you through a one-page people tool to help assign specific accountabilities and then link it back to a variation of the traditional organisational chart. What these tools will also do is help you to think about the structure of your business (as it is now and as you want it to be), identifying roles that you may want to recruit for next as you scale, as well as the roles that you want to delegate yourself out of next. It is a similar concept to that described by Michael Gerber in his book *The E-Myth Revisited* where he encourages the characters in the story to define the key positions or functions required by their business. Even though there are only the two of them in the business, they identify 12 key positions. They then write a 'Position Contract' for each position that details the key accountabilities and metrics for each role.[77]

The first tool focuses on making sure you have the right people in the right seats at the top of the organisation. It is based on the Function Accountability Chart developed by Verne Harnish and the Gazelles.[78] This is the 'right people doing the right things' bit. And it helps to see whether we have clear roles and accountabilities.

Every business requires 5 primary functions to be done – regardless of whether you are a one-person business or have several employees. Every business has to do these things and we have adapted the framework to include these as well as our BAUD rate that we will explain shortly.

The adapted framework lists the functions that exist in every business under 5 headings – essentially BRING IT (i.e. bring in business), DO IT (make or deliver whatever your business does for clients), COUNT IT (all the business administration that needs to be done to support the business), LEAD IT (all the big picture stuff) and ENABLE IT (as in 'make it happen').

Bearing in mind that most of us reading this are small or medium sized businesses, we still have to do all of these functions even if we only have a few people, or even if we are on our own. The difference is that we might be the one doing everything!

So I'm going to take you through step by step how to use it and how to get the most out of it, but first, a quick summary. You can see a space for the functions to be listed down the left hand side with then three further columns headed Person Accountable, Leading Indicators, Lagging or Results Indicators and then the big one – would you 'Enthusiastically Rehire?' In scaling up the business, this can help us to work out which function to delegate next – so it can give us a roadmap for scaling our business. For example when Ivan Misner speaks about how he started BNI, he talks about doing a very similar exercise at the beginning of his journey when he worked out what he wanted to delegate next and what needed to be in place for each delegation. In his case, one of the first was delegating the packing and distribution of member welcome packs.

The first thing to do is to insert the key functions of your business in the first column – the big things that need to be done in order for your business to exist. You may have subcategories – so under Bring It we would include Marketing, and under Marketing you might include Promotions, Pricing, New lead generation for example.

Functions	Person Accountable	How do we know if the role is being done well?		
		Leading Indicators (Actions/ Behavioural KPIs)	Lagging Indicators (Results KPIs)	Enthusiastically Rehire? BAUO Rate
Bring it				
Do It				
Count It				
Lead It				
Enable It				

Fig. 46

So as examples (you will have some or even all of these, and you may have other specific functions you wish to include):

Bring It e.g. Marketing (Promotion, Pricing, Client retention, New lead generation), Sales (New account sales, Upselling existing accounts), Customer service etc

Do It e.g. Operations (Sourcing, Design, Production, IT, R&D/Innovation, Quality), Distribution/Delivery

Count It e.g. Finance (Funding, Managing budgets, Accounting, Financial controls and audits), Human resources (Recruiting/Onboarding, Training/Development, Evaluations, Benefits), Audit control (ISO/Regulatory)

Lead It e.g. Vision, Culture, Strategy, Strategic Relationships (e.g. Investors, Partners), Ensuring right people in right seats, Chairing the leadership team/board of directors

Enable It e.g. Business planning, P&L, Strategy implementation/Execution (e.g. Business Rhythm), Special projects, Problem solver/removing obstacles, ensuring the right people are doing the right things

Then you complete the second column with who is accountable (this can be an outsourced function – so include outsourced also).

If you do have a number of senior managers, then get them to do this individually and compare results! This can sometimes lead to some interesting situations and shows very quickly if there is confusion within the team over accountabilities. You may have more than one person in a box, you may have gaps and you may have one person (normally you as the owner!) appearing in too many boxes. This can lead to some great conversations and thinking, such as which role you should be looking to delegate yourself out of next.

Then you can list up to 3 'leading' and 'lagging' KPIs for each of the listed functions – not too many, 1, 2, or 3 that help you answer the question 'How do we know if that role is being done well on a day-to-day basis?'

Leading KPIs – measuring daily and weekly activities that should lead to the desired results – should be the day-to-day behavioural KPIs that help us to know if the function is being done well. Lagging KPIs are the results you hope to achieve such as turnover, profit, sales etc.

When you do this, it is important to separate the individuals from the KPIs – so don't ask yourself what does Geoff do each day if Geoff is the accountable person. Ignore the fact that it is Geoff and ask what the leading KPIs should be for the function to be done well.

Now you can go back and ask the killer question, 'Would we enthusiastically rehire this person in this role knowing what we now know?' in the light of the Key Performance Indicators but also using the BAUD rate.

As a double-check, take your Profit and Loss, Balance Sheet, and Cashflow accounting statements and make sure nothing is missing – in other words that each key line item has a person accountable.

So we can then translate this into an accountability org chart which is like a more traditional org chart but you notice we have the key accountabilities included. Early on your accountability chart may look like the one that follows.

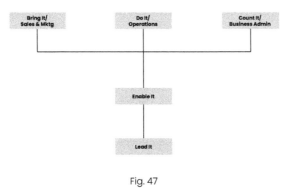

Fig. 47

The first thing that you will notice compared to the traditional organisational chart is that it is upside down! There are a couple of reasons for this; firstly the rest of the organisation exists to support the customer facing roles, not the other way around. The customer facing roles/the delivery of what the customer will see tend to be at the branches, so let's make that clear by reversing the chart. Also it is like a tree now, with the roots at the bottom that support the branches and leaves.

When I came out of the Royal Air Force to become a sales representative in a pharmaceutical company, I was struck by the difference – in the air force, everything is organised around making sure the pilots can do their job – the pilots (although by no means the senior ranking officers) are the ones that are respected and everyone else understands that what they do in some way contributes to keeping the pilots in the air and enabling them to be effective.

In the pharmaceutical industry, the sales rep is the equivalent of the pilot – but do you think they were perceived in the same way?

Another reason for turning things upside down is that initially (when you start and are small) you will be starting at the customer interface. As you scale, you develop processes, automate, delegate and hire to enable you to vacate that role and move more towards the roots of the tree – increasingly playing a supportive role to enable your frontline teams to do their roles effectively.

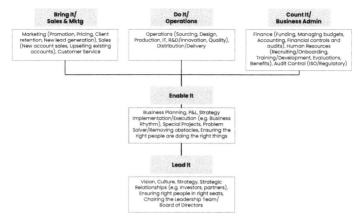

Fig. 48

Initially you will have your name in most of the boxes – which is fine but we know not sustainable. So we use the concept of the accountability org chart to map what the business needs to look like at the next step on your ScaleUp Journey – maybe two or three years ahead.

You may use this idea in conjunction with your SmartWeb 3-year plan to work out the key roles you need in the future (see the example below). Do it without names to begin with even where you think you have a role filled, and then map who you have now. Where you think you might have more than one of a role, just include the one box with the number of people in it – e.g. Sales Representative 3.

This should help you to work out where you need to recruit next, or develop someone towards – and most importantly where you can remove yourself.

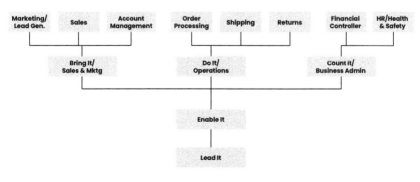

Fig. 49

In addition to including a few key accountabilities of the role, you can also create a one-page Job Scorecard for each role and then you have the ultimate clarity in roles and accountabilities.

We often get asked about the 'Enable It' role and what it is, why we need it and when it needs to be a separate role. Clearly in the very early stages the business owner needs to do most things, certainly setting strategy and making things happen. As we progress beyond the 3–5 level we start to get to the point where it is extremely hard (nearly impossible) for one person to keep control as well as be able to do all the things a good leader needs to be able to do. This is the point where we need what is effectively a second-in-command or XO.

In many militaries and police forces, an executive officer, or 'XO', is the second-in-command, reporting to the commanding officer. The XO is typically responsible for the management of day-to-day activities, freeing the commander to concentrate on strategy and planning the unit's next move. In other words they are the enabler, enabling the leader to get on with leading whilst enabling the rest of the team (mainly implementors) to do the right things well.

Enablers are the people who help the implementors focus on implementing. They make sure all of the implementors are working towards the same end result and deal with things that take time away from creating and delivering value.

HIRING

Punching above our weight class

RHYTHM 90

10. Our ability to retain and hire good people is a strength of the business	SUBTOTAL
We have a retention, development and succession/contingency plan for every key employee (score 1 if just you in the business) and hold regular (quarterly) 'retention discussions' with key employees	
We have a clear view of organisational needs/structure over the next 3 years and whether we are hiring in or developing internally for each role	
We are clear on our Employee Value Proposition and are able to attract sufficient good candidates (we are able to 'punch above our weight' in recruitment)	
We have a robust hiring process in place that minimizes the chances of making a bad hire	

One of the most common and biggest challenges we see with growing businesses is finding the right people and getting them on board.

This has always been a challenge for small and medium-sized businesses competing for talent with bigger names.

And often we leave it until we need someone urgently – which of course puts extra pressure on us and is likely to lead to taking anyone with a pulse!

We are never going to be able to outspend a big company – either in terms of our recruitment spend or probably the salary that we are able to offer – so we need to think differently and systematically and give it the attention it requires.

We also need to be mindful of the 'costs' of making a bad hire.

According to an in-depth report conducted by the REC (Recruitment and Employment Confederation):[79]

- 85% of HR decision-makers admit their organisation has made a bad hire, and a third (33%) believe that these mistakes cost their business nothing
- A poor hire at mid-manager level with a salary of £42,000 can cost a business more than £132,000
- The hidden costs involved in bad recruitment include money wasted on training, lost productivity, and increased staff turnover
- Four in ten employers (39%) admit that the interviewing and assessment skills of their staff should be improved.

So we need to get it right. We need to approach recruitment with the same focus we might approach finding new customers. In some sectors finding the right staff may be so critical that one of your Critical Paths is your recruitment and you may even aim to have recruitment as one of your key differentiators – one of the things that you can be the best at in your sector.

Three overarching hiring principles

Before we get into the detail, there are three overarching principles to punching above your weight class in hiring, followed by five to minimise the risk of a bad hire:

Fig. 50

Think and act differently

Think and act differently; don't limit yourself to what everyone else does. Recruitment platforms such as Indeed and other tactics can be great, but what can you do that would get you in front of hard-to-find people earlier? Are you regularly going after people with a particular skill set? Where do they get trained? Could you offer your time to train, and could you even run your own training?

Here are a couple of examples of businesses thinking differently:

First, Paul Rhodes of Green Gorilla Software. His scarce resource is Ruby on Rails qualified developers. They are available but at exorbitant rates. So firstly, Paul accepted that he would likely be a stepping stone on a Rails's career – that they would probably leave after 2–3 years once they had built up experience with him. Secondly, he found a Ruby on Rails bootcamp where developers learn to code in Rails and he offered to teach a module or two, leading to a number of successful hires.

Another example is in the health and safety sector. A West Midlands (UK) company recognised that newly qualified consultants often went to work in the public sector for their first job to gain experience, but grew dissatisfied after a couple of years. So they effectively developed a poaching strategy targeting disillusioned health and safety executives in the public sector.

Both of these are great examples of thinking a little differently instead of just spending more on recruitment platforms or with recruitment agencies.

Also – and this is a tactic for getting comfortable that you can afford to make the hire (and links with the 'profit first' ideas explained later in the 'Cash' chapter) – the moment you decide you want to start recruiting, you should start putting the money aside as if you were paying them already. This will show you that you can afford them (or make you do something different now!) but it will also mean that by the time you have them on board, you should have saved at least a couple of months' salary for them!

Make the job appealing

Making the job appealing reflects the paradigm shift that has been happening for a while – namely that the attitude of 'they should be grateful for a job' has been turned on its head. Recent stats suggest that every candidate has the choice of around 38 jobs and as employers we need to the have the mindset of 'What's in it for them?' In Paul Rhodes's example above, I mentioned that he has changed his mindset to accept that they are on the beginning of the career path for a 'Rails' developer, and that they may well lose them in a couple of years.

So this is also about how you can appeal to the type of candidate you are after – what do you offer that they might value that they might not get elsewhere? This is where the idea of the Employee Value Proposition (EVP) comes in and aims to answer the question 'Why should I work for your company instead of somewhere else?' And to be clear, we are not talking about specific compensation plans here – this is much more about appealing to their desires and passions.

You can pull on a lot of the work you did earlier around Core Values and purpose – clearly these are what you stand for and should appeal to the right candidates. Your best source of ideas will be your existing employees and potentially ex-employees – why do they love working in your business? You can google great examples online, but don't get sucked into just copying someone else's – it needs to be authentic.

We suggest you start internally with the same types of questions you would need to answer for your customer value proposition which we define in more detail in Execution – Business Development. The key areas are:

- Who is your ideal candidate? Describe them in as much detail as you can. Create an 'avatar'.
- What are they looking for/what do they need?
- What are you offering and how does that help them meet their needs – what are the benefits to them?
- What are their alternatives/who else might they work for?
- Why are you different/what is different about working with you?
- How can you show that?

If you can answer all these questions well, then you will have a strong idea of how to position your company in a way that is likely to appeal to the kind of candidates you are seeking.

Always be recruiting

The key to this is having a forward view of what kinds of roles and people you will need for the next stage of your ScaleUp Journey. We covered this in accountabilities with the 'accountability org chart' – put one together for the business as it is now, and as you think it will need to be for the next step – which might be in three years, for example.

If you define the key accountabilities of that role as part of this, then you will be able to keep a lookout for promising candidates in the meantime and in advance of when you may actually need them. You may have a permanent recruitment page on your website which not only includes any current vacancies but a distilled version of your EVP along with an encouragement to get in touch even if you don't see a precise job that matches your CV.

This links with the idea of a 'people bank' which I'll cover in a 'best practice' 10-step hiring process shortly.

So now we have started to think and act differently, we need to make sure we minimise the risk of a bad hire.

Five steps to minimising the risk of a bad hire:

Define	Have a clearly defined Job Scorecard with KPIs
Create Choice	Make sure you have a choice – think and act differently
Don't Rush	Hire Slow Fire Fast
Discard Chaff Fast	Have a 'system' to weed out quickly – spend the time with the best
Onboard Well	Have a defined and agreed onboarding programme with reviews – what does good look like?

Fig. 51

1. **Define** the 'mission' of that role, identifying the key accountabilities and Key Performance Indicators for the role along with the behavioural expectations (these should include Core Value behaviours).
2. **Create choice:** Don't put yourself in the situation where you only have one candidate to choose from. Use the three overarching principles discussed above to increase your chances of having a good choice – in particular the 'think and act differently'.
3. **Don't rush:** Remember the cost of a bad hire. This is a mindset as much as anything. Take your time getting them on board but make sure you don't get stuck with a bad hire for any longer than necessary – see 'Onboarding' later in this section for where the 'fire fast' comes in.
4. **Discard chaff quickly:** Ensure you have a recruitment 'system' that prequalifies candidates without you spending lots of time. For example ask

them for a cover letter explaining why they think they are the right candidate and discard any candidates that don't do it (don't even look at their CVs). Get rid of the chaff quickly so you can spend quality time with a shortlist of strong candidates.

5. **Onboard well:** Set expectations and agree an onboarding programme with the new recruit. You should have mapped out the key milestones beforehand, but it is so much more powerful to develop this further with the new recruit. What does good look like when they are up to speed? When is that by – is it 3 months, 6 months? Work back and agree milestones and any training needs. Agree it with the chosen candidate and ask them what they would expect to happen if they fall behind.

A 10-step hiring process

So having set the overall principles of punching above our weight class in recruitment, I'm going to take you through 10 steps that will help you to attract and hire the right people (What you might call the A-players – where the A really should stand for 'Attitude'). These 10 steps are a combination of what we consider best practice. You may add to these depending on the level of the role. The only thing we would think remotely sensible to shorten might be the combination of steps 6 and 7 for more junior roles but we wouldn't recommend it. Think about the wasted time and money of a bad hire if you are tempted to short circuit the steps...

I'm not going to tell you that this will mean you get it right every time – there will always be a margin of error just like you won't always win that new customer – but this has been shown to help hire the right person most of the time, maybe even 90% of the time.

Any recruitment process will have three potential outcomes:

- You hire the right person
- You hire the wrong person (false positive)
- You reject the right person (false negative)

We've seen the cost of hiring the wrong person so contrary to what you may have thought before, you want a process that is biased more towards the false negative – so just like good selling, you want to qualify hard upfront before you jump and say yes. Qualifying hard is about making sure you spend your time with good prospects, and weed out the others early on. I explain more in 'Weed out' below.

Here are the 10 steps:

1. Develop a Job Scorecard and your EVP (Employee Value Proposition)
2. Build a people bank
3. Create/place a distinctive job ad
4. 'Weed out'
5. Telephone screen
6. Job Scorecard interview
7. Flight test
8. Reference check
9. Will, values, results and skills (WVRS)
10. Offer interview

Develop a Job Scorecard and your EVP (Employee Value Proposition)

We suggest a Job Scorecard rather than a job description. This tool is a key element in Topgrading, a methodology for hiring A-players, co-created by Brad and Geoff Smart.[80]

Writing a scorecard has to be the first step and it will help you throughout the process. Ideally you do this well in advance of the actual need to fill the role, once you have defined what roles you will need to fill next as you grow. We went through this in the module on Accountability.

A Job Scorecard details the purpose of the job (the mission), the desired outcomes for that individual/role and the behaviours/competencies (including cultural) required.

It is much more powerful than a typical job description – particularly because of the emphasis on outcomes. In one sense it is simpler (shorter) but that doesn't necessarily mean easier; it will require more thought to make it simple and will then be all the more powerful for it.

Another key section of the Job Scorecard is the Behaviours/Competencies that link with your Core Values/Culture – which we went through in the Core Values module in the 'Strategy' chapter.

Based on the vital question, 'Would you enthusiastically rehire ...' as detailed previously, we have included the BAUD rate assessment in the Job Scorecard – Behaviour, Aptitude, Understanding and Desire.

Position/ Role:

Location:

Reports to:

Mission:

e.g. to increase revenues of our .... Service/ product from existing and new customers – you'll be expected to follow-up on leads from marketing activities as well as develop and carry out a prospecting call plan including cold calls and emails

Outcomes

Accountabilities	Metrics	Rating (A,B,C)	Comments/ BAUD Behaviour, Ability, Understanding & Desire
Increase Sales with existing customers	To/ by x amount within 3 months To/ by y amount within 12 months		
New customer sales	Close x amount of new sales/ new customers within 3 months Close y amount of new sales/ new customers within 12 months		
Activity	Make x many cold calls per day Schedule x many appointments		
Admin	Provide weekly/ monthly reports Keep CRM system up to date – daily		

Key Behaviours/ Competencies (including link back to core values):

e.g

	e.g. 10 things you can do with zero talent	
	Being on time	Attitude
	Work Ethic	Passion
	Effort	Being coachable
	Body Language	Doing extra
	Energy	Being prepared

Fig. 52

A scorecard contains three main parts:

1. Mission/Purpose of the job (e.g. to increase revenues of our .... from existing and new customers – you'll be expected to follow up on leads from marketing activities as well as develop and carry out a prospecting call plan).

2. Outcomes – Examples include:

Increase sales with existing customers

- To/by x amount within 3 months
- To/by y amount within 12 months

New customer sales

- Close x amount of new sales/new customers within 3 months
- Close y amount of new sales/new customers within 12 months

Activity

- Make x many cold calls per day
- Schedule x many appointments

Admin

- Provide weekly/monthly reports
- Keep CRM system up to date – daily

3. Key Behaviours/Competencies – Examples might include:

- Displaying a positive 'can-do' attitude
- Being coachable
- Being on time/showing a strong work ethic
- Being prepared etc.

These key behaviours should have a strong link back to your Core Values.

The Job Scorecard is an excellent first step in helping you define what you are looking for, but it is also a key guide/reference to help you define the kind of questions you might want to ask the candidate during interviews as well as helping to guide their onboarding and reviews when they have started. We recommend our clients develop Job Scorecards for existing as well as new staff – preferably in conjunction with the staff member, for example during their appraisal.

As a final point, you should get each person to sign their scorecard along with their manager right from initial onboarding and then subsequently each year during their annual review.

I covered the EVP earlier so make sure this is considered with the Job Scorecard.

Build a people bank

Now you have in mind the kind of roles you want to fill and the kind of people you are looking for, you need to keep an eye out even if you are not ready to recruit. This is such an easy thing to do but very few businesses do it well. Of course it needs time to develop, but imagine having a decent starting list of people you already know something about when you are ready to recruit.

There are great tools out there to manage recruitment that include you being able to keep track of prospects and build a people bank – for example Smart Recruiters. David Lynes, the founder of Unique IQ, has been using them for around three years now and has a 'bank' of over 4,000 people that have expressed an interest in various roles. These are now a pool of people that could be gone back to over the years – their careers and experience will change as will your needs over time, so even rejected candidates may become priorities (as long as they were not rejected on values!).

Even if you don't use an app, you may like to keep a simple tabbed spreadsheet for each type of role and include people who have impressed you (whether they be contractors, customers – whoever might be relevant for the role). If you have a CRM then why not add a separate category for your people bank?

Once you know what you are looking for, if you spot someone you think might be a strong fit then make time to explore further, for example over a coffee, or at least a telephone call. It will be time well spent. You can approach it along the lines of 'We're always on the lookout for great people – you may not be looking right now and we're not recruiting at this moment but things might change. Would it be worth a coffee to find out more about each other?'

Ideally you then rank them. Consider recording the following as a minimum for each prospect:

- Name
- Ranking – 1 (top tier), 2 (mid-tier) or 3 (low-tier).
- Current job title
- Last contacted
- Notes

You might like to add fields such as source/how you met them.

Of course you need to keep in mind the data protection regulations under GDPR and make sure you have a policy for permissions and how long you are going to keep the data before you delete it!

And remember to consider having a permanent section on your website about the kind of roles/people you are looking for so you can build this into your people bank approach.

Create/place a distinctive job ad

Now that you are ready to think about going out to a wider audience to recruit, we will need a job ad and we will need to think about where to post it. And remember the idea of thinking differently.

Don't just do what everyone else does – try to stand out with your job ad.

Go back to the EVP in step 1. What is different about the way you do things and what is in it for them?

What is the ideal kind of person you are looking for and where could you best reach them? (Maybe not traditional job boards.) Where do they hang out?

What characteristics describe our ideal workforce that our competitors would or could not use to describe theirs?

What benefits can you offer over your competitors (and by this I don't mean financial)? It might be as simple as coming to work in jeans, wanting to work for David not Goliath (!) or it might be training for a particular qualification – or even the idea of 'cutting your teeth with us...'

Being upfront about your Core Values and your culture will really help you identify candidates who share those values and are not just looking at the size of the pay cheque!

Once you've done your job ad, the question becomes where to put it?! I refer you back to thinking differently in your recruitment. Sure, you can place it in all the 'usual' places, but where else might make you stand out with the right kind of candidate?

There is one spin-off benefit you may not have considered of having a consistent social media strategy. We've had examples where potential candidates have been following the business on social media well in advance of jobs becoming available – so think of this as another reason for your social media activities and potentially build this into your people bank approach.

'Weed out'

As candidates begin to contact you, it's important that you weed out ones that are not worth your time – before you spend time on them! This refers back to weeding out the chaff mentioned earlier.

We want to create choice, but we want to spend the most time with the best prospects – not reading through dozens of CVs to find one good one. So we want to create a way of 'qualifying' quickly and not get hung up on whether there is a chance we miss a good candidate.

For example you might give them a basic instruction to start with in the job ad – such as 'visit our website and apply from there using the contact form'. Or you might ask them to submit a cover note with their CV that outlines what they think they will bring to the role, or simply what interests them about the role. Maybe get them to record and send you a 60-second video about themselves rather than send a CV – you'll weed out at least half of applicants just by doing this. Reject any that can't follow the instruction!

Then ask them some 'killer' questions by email that link with the Job Scorecard and would enable you to filter/weed out those that either don't bother to reply or answer in a way that shows they are not a good fit. You should obviously tailor these according to the role.

Example questions:

- What's the closest role you've had to (this role) and explain how this will be relevant/help you succeed in this role?
- What's an example of where you've grown an existing client base (assuming that was part of the accountabilities of this role!)?
- What do you think we mean by being 'coachable' and give an example of where you have shown that you are.

- Pick one of your Core Values and give an example where you have shown qualities that support the value.

Remember, the purpose here is to 'weed out' candidates, not to rank them necessarily – you are trying to make sure you don't waste time on 'no hopers'.

If you managed to get 20 applications, this step should get you down to around 10 – or maybe lower!

The telephone screen – 'fit'

The next step is the telephone screen. This is an absolute killer. It's the first time you will speak to the candidate (unless they are from your people bank and you've previously had a coffee with them) and the first time they will have spoken to you.

For those candidates who make it past the 'weed out' questions, then do a short phone screen. Again the operative word is 'short' – we are still qualifying hard to get us down to the really good prospects quickly.

The purpose of this is to decide whether they are able to think and communicate in a way that supports their answers from the 'weed out' stage – and that they display the kind of competencies, values and desire that you are looking for – not really to see if they have all the technical expertise you are looking for. You will interview suitable fit candidates on the actual projects you have in mind at the next step. You know that if I asked you whether you would rather have someone with the right technical skills and knowledge but the wrong attitude, or someone with the right attitude but perhaps not all the technical skills and knowledge, you would want the right attitude. So the aim of the telephone screen is to screen out the ones with the wrong attitude or fit.

The firmer you are about your Core Purpose and the core behaviours/values and competencies that the person needs to display, then the easier you should be able to develop a few questions to test them. For example, I've previously mentioned one of our clients who runs a call minding service and defined their Core Purpose as 'Making the right first impression for our customers'. This led to a really key element of the telephone screen which was if the candidate did not make a great first impression with the interviewer then the application was politely terminated.

We suggest you introduce the call and explain that 'the purpose in the next 30 minutes is to agree whether we both think it is appropriate to proceed to the next step of a face-to-face interview and I have some questions I'd like to ask you and you probably have some questions you'd like to ask me to help decide that – are you OK with that?'

You need to put your own questions together to help you weed out a further 50% or so of the candidates to leave you with five ideally. You should definitely further explore their written responses to your 'weed out' questions and then include questions such as:

1. What are your career goals?
2. What would your current boss say you are really good at?
3. What would you say you are not so great at or not interested in doing professionally?
4. Who were your last bosses (go back 5 if you've had that many) and how will each of them rate your performance (1 to 10 (with 10 being high)) when we talk to them?
5. Why are you thinking of leaving?
6. What are your most important considerations in taking on a new role? (This might lead you into compensation questions – such as 'How much pay do you need to live on?')

Question 4 is critical – a top candidate (sometimes referred to as an A-player) is going to answer with a mix of 7s, 8s, 9s and 10s. If they have a 6 or lower, it is likely to be the exception and they will have a very clear explanation for it. The implication of the way you phrase the question is that you are likely to be asking their boss, so there is no point in just saying a 10!

Give the candidate a chance to ask their questions; if they don't have any then unless they have asked questions as you went along you would have to question whether they are really interested in what you have to offer.

You should now have a much better idea of whether to proceed to the next step – you may want to close the discussion with a 'We'll get back to you in the next x days to let you know if we'd like to invite you in for an interview'.

Just a reminder as to where we are!

We are half way through reviewing a 'best practice' hiring process that you can adapt to help make recruitment a competitive advantage for your business so you can 'punch above your weight' in hiring.

We are treating recruitment like any other of your core business processes or habits, and making it just that – a process that can be repeated and tweaked or improved as time goes on and we learn what works best and what doesn't.

We are trying to make sure also that we spend the least amount of time with the wrong candidates and focus our efforts and time on the real potentials.

So far we have filtered our candidates down to a handful without wasting time on meeting them or, you will notice, poring over CVs.

Now is the time to meet them face to face.

Job Scorecard interview

By now you should be down to 3–5 candidates who you believe have displayed the right attitude and fit for your business.

This next step is an interview focused on the actual projects/role you have in mind for the candidate. The ideal approach here is that you take an outcome you want from the Job Scorecard and focus on it.

For example, one outcome might be 'Increase sales with existing customers to/by x amount within 12 months or by 50% within 12 months'.

Some good questions to ask might be:

- Can you give me some examples where you have succeeded in growing sales 50% or more?
- What are some mistakes and lessons you've learned in growing sales by 50%?
- How would you go about delivering/where would you start?

Depending on the outcomes you are looking for you may have a number of questions you could ask to get a strong view of how you and the candidate are starting to envision the actual work you would be doing together and the conversation should be quite natural.

This would be a great time to involve the rest of the leadership team and the team that they will be working with – with the aim of further establishing fit.

Ideally you will now be able to get down to 2 or 3 candidates you can invite back for a deeper assessment interview.

The flight test

The aim of this step is to 'test-fly' the potential employees.

The best way would be to have the candidates work for you for a few weeks before offering the job. In most cases this is not practical (although think about it and whether there might be a way – for example if you subcontract work why not subcontract some to a potential candidate, or would an apprentice work?) so you need to find a way to flight test them in an interview.

If you have a specific skill set requirement that they are expected to have, this is the step where you might want to give them a practical test, for example build a web page, or role play a customer opportunity or complaint, role play a cold call etc.

This is a great opportunity to get others in your team involved. Who do you value the opinion of/who is it relevant to include and are they to help with the team fit decision or with the technical skill decisions?

You may also like to consider conducting a personality and behavioural assessment using something like DISC that we discussed in the 'Cohesive Teams' section earlier in this chapter.

If you get the candidate to do this in advance of the interview then you will have some more information to help cross-check with what they say about themselves in their CV. It is not expensive – particularly as you are now down to a couple of candidates – and will give you some great insights.

Whether you do or don't do a 'practical' you should now really explore in depth their education and work history and ask questions about who they reported to at each job, including making sure you have the correct spelling of the boss's name to show that you are serious about taking references.

Here are some useful questions for each role in their career history:

- What were you hired to do?
- What accomplishments were you most proud of, and what were your low points?
- Who were the people you worked with and how would you rate them and they rate you?
- Why did you leave that job?

Reference check

If the candidate still looks like a good fit, it is then key to get in touch with at least a few of the candidate's references. You won't usually be able to approach the current employer at this stage but you should be able to talk to previous employers.

A mistake many people make is to leave the reference check until after making the offer, or even miss it out altogether – don't make that mistake. I've known people to completely fabricate a previous role and not be found out until six months later.

Make sure you cover things such as:

- What was their role?
- What were they good at and what were they not so good at?
- How would you rate their performance on a scale of 1 to 10?

Then, describe the role you envision for the applicant and ask them what they think of the fit.

Clearly you are looking for consistency with what the candidate has told you. You might even like to get the candidate to arrange the reference check discussions.

These days it is harder to elicit detailed references from previous employers so you may have to consider ways to 'bypass' the written reference, perhaps picking up the phone if the previous employer is open to it.

Will, values, results and skills (WVRS)

Now you should have enough information to hire the best 'A-player' you can find – to make the final decision.

Here are four criteria to help you make that decision – in rank order!

- Will – Do they show a desire to excel at the role, including learning/improving?
- Values – Do they align with your Core Values?
- Results – Have they convinced you they can deliver on your outcomes?
- Skills – Do they have the basic skills required? This is the least important as skill-sets need to be updated frequently and if they show 'will and values' they will acquire the necessary skills anyway.

What you are looking for in response to asking yourself and your team whether the candidate should be hired is a 'Hell yes'. Anything less and you really shouldn't be hiring – because those niggling doubts you have will turn out to be correct. You are after the 9s and 10s, not the 7s or 8s.

So you should be in a position to make the offer... but hold on just a second!

The offer interview

Bring them in for one final session – 'We'd like to offer you the role and would like you to come back in for the offer interview'.

Don't skimp on this last important step. Try to think through all the responses your candidate will have and the scenarios that might come up. Consider role-playing 'the offer' conversation with a friend or colleague ahead of time.

If you have an A-player on your hands, you want to close the deal as soon as possible.

Ideally you would invite them in again for this final step – or perhaps meet them elsewhere. It can be done by telephone but we'd recommend not if possible.

Bear the following in mind:

- Move fast – A-players are rare so don't waste time once you have decided.
- Compensation – You should both feel comfortable by now talking money and you should know what they need/are expecting and what else besides money is important to them.
- Agree that one of the first actions will be for the two of you to agree an onboarding plan, which will include milestones and key behaviours en route to the desired outcomes in the Job Scorecard.
- Get their permission to fire them! What do I mean by that? Ask them what they would expect to happen if they fall behind the milestones – first time, second time? The A-players will have no problem with this; it will be the weaker candidates who will be uncomfortable here – and you should have got rid of them by now!
- Counter-offers by the A-player's boss – Ask your candidate what they expect to happen when they tell their boss. You should expect the boss to make a counter offer – if the person you are offering the job to is truly an A-player then it is only natural the previous employer will want to keep them! 'What will you say if they offer you more money/increase your benefits?'
- Show them you care – Go out of your way to close the deal, making them feel welcome.

So there you go, 10 steps to recruiting the best people and punching above your weight.

If you do all of this you will build internal momentum and strength that will pay dividends for years to come. Hire the right people and you and your business will be great – hire the wrong people and things will be miserable!

Onboarding

The final step of hiring is the onboarding. I'm not talking about making sure they have a place to sit and a company email account (of course you need to do these things) but ensuring that everything is in place to get them up to the point of being a 'Highly Capable individual' in their role.

It has started with the offer interview above. You have already begun to develop the onboarding plan and get the candidate to buy into it. Ensure that this is captured fully in the Job Scorecard for their role – effectively this now becomes 'what good looks like' when they are performing as a highly capable individual in that role.

Next put a date on it – is it three months away, six or something else? This should ideally tie in with their probationary period. Once you have agreed this with them, work it back, identify key milestones – monthly first and then backfill weekly. Make sure you identify with the new hire any developmental or training needs and build them in.

Get the candidate to sign it off with their manager, making sure that the candidate takes 'ownership' of it so that they are the ones coming to you (or their manager) with what they need to reach the milestones.

This gives you a structure to get them up to speed in a timely fashion. Do not forget that one of the first things you need to do is to inspire them with the vision of where you are taking the business and how they can contribute to that vision through their role. There is no substitute for you doing this personally for as long as is feasible as you scale up with each and every hire.

FEEDBACK

RHYTHM 90

Of course, just as when we think about acquiring customers and the easiest customer to acquire is the one we already have, we need to think about employee retention. Think back to the drivers of value also, and the employee element of the Switzerland structure (see Chapter 4). We need to make sure that we are not over-reliant on any one key individual – a part of which is doing everything we can to retain them as well as having a contingency plan.

The relevant questions from the InFlight Checks for this section are:

	SUBTOTAL
10. Our ability to retain and hire good people is a strength of the business	
We have a retention, development and succession/contingency plan for every key employee (score 1 if just you in the business) and hold regular (quarterly) 'retention discussions' with key employees	
We have a clear view of organisational needs/structure over the next 3 years and whether we are hiring in or developing internally for each role	
We are clear on our Employee Value Proposition and are able to attract sufficient good candidates (we are able to 'punch above our weight' in recruitment)	
We have a robust hiring process in place that minimizes the chances of making a bad hire	
11. We actively listen to our staff and track engagement	SUBTOTAL
Managers actively seek ongoing feedback from team members – e.g. all managers have a 'Stop, Start, Continue' discussion with at least one employee each week and feedback is shared at weekly leadership meetings (score 1 if just you)	
A 'Balance Wheel' or equivalent personal and professional 'happiness' discussion is held monthly with all team members (or you if you are on your own)	
We have a working process for informing staff on actions taken following feedback	
We track and work to improve employee engagement levels (e.g. NPS, Gallup12, TPS)	

The best retention plan of all is to ensure that all team members are happy and engaged at work – and much of this comes down to whether people feel listened to and valued. We have covered the key principles of cohesive teams which will help to drive engagement and happiness. But what is engagement really and how do we know if we have it?

Engagement

According to Gallup[81], typically around a third of employees are 'engaged', and about 15% are actively disengaged with the remainder (around half) disengaged.

1. **Engaged Employees** – 'Engaged employees work with passion and feel a profound connection to their company. They drive innovation and move the organisation forward.'
2. **Disengaged Employees** – 'Not engaged employees are essentially "checked out". They're sleepwalking through their workday, putting time – but not energy or passion – into their work.'
3. **Actively Disengaged Employees** – 'Actively disengaged employees aren't just unhappy at work; they're busy acting out their unhappiness. Every day, these workers undermine what their engaged co-workers accomplish.'[82]

In many respects this is a similar way of looking at customers as when we raised the concept of Net Promoter Score (NPS) in the section on Value (Chapter 4). This categorises customers into Promoters, Passives and Detractors.

Our research into the challenges of scaling up showed, as mentioned previously, that staff challenges rose to the top of all challenges preventing growth with businesses over £500k turnover, the main aspect being 'Getting staff to think and act for themselves and take responsibility in the way that you would'. This was reported as the number 1 challenge by businesses with a turnover between £3m and £5m – and part of this is around engagement. Despite this, only 4% of the top 5 reported Key Performance Indicators related to staff KPIs such as engagement and satisfaction, suggesting that we struggle to find ways to measure it.

If you are wondering whether improving engagement can impact the bottom line, then Gallup's own research shows that the most engaged teams show 41% lower absenteeism, 10% high customer metrics and 21% higher profitability.[83]

Measuring teamwork

Teamwork is essential for the success of your business – but how can you measure, track and develop it?

You know that creating and developing the right culture in your organisation is so important, not just for performance but so many considerations: recruitment, retention and customer satisfaction to name just three. The challenge is not only working at creating a positive culture that unleashes the power of your people but also maintaining and developing it as your business grows and the inevitable pressures and challenges occur.

I'm going to take a brief look at a few ways you might like to consider keeping your finger on the pulse with regards to teamwork and engaged team members. In terms of quantitative measurement, there's the employee Net Promoter Score (eNPS), the Gallup 12 and something we have recently found particularly insightful – Team Performance Scan (TPS). In terms of more qualitative measurement, you could utilise Stop, Start, Continue 'retention interviews', including something called the 'Balance Wheel'.

eNPS – employee Net Promoter Score

This is a really simple measure based on the Net Promoter Score that we covered in the section on Value (Chapter 4) and links in with the Gallup definitions above of Engaged, Disengaged and Actively Disengaged Employees.

The key question to ask is 'On a scale of 1 to 10, how likely is it you would recommend this company as a place to work?' You should do this on a regular basis – at least every six months but we would recommend every quarter – and track trends over time. Simply measuring it will focus your mind on thinking of ways to improve it. It should be anonymous so that you don't skew the responses.

This enables us to separate out three groups, those that are **Engaged** (scoring 9 or 10), those that are passively **Disengaged**/neutral (scoring 7 or 8), and those that are **Actively Disengaged** (6 or lower). The 'net' bit, remember, comes from subtracting the number of actively disengaged from the number of engaged (ignoring the passively disengaged). So if out of 10 responses we have 2 engaged and 3 actively disengaged (5 passively disengaged), we have an NPS of minus 10 (percent). It would blow the mind somewhat, no doubt, to have a negative score! It is quite sensitive as an employee measure because the overall survey size is generally low – but this is good as it highlights changes in engagement.

To provide a little more insight, you can easily add a question each time such as 'What one thing do you like most about working here?' and 'What one thing can we do to improve?' for example.

You can do this yourself really easily with tools such as Survey Monkey and a quick spreadsheet calculation.

The Gallup 12 questions of employee engagement

If you want to go a little further, Gallup have put together a set of 12 questions (Q^{12}®) that they have found correlate with employee engagement. They are:

1. I know what is expected of me at work.
2. I have the materials and equipment I need to do my work right.
3. At work, I have the opportunity to do what I do best every day.
4. In the last seven days, I have received recognition or praise for doing good work.
5. My supervisor, or someone at work, seems to care about me as a person.
6. There is someone at work who encourages my development.
7. At work, my opinions seem to count.
8. The mission or purpose of my company makes me feel my job is important.
9. My associates or fellow employees are committed to doing quality work.
10. I have a best friend at work.
11. In the last six months, someone at work has talked to me about progress.
12. This last year, I have had opportunities at work to learn and grow.[84]

Again you can run these in Survey Monkey and chart up the results to give a benchmark and identify weaker areas, or if you want to benchmark against other companies then Gallup provide that service through their Q^{12} survey in Gallup Access[85].

Team Performance Scan (TPS)

TPS has been developed by a group of team performance experts led by George Blakeway and Stuart Preston[86] through their research and experience with hundreds of clients including IBM, Amazon, McLaren Formula 1 and Round the World Yacht Racing. We have found it a great tool to facilitate team development within scaling businesses.

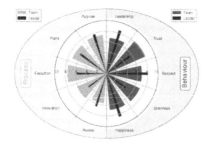

Fig. 53

Every business has a unique culture, derived from 'how we do things round here'. It's created through many factors: your environment, legacy, leadership, people, diversity, processes, customers, brand and so on. George and Stuart discovered there were 10 consistent elements that appeared in all these groups.

Team Performance Scan measures these 10 key themes of team performance – five themes that are process based and five that are behavioural. There are 40 individual indicators that are measured and collated. All team members are invited to participate and the resulting report provides key insights to help identify areas to consolidate and areas to act on. George describes it as a 'People P&L' – and just like your financial P&L, it should be updated and reviewed regularly to identify focus improvement areas. We build it into the thinking around the Smart90-day planning.

SME case study: finance consultancy (circa 30 employees)

This SME (let's call them Company A for the sake of confidentiality) is a young, vibrant and progressive finance consultancy providing advice and analysis mostly for mergers, acquisitions and IPOs. Whilst they are a small business, they punch well above their 'weight' through attracting and retaining talent, focusing on being responsive and developing a high-performance culture. This is especially important as for each client project they create a team that need to collaborate and work very closely with the rest of the business in order to achieve the high expectations the client (and themselves) have.

In this case, Company A were performing very well. The culture was strong and the leadership invested time and effort in ensuring everyone felt engaged and rewarded. An annual company trip was just one example of some of the team 'perks'. However, they knew that their expansion and plans for the future meant that they needed to be ever better. The owner/manager also wanted to ensure they'd read the situation right – that the culture really was as good as he thought it was.

The first Team Performance Scan highlighted a number of strengths that reassured the leadership team that they had the majority of things in a good place – especially around having clear purpose, goals, roles and responsibilities. The team was motivated and engaged. There were a couple of relatively low scores and a lack of consistency on some indicators. The most significant one was around openness and specifically creating a culture where team members can be more honest with each other including offering and receiving feedback. We know this is important as without it teams can stifle empowerment and proactivity if they feel they can't speak up.

So in agreement with the leadership team, some simple actions were introduced – a suggestion box where each contribution was acknowledged and explored; specific listening and feedback conversations; more 'MBWA'[87]; agenda items on meetings that invited feedback. All this was underpinned by a greater appreciation of each other and their situation. This trust is a vital basis (see the Five Behaviours of a Cohesive Team model earlier in this chapter).

Six months later Company A ran the Team Performance Scan again. The specific score for openness had significantly improved and team members felt that the culture of being frank with each other had really improved. The vast majority of scores on all the themes had improved, however it did highlight the next priority to focus on. Working on developing and maintaining a high-performance team culture should be a constant.

We have included access to TPS through esusgroup.co.uk and you can find out more also by visiting www.team-performance-scan.com.

Stop, Start, Continue and retention interviews

On the theme of listening to our employees and gaining feedback, two great habits you can implement are the Stop, Start, Continue discussions and retention interviews – in addition to ensuring that all team members are actively asked for their feedback during all team meetings.

The idea of the first is that each leader and manager should have at least one discussion with an employee each week (the outcomes should be fed back as part of the weekly Smart7 team meeting) that covers:

- What things are we not doing that we should start doing?
- What things are we doing that we should stop doing?
- What things are good that we should continue doing?

Simply getting into this habit and reporting weekly will keep employees feeling listened to and valued – as well as providing a wealth of ideas for improvement and efficiency gains.

The retention interview is another great habit to get into with all key employees, those that if they were to leave would have an impact on the business and be hard to replace. This should be done every quarter and is not to be confused with an evaluation – the aim is to find out how 'happy' the employee is and what they need to do their role effectively. Done well this will not only give early warning of any disgruntled key employees, but it can prevent even getting to this stage and also drive a really supportive culture in the business.

County Battery of Nottingham have implemented this brilliantly. They have developed a 'Balance Wheel' based on eight areas of 'balance' that they check with every employee monthly to get a measure of how the employee is feeling. They can then identify priority areas to help the employee. Note that these eight areas cross over home and work life – on the basis that each impacts the other. They are:

1. Family
2. Relationships
3. Career
4. Health
5. Money
6. Personal growth
7. Fun/Social
8. Physical environment

Each employee is asked to rate each of these out of 10, and identify areas that they would like to improve over the month. They can then be helped to identify one or two things they will do that month to improve their 'balance'. For example it could be to do with personal growth, maybe to learn a language – so what would be the next step to move you towards that goal?

County Battery combine the Balance Wheel with a personal 'bucket/goal' list that encourages employees to think about big things they wish to achieve and identify when by and what the next step towards achieving it will be.

We actively listen to our customers

Whilst we are on the track of listening, then we should also build in listening to our customers in much the same way. So implementing NPS or equivalent and tracking as a Key Performance Indicator should be a habit you develop.

Refer back to the 8 Drivers of Value in the 'Strategy' chapter, and the section on 'Customer satisfaction or customer "delight"'.

Key elements from the InFlight Checks include:

12. We actively listen to our Customers	SUBTOTAL
Net Promoter Score or equivalent is tracked as a KPI	
All managers have a meaningful discussion with a customer each week (How are things going, What's the latest in your industry, What do you hear about our competitors, How are we doing?)	
Insights from these discussions are shared at the weekly leadership meeting	
One of the leadership team is accountable for actioning and reporting on customer feedback – positive and negative	

In the same way that we should have Stop, Start, Continue Discussions with employees every week, all leaders and managers should have a similar discussion with at least one customer each week and report back to the Smart7 meeting. This should also include asking questions about the customer's 'world' included in the InFlight Checks above.

It's good to share these in the Smart7 meeting; it's great to have someone identified as being accountable for actioning and reporting on customer feedback. If you want to champion customer experience, make it an accountability of someone on the leadership team!

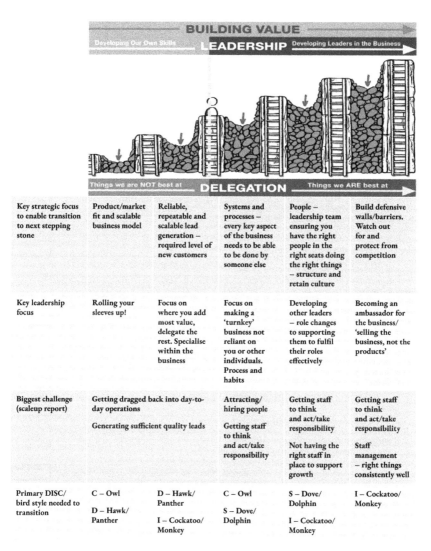

BUILDING VALUE					
Developing Our Own Skills	**LEADERSHIP**		Developing Leaders in the Business		
Things we are NOT best at	**DELEGATION**			Things we ARE best at	
Key strategic focus to enable transition to next stepping stone	Product/market fit and scalable business model	Reliable, repeatable and scalable lead generation – required level of new customers	Systems and processes – every key aspect of the business needs to be able to be done by someone else	People – leadership team ensuring you have the right people in the right seats doing the right things – structure and retain culture	Build defensive walls/barriers. Watch out for and protect from competition
Key leadership focus	Rolling your sleeves up!	Focus on where you add most value, delegate the rest. Specialise within the business	Focus on making a 'turnkey' business not reliant on you or other individuals. Process and habits	Developing other leaders – role changes to supporting them to fulfil their roles effectively	Becoming an ambassador for the business/ 'selling the business, not the products'
Biggest challenge (scaleup report)	Getting dragged back into day-to-day operations Generating sufficient quality leads		Attracting/ hiring people Getting staff to think and act/take responsibility	Getting staff to think and act/take responsibility Not having the right staff in place to support growth	Getting staff to think and act/take responsibility Staff management – right things consistently well
Primary DISC/ bird style needed to transition	C – Owl D – Hawk/ Panther	D – Hawk/ Panther I – Cockatoo/ Monkey	C – Owl S – Dove/ Dolphin	S – Dove/ Dolphin I – Cockatoo/ Monkey	I – Cockatoo/ Monkey

Fig. 54

That now completes the main elements of 'People' around scaling up. You should now be able to see how you can work towards being strong at the habits and questions from the InFlight Checks.

Now that you understand a little more behind each of these, take a moment to re-rate yourself/your business on each of the key questions on a 5-point scale where 1=Very weak/'We don't do this', 2='We sort of do this a bit', 3='We're OK but not great at this', 4='We're quite good at this but not perfect', 5='We've got this nailed'

Now take a look at where you think you are weak and prioritise one or two of them that you think would make the most impact on your business if you were to improve them.

		SUBTOTAL
8. All teams function Cohesively		
Team members understand each other's styles, differences and priorities		
Team members trust each other enough to admit mistakes		
Team members feel able to challenge each other and engage in constructive debate		
Team members are motivated to and work well to achieve the team goals		
9. We have a culture of Individual Accountability and Joint Responsibility		SUBTOTAL
We have the right people in the right roles with clear roles and accountabilities		
Individuals are empowered to make decisions for their area of responsibility		
Teams are focused on achieving collective results and we celebrate team success		
Everyone has visibility of and religiously track progress against 'Rocks' and Critical Numbers		
10. Our ability to retain and hire good people is a strength of the business		SUBTOTAL
We have a retention, development and succession/contingency plan for every key employee (score 1 if just you in the business) and hold regular (quarterly) 'retention discussions' with key employees		
We have a clear view of organisational needs/structure over the next 3 years and whether we are hiring in or developing internally for each role		
We are clear on our Employee Value Proposition and are able to attract sufficient good candidates (we are able to 'punch above our weight' in recruitment)		
We have a robust hiring process in place that minimizes the chances of making a bad hire		
11. We actively listen to our staff and track engagement		SUBTOTAL
Managers actively seek ongoing feedback from team members – e.g. all managers have a 'Stop, Start, Continue' discussion with at least one employee each week and feedback is shared at weekly leadership meetings (score 1 if just you)		
A 'Balance Wheel' or equivalent personal and professional 'happiness' discussion is held monthly with all team members (or you if you are on your own)		
We have a working process for informing staff on actions taken following feedback		
We track and work to improve employee engagement levels (e.g. NPS, Gallup12, TPS)		
12. We actively listen to our Customers		SUBTOTAL
Net Promoter Score or equivalent is tracked as a KPI		
All managers have a meaningful discussion with a customer each week (How are things going, What's the latest in your industry, What do you hear about our competitors, How are we doing?)		
Insights from these discussions are shared at the weekly leadership meeting		
One of the leadership team is accountable for actioning and reporting on customer feedback – positive and negative		
People Pillar – add all the yellow subtotals above		SECTION TOTAL

(Left margin label: **PEOPLE**)

CHAPTER 6

EXECUTION

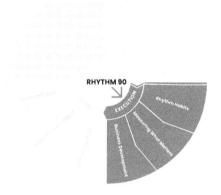

RHYTHM 90

Setting the scene for Execution

So we've looked at making sure we have the right Strategy, we've explored how to harness the power of our People – now we need make sure we 'champion' Execution! Execution is about 'executing' the strategy. Whereas Strategy is primarily around ensuring we are 'doing the right things', Execution is about 'doing things right' to deliver the desired outcomes.

The relevant elements of the InFlight Checks are:

EXECUTION		SUBTOTAL
	4. 90-Day Planning is a strong habit within business	
	The Leadership Team (or you if you are on your own!) meet quarterly (offsite) to work on and set robust/well considered 90-day priorities working to a structured agenda	
	The critical number is identified along with 3-7 supporting SMART priorities	
	The above are rolled out to the rest of the team, tracked and visible to all along with an overarching 'theme' for the quarter	
	All staff (or you if on your own) identify their own supporting critical number and 3-5 'Rocks' that include personal and development priorities	
	5. Everyone in the business is clear about what good looks like – daily, weekly, monthly, collectively and individually	SUBTOTAL
	A Balanced Scorecard is in place and visible along with KPI dashboards for tracking daily and weekly metrics	
	All staff have developed supporting actions for their 'Rocks'	
	All staff can state their goals for the week and for the day towards achieving their individual and team 'Rocks' (they can state 'what good looks like' for the end of the day/week)	
	Each team celebrate successes and the business celebrates achieving the quarterly theme	
	6. There is a well-functioning Business Rhythm supporting the 90-day habit	SUBTOTAL
	All teams (including the Leadership Team) have a weekly meeting that includes progress against 'Rocks' (or you if you are on your own!)	
	All staff are in a short (less than 15 minute) daily huddle/standup	
	The Leadership Team meet monthly for at least half a day to include progress against the 90-day plan and work on an improvement initiative	
	The Leadership Team meet annually to reset against the 3-yr plan and work on the 4 Pillars (Strategy, People, Execution and Cash)	
	7. Business development activities provide a predictable stream of focus/'on profile' clients	SUBTOTAL
	A value proposition is defined and validated (with customers) for the key service/product offerings	
	There are proven processes for lead generation and conversion 'funnels' that are followed and monitored/improved regularly (you know your pipeline and the success/conversion rates at each key step of the funnels)	
	Those accountable for marketing and sales have individual 'cookbooks' (activity plans) that are tracked and reviewed	
	Budgets are in place and monitored against results for all lead generation activities	
	Execution Pillar – add all the green subtotals above	SECTION TOTAL

Remember how few businesses manage to be good at both defining and executing their strategy? Only about 10% manage to be good at both, and these are the ones that outperform their peers.

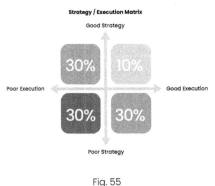

Strategy / Execution Matrix

Good Strategy

Poor Execution — Good Execution

Poor Strategy

Fig. 55

Even if you have a great strategy, if you suck at getting things done and delivering on that strategy, then you will not thrive. In fact, the real danger here is that you don't know you are failing from an execution perspective – a good strategy poorly executed can lead to a long and painful death. If you are great at executing and lousy at strategy, at least you will probably fail fast!

Our own ScaleUp Challenges research shows that the challenge of 'getting staff to do the right things consistently well' increases as the business scales and was cited by 60% of businesses with turnovers between £3–£5 million as one of the top 5 challenges. In addition, and perhaps not surprisingly, it also increased as a challenge for those businesses that are in rapid expansion mode.

So Execution is absolutely about execution habits (in particular Business Rhythm of which 90-day planning is critical); it's also about knowing our numbers and making sure we have a predictable and consistent process for generating high quality on-profile leads in sufficient numbers. So these are the areas we will look at in this chapter.

RHYTHM HABITS

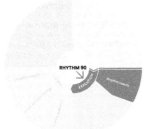

Now we come onto arguably one of the most important sections of all, the Business Rhythm, of which the 90-day planning outlined previously is a fundamental part.

This is something you can start right away, regardless of whether you are a one-person band or a much larger business.

Get the rhythm right and you can begin to work on all the other areas and gradually change the way you do business as you go along.

The Business Rhythm is literally the 'heartbeat' of your business, and it is vital to implementing your strategy and to reaching your Smart Stretch as you scale up your business. Just like your heartbeat, there may be times when you need it to speed up and times when it can slow down – but the right rhythm is vital if we are going to remain healthy and able to do the things we want to do.

We all know that getting the balance right between working in and on your business is critical, but it is not easy. How do we make sure as business owners that the business keeps on top of the day-to-day activities as well as the key strategic priorities? At the heart of the answer to this dilemma is finding an appropriate Business Rhythm for your business.

So what do mean by Business Rhythm? Essentially it refers to a well-structured 'rhythm' of daily, weekly, monthly and quarterly meetings.

But not meetings for meetings' sake, and depending on the type of business and the pace of growth, the rhythm will need to be different – like our heartbeat.

At this point you may be thinking this sounds like a load of unnecessary meetings – and frankly we have all had our fair share of poorly run meetings. You may share some of the common objections that we hear about meetings:

- Maybe you simply hate meetings
- You believe they would get in the way of 'doing the business' and take up too much time – you simply don't have time for meetings
- Maybe you don't think they would work in your business
- Perhaps you feel meetings are just an excuse to chat
- And most common of all in smaller businesses – 'We see each other all day anyway'

All of these are perfectly understandable. Have you stopped to consider though that your opinion may be clouded by previous bad experiences of meetings? If you have spent any time in large businesses, you will have sat in meetings wondering why you were asked to be there, frustrated when the meeting goes off track (assuming there was a clear track and purpose in the first place) and afterwards wondering if anything will change or get done as a result of the meeting.

Most of the bad experiences around meetings come down to a few common issues such as a lack of a clear agenda, purpose and expected outcomes.

A correct meeting rhythm will actually save time (and avoid constant interruptions) and will provide a forum for tabling and discussion of issues where they can be addressed properly and within agreed time limits. It will save revisiting something several times and clarify what needs to be done, by whom and by when.

Furthermore, and this is nearly always missed, casual encounters do not take advantage of gentle peer pressure or collective intelligence, do not support alignment and do not provide clear and unambiguous communication.

Most meetings are led by someone who essentially does the 'driving' and feels under pressure to identify where things need fixing, whether people are on track and to provide actions for the others. This is a recipe for embedding that 'owner's trap' we raised earlier and also for why so many business owners feel the biggest challenge as they scale is getting their staff to think and act in the way that they would like them to. Most people have good intentions and want to do a good job and to contribute – so let's make sure our meeting environment (for one) encourages that. Let's build into our meetings a requirement for team members to bring information and account for whether they are on track for their 'rocks', for example. In other words, let's put the onus on them to take ownership of reporting how they are doing and proposing corrective actions rather than us feeling burdened to keep them on track. Let's also build in time where we work together on a challenge (issue or opportunity) so that we can make use of the collective brain power in the room – remember the submarine captain vowing never to give orders again because he realised that he couldn't possibly come up with better solutions on his own compared with having his whole crew thinking for themselves? And let's make them responsible for summing up and committing to their own takeaways and actions at the end of every meeting. Now we might be getting somewhere!

If you're still not convinced about introducing or improving your meetings, have a think about whether you recognise any of the following:

- Interruptions from staff coming to you asking for advice/solutions/what to do
- Feeling of constant fire-fighting
- Things getting missed/information not passed from one person or team to another
- Targets not being met and not realised until too late
- Some people seem overworked whilst others not
- Deadlines missed
- Feeling that no-one else has the 'big picture' in mind
- Feeling disorganised
- Peaks and troughs of activity
- Not everyone clear on the priorities
- You are getting sucked into the day-to-day activities and unable to spend the time you'd like planning the future
- You discover late about customer, competitor or employee issues/information

All of these things can be helped and overcome with the right Business Rhythm and if you are recognising more than one or two of these on a regular basis, then you need to think about working on your Business Rhythm.

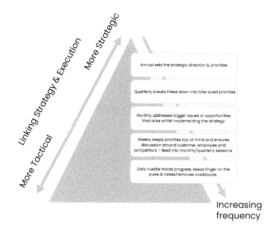

Fig. 56

The idea is to link the strategy with the execution with appropriate frequency or rhythm. So we need to do our strategic planning – but not every day. The more tactical the meeting the more frequently we want to meet, the more strategic the less frequently we meet.

So we are after something like this:

- The annual sets the strategic direction and priorities.
- The quarterly breaks these down into bite-sized priorities – remember our quarterly focus through 90-day planning.
- The monthly addresses bigger issues or opportunities that arise whilst implementing the strategy.
- The weekly keeps priorities top of mind and ensures discussion around customers, employees and competitors – and the outputs feed into monthly/quarterly sessions.
- And the daily huddle tracks progress, keeps fingers on the pulse and raises and removes any roadblocks.

So turning that on its head and starting with the most tactical, here's an example of a typical Business Rhythm, designed to support disseminating information around the key priorities and targets. It may vary slightly from business to business but not much because each plays an important role.

The most important thing to start with is to schedule them and get them in your diary – and your team's! They won't happen otherwise – or certainly not on a regular basis.

So the key elements are some form of daily, weekly, monthly and quarterly and annual meetings.

The daily huddle – SmartDaily

- Who – everyone in appropriate groups/could be by project or functional team
- How long – 5–10 minutes (2 minutes each typically)
- What for – tactical issues and updates
- Where – on site, ideally in the same place every time appropriate to the team

The weekly team meeting – Smart7

- Who – by team
- How long – typically 60–90 minutes
- What for – review progress on quarterly 'rocks' and market intelligence
- Where – on site

The monthly management meeting – Smart30

- Who – leaders/middle management
- How long – typically half-day for small and medium businesses
- What for – review key metrics of the business and collaboratively address one or two key issues
- Where – ideally off site

The quarterly and annual planning meetings – Smart90 and Smart365

- Who – leaders plus an update for employees
- How long – ideally full day
- What for – update the plan and establish the theme/focus for the next quarter/year
- Includes an update for all employees
- Where – off site

If you have been in business for more than a year, you will almost certainly have an established Business Rhythm that is functional – otherwise you will not have got this far. What we see with the vast majority of businesses that we work with is that the rhythm is tactical. It is all about day-to-day operations and making sure that we deliver against what we promised to clients. Rarely do we see a rhythm that achieves the balance between this and moving the business forward towards our longer term goals, and rarely do we see a rhythm that capitalises on peer pressure and collective intelligence. Remember the strategy:execution divide and the small number of businesses that are good at both – this is about getting into that top 10%.

A tip to help all the various meetings run smoothly: assign roles in advance or at the start of the meeting at the latest. Roles required: leader (not always the most senior person), timekeeper (accountable for keeping time and letting the leader know when time is up for each item), action scribe (accountable for noting What, Who and When actions – not required for daily huddles), 'hangar manager' (accountable for tracking any items that are 'put in the hangar' for discussion later in the meeting or outside the meeting and adding to the TALis where appropriate). TALi stands for 'Think About List' and is a mechanism for addressing important but less urgent things that arise, and feeding them in to the appropriate part of the Business Rhythm. If they need to be addressed in the next weekly meeting, then they go on the TALi 7 and are discussed at the appropriate time on the weekly meeting (Smart7) agenda. If they can wait for the next monthly meeting (Smart30), then they go on the TALi 30, and similarly for the TALi 90 to be raised at the next quarterly meeting (Smart90).

So let's take the different meetings in turn:

The daily huddle or SmartDaily

Do not underestimate the power of the daily huddle. You may have heard it referred to with a different name – scrums or standups to name two.

We have often had initial resistance to the idea but invariably business owners come around to it and never look back. You will get so much more visibility on what is going on, keep on top of issues before they become issues and generally be so much more productive as a team – even if there are only one or two of you!

It works equally well in manufacturing or in service businesses. We have some clients who have even found it useful to have more than one 'daily' huddle especially during busy periods or if your throughput is high. Sometimes the beginning and end of day, or others add one in the middle of the day.

The trick is to keep to the very simple structure and be religious about holding them at the agreed time, day in day out. If someone is late, then they are late. If the usual person who leads it is not available, then make sure someone else is briefed to run it in their place. The moment you either allow it not to happen, or you allow people to wander off from the set structure, is the moment that it will lose its 'power'.

Remember the ideal team sizes from before. These can work with up to 12 people at a push – but you will really need to make sure they are well controlled. They should be relevant teams which could be around specific projects or functional teams such as marketing or production.

The 3-step daily huddle agenda

1. How did you do against yesterday's priorities/targets?
2. What are your priorities and targets for today?
3. Where are you stuck/where do you need help?

Question 2 is basically getting them to answer, What does a good day today look like? What has to happen today for you to consider today a good day?

Note the element of peer pressure created with the onus on individuals to own their priorities. Note also the element of harnessing the power of the room by raising areas where help is required, and note the clarity of communication that comes from this – everyone knows each other's priorities for the day and can potentially work together to help achieve as a team.

Daily huddles are really simple – but it is easy to go wrong. Some golden rules to help you implement them well and ensure that everyone continues to get value from them:

- Hold them the same time every day/to fit in with the business.
- Have them in the same place – ideally with any physical dashboards, whiteboards etc.
- It should be standing only – no sitting down.
- Start on time whether everyone present or not – people will soon realise they need to be on time.
- Plan one minute per person – maximum two. It is only three questions, remember!
- Include remote workers – e.g. Zoom!

- Time the meetings and make sure to keep control. Take things 'offline' where necessary for example if something is raised that requires in-depth discussion and/or does not involve everyone.
- It is *not* a ramble about what everyone did yesterday, it is *not* a planning meeting, and minutes are *not* required. The most you might want to do is capture key priorities on a whiteboard to help with visibility and also the next day when asking the first question.

The weekly or Smart7 meeting

Next is the weekly meeting. For some businesses this is the main beat of the rhythm, particularly if daily huddles are not key to your business, for example with smaller service businesses where a daily huddle may not be so appropriate. We refer to this as the Smart7 meeting, the 7 referring to the frequency of every seven days – it also happens to have seven agenda items to the structure.

It is the first of the most frequent meetings that brings in aspects of the longer term goals and the first that includes time to work on something as a team.

This remains a simple structure, typically along these lines:

The Smart7 meeting agenda ~ 60 minutes
1. What went well/highlight of the week? – 30 seconds each
2. What did not go so well/is an area for improvement? – 30 seconds each
3. Progress against critical numbers, rocks and Smart Actions – 30 seconds each – on track or not for each rock, if not whether need help
4. Learnings from the week – feedback/intelligence from customers and employees (e.g. Stop, Start, Continue) – 10 minutes
5. Focused challenge – e.g. major event, opportunity or issue or addressing off-track rocks where help needed – 30 minutes
6. Smart Actions from above – What, Who, When, Measures – 5 minutes
7. Key takeaways from each member and priorities for the week (What does a good week look like?) – 1 minute each

Again note the peer pressure and accountability elements, the increased opportunity for collaborative thinking and gathering intelligence/feedback along with the clarity of communication. In particular note the onus on the individual to sum up their own takeaways at the end rather than the leader summing up.

A few things to note on making these sessions work effectively:

Keep to time – you might find it flows better to combine 1–3 for each team member – so give them 90 seconds to cover all three. It should be one highlight, one area for improvement and for each rock (or action from the previous week) whether they are on track or not – not chapter and verse about what they have and have not done! If they are not on track with a rock, then do they need help to get it back on? If it needs group input to overcome a barrier for example, then 'hangar it' for item 5.

Item 4 is where we update the team on what we have learned during the week from our discussions with customers and employees in particular. Refer back to sections 11 and 12 on the InFlight Checklist:

11. We actively listen to our staff and track engagement	SUBTOTAL
Managers actively seek ongoing feedback from team members – e.g. all managers have a 'Stop, Start, Continue' discussion with at least one employee each week and feedback is shared at weekly leadership meetings (score 1 if just you)	
A 'Balance Wheel' or equivalent personal and professional 'happiness' discussion is held monthly with all team members (or you if you are on your own)	
We have a working process for informing staff on actions taken following feedback	
We track and work to improve employee engagement levels (e.g. NPS, Gallup12, TPS)	

12. We actively listen to our Customers	SUBTOTAL
Net Promoter Score or equivalent is tracked as a KPI	
All managers have a meaningful discussion with a customer each week (How are things going, What's the latest in your industry, What do you hear about our competitors, How are we doing?)	
Insights from these discussions are shared at the weekly leadership meeting	
One of the leadership team is accountable for actioning and reporting on customer feedback - positive and negative	

Item 5 is where we look to make use of the combined brainpower in the room by prioritising and addressing an issue or opportunity either from the TALi 7 or from a rock that needs help. Encourage people to keep the TALi updated rather than 'spring' an issue during the meeting. The idea here is to use the 30 minutes (no more) to progress one or more 'challenges' to a next step that would move it forward. If it takes all 30 minutes for one topic then the remainder stay on the TALi until next week. If it is so urgent that it cannot wait, then arrange a separate time to progress it. If you progress one challenge to a logical next step within the 30 minutes, then move on to the next.

Use the approach outlined in the Smart90 planning section to work on a challenge:

- Define the challenge in one sentence ('owner' of the challenge)
- The current situation – what is happening now?
- What does good look like/what are the desired outcomes?
- 'Walk the room'/each person gives their thoughts/opinions around the challenge description – **once only** – more than once is politics!
- What are the root causes of the current situation – not just the symptoms (keep asking why!)
- What information are we missing to move forward?
- How can we move forward – what are some tangible next steps?
- The 'owner' defines the next steps (so they retain ownership of the challenge)

Item 6: During this, capture any actions – it only needs to be in the form: What needs to be done, Who (clear ownership) by and When. These can be circulated afterwards and referred back to the following week in item 3.

Item 7: Finally, go around the room and ask everyone individually for their highlights and key takeaways from the meeting.

Following this there should be no doubt from anyone as to what is expected for the coming week –what good looks like for them but also the rest of the team. Everyone should feel part of the meeting, that they have contributed and that they are valued as well as feeling a sense of ownership.

The monthly or Smart30 meeting

No prizes for why we call the monthly meeting our Smart30!

This is now moving into more strategic territory – not so much from a planning perspective but from a progress against strategy implementation perspective. So the aims are essentially to review where we are against implementing the quarterly priorities (and address as required) and to work on more significant issues or opportunities than would typically be addressed in the Smart7. The people involved are the leadership and management teams.

Ideally half a day is devoted to this away from the workplace. (I know you will think this is a lot but trust me and look back at the reasons why these are so important. It is a challenge to take your senior team 'offline' for a few hours, but it will be worth it!)

The structure of the meeting is similar to the Smart7 with a couple of extra items and more time allocated to work on more significant challenges.

The agenda should be circulated at least a week in advance with the focus for item 7 already identified and any preparation for it included.

Smart30 agenda

1. What went well/highlight of the month? – 30 seconds each
2. What did not go so well/is an area for improvement? – 30 seconds each
3. Progress against quarterly theme, critical number(s) and priorities
   - The owner of each priority to lead – 5 minutes per priority
4. Progress against last month's key focus for improvement – topic/process/issue – 10 minutes
5. Progress against Key Performance Indicators/Balanced Scorecard – 5 minutes per area – 45 minutes
6. Group solve of 'hangared' items – 30 minutes
7. Work on this month's key focus for improvement – topic/process/challenge pre-identified – 60 minutes
8. Identify an individual who deserves recognition from the 'leader' for their contribution – 5 minutes
9. Confirmation of priorities and actions for this month – 10 minutes
10. Key takeaways – 5 minutes

A few things to note on making Smart30s work effectively:

Again, keep to time – you might find it flows better to combine 1–2 for each team member – so give them a minute to cover both. It should be one highlight, one area for improvement.

For item 3, we want to know where we are against the 90-day aim for each core priority as well as for the process and cash improvement initiatives. A simple overview is fine as the starting point; in the Smart90 software we use the following categories:

- Not started or hit a problem
- Early days but progressing
- Making headway
- About half way
- Objective in sight
- Final approach
- Completed

A short summary to add some context behind the rating including where we are against the supporting rocks for that priority is then given to enable a fuller picture of progress and to enable consensus from the group as to whether it is on track or not. As with the Smart7, if we are not on track then the follow-up question is whether help is needed or whether corrective action is already in place (and outline what that is). If help is needed, then it is 'hangared' for potential discussion in item 6 on the agenda.

Item 4 is straightforward. The accountable 'owner' of the key focus for improvement identified last month gives an update of progress against the actions agreed and recommendations for any next steps.

Item 5 is where we review progress against the Key Performance Indicators for the business. Our Smart Scorecard follows a 'Balanced Scorecard' approach to ensure a 'balanced' look at the business performance – all too often businesses set KPIs that are too narrow, focusing on financial and operational 'result-based' or 'lagging' measures and missing vitally important aspects such as culture and team engagement/morale, for example. We address this later in the section on 'Measuring What Matters'.

For now the nine key areas we consider in the Smart Scorecard are:

1. Financial performance
2. Team/People/Internal communications
3. Marketing/Lead generation
4. Operations/Production
5. Sales
6. Stability and value growth
7. Business admin

8. Continual improvement

9. Customers

No more than a handful of measures for each (3–5 max) should be set in light of the 1-year Critical Paths and our Core Purpose and then reviewed here on the Smart30 agenda. For each area there should be an 'owner' who summarises:

- Actual against target
- Reasons for any variance
- What have we learned this month/what new information do we have? Particularly relevant about customers and employees but applies to all
- Whether corrective action is required and if so what and whether in hand
  - If help is needed then this is 'hangared' for item 6

Set 5 minutes for each area which should result in this item taking 45 minutes.

Item 6 is where we prioritise and work on any help required items in the 'hangar' from agenda items 3 and 6. Allow a maximum of 30 minutes and prioritise them first. Take them one at a time with the aim of identifying a tangible next step for each that is believed likely to make most progress towards addressing the issue. In most cases 30 minutes should be enough as you should only consider those areas where the owner of the priority or KPI area has not been able to propose corrective measures themselves and has requested help – or the team feel extra focus is needed.

Use the same 'challenge solve' approach as in the Smart7:

- Define the challenge in one sentence ('owner' of the challenge)
- The current situation – what is happening now?
- What does good look like/what are the desired outcomes?
- 'Walk the room'/each person gives their thoughts/opinions around the challenge description – **once only** – more than once is politics!
- What are the root causes of the current situation – not just the symptoms (keep asking why!)
- What information are we missing to move forward?
- How can we move forward – what are some tangible next steps?
- The 'owner' defines the next steps (so they retain ownership of the challenge)

Item 7 is where we work together on a key focus for the month. It could be a big event coming up, a major opportunity or a big challenge for example. It should have been pre-agreed and circulated at least one week beforehand with any required preparation.

An hour should be devoted so that we can do justice to what should be a 'meaty' challenge.

Item 8 is where we agree on an employee who deserves recognition. It could be for outstanding performance in their role, but this is a really great opportunity to use it to reinforce the values of the business. Ideally identify someone who has exemplified one of the business Core Values in their actions and then agree the appropriate recognition. It is a great way to remind of and reinforce Core Values with all employees. Private recognition does not have to be monetary or even 'big'; a simple personal 'thank you' from you as the leader of the business will go a long way, ideally verbally backed up with a handwritten thank you note, for example.

Item 9 is where we ensure we have captured all the actions – what, who and when, for the previous items. As for Smart7, a simple sheet with columns for the above and rows for each item is perfectly fine. A maximum of 10 minutes should address this as ideally they have been tracked during the meeting and it is simply a case of confirming.

And then item 10 is where we go around the room asking for individual highlights and takeaways from the meeting. Thirty seconds each is all that is needed – so no more than 5 minutes in total.

In total this represents approximately 3 hours and 20 minutes of 'working' time. Allowing for a couple of 10-minute breaks will mean realistically 3¾ hours to do the Smart30 justice. Think back through the items and imagine what it would be like to come away from this each month with everyone crystal clear and taking ownership on what they and the business need to do in the next month, everyone understanding the role they are playing and contributing as well as understanding that of the other members of the leadership team. Take a moment to think about how this structured agenda is ensuring those fundamentals of peer pressure, 'groupthink'/collective intelligence, alignment and clear communication. It will be worth every minute of those 3¾ hours once a month!

The quarterly meeting or Smart90

This of course we have already addressed at length (Chapter 3)!

The annual or Smart365

The structure of the annual planning meeting is similar to that of the 90 day in terms of the strategic areas to be addressed – the only real difference is that additional emphasis needs to be placed on where we are against the 3-year plan (see SmartWeb) and to identify the Critical Paths and objectives for the next 12 months.

It is an ideal opportunity to spend more time with your senior leadership team and combine with an annual update to the team. Ideally this should be an off-site meeting spread over two days – perhaps starting and ending with lunch and including an evening meal and social event.

There is no real difference between the Smart90 and the Smart365 agenda except for allowing increased time for the above areas. So a typical Smart365 would look like this with the first 'day' focusing on reviewing the previous year, and the second 'day' focusing on the coming year:

- Arrive for informal lunch – 13.00
- Meeting start – 14.00
- Objectives/setting the scene – 14.00–14.20
- Last quarter performance against priorities and KPIs – 14.20–14.40
- Last year learnings – 14.40–15.10
    - Markets and internally
    - Trends and our inherent strengths and weaknesses
- Performance against plan – 15.10–15.40
    - Hedgehog/Focus, Smart Stretch, 3-yr and 1-yr
- Tea break
- How is the culture? – 16.00–16.30
- How are we doing against the ScaleUp Pillars? – 16.30–17.00
- Team challenge solving – 17.00–17.30

- Team cash challenge – 17.30–18.00
- Close for the evening – personal time followed by drinks, dinner, social

Next day

- Day 2 objectives/scene setting – 09.00–09.10
- Team energising exercise (they might need it after the night before!) – 09.10–09.30
- SmartWeb review/reset as required – 09.30–11.00
    - Identify 12-month Critical Paths
    - Identify KPIs/Smart Scorecard measures
- Coffee – 11.00–11.15
- First quarter priorities 11.15–11.45
- Personal goals – 11.45–12.15
    - Individual goals for the year – personal and professional
    - Identify new skills to be learned/CPD
- Individual rocks for the quarter – 12.15–12.45
- Meeting close/wrap-up – 12.45–13.00
    - Individual highlights/takeaways
- Lunch – 13.00

Not every business will feel able to take an overnight at the beginning, so this may be something you work towards as the need develops.

It may be that you invite the rest of the business to join everyone for lunch and then include a company social activity for the afternoon, perhaps following a company briefing summing up the outputs from the planning session. There are pros and cons of doing this immediately after the planning session; the pros are that it is all fresh and it should be a great motivational time to do it whilst the energy is high, and you have already assembled everyone together. The obvious con is that you will have little time to prepare and it will likely be 'off the cuff'. So it comes down really to whether you feel able to deliver something of value without being overly prepared.

So there you have it – a structured set of meetings for you to develop the perfect 'rhythm' for your business and bridge the strategy:execution divide!

	SUBTOTAL
6. There is a well-functioning Business Rhythm supporting the 90-day habit	
All teams (including the Leadership Team) have a weekly meeting that includes progress against 'Rocks' (or you if you are on your own!)	
All staff are in a short (less than 15 minute) daily huddle/standup	
The Leadership Team meet monthly for at least half a day to include progress against the 90-day plan and work on an improvement initiative	
The Leadership Team meet annually to reset against the 3-yr plan and work on the 4 Pillars (Strategy, People, Execution and Cash)	

MEASURING WHAT MATTERS – KNOWING OUR NUMBERS

The next component of the 'Execution pillar' is around measurement and knowing our numbers. But not just measuring for measuring's sake; we want to make sure our focus is on Measuring What Matters!

We all know we should be keeping a close eye on our business performance.

But what should we be measuring? How do we strike the right balance between getting bogged down in measuring everything and not measuring enough?

We've also no doubt heard this: 'What gets measured gets done'.

But we know we can't do everything – therefore by definition we can't and indeed don't want to measure everything!

So deep down we know we should be reviewing things regularly – so we know we should be making a habit of it. But to make something a habit, we have to get started somewhere, and that's what I'm looking at here. In this section I am going to introduce two key concepts – the idea of leading and lagging Key Performance Indicators, and something called a 'Balanced Scorecard', or our Smart Scorecard. We mentioned this in the previous section.

We know that it is important to know our numbers so I hope I don't need to convince you of that. However, our research highlighted a few interesting things on measurement.

We asked business leaders to tell us their top 5 KPIs that they measure. There turned out to be a far greater weight on finance and cash-based challenges for smaller businesses when compared with larger organisations, however the challenge of hiring, retaining and securing the right people who work in the right way to support growth is apparent for all businesses when they exceed a £500k turnover, regardless of where they are on the ScaleUp Journey.

Despite this, most respondents fail to create and measure themselves against people-related KPIs and focus on financial indicators:

- The most frequently reported KPIs are financial; 43% of the top 5 reported measures are financial
- Despite accepted wisdom on the importance of our people, only 4% of reported KPIs related to team engagement/satisfaction
- Equally only 10% related to customer engagement/satisfaction
- Only 4% of measures directly related to resilience/stability and value – particularly interesting given the recent pandemic

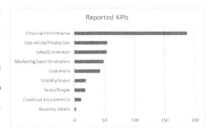

Fig. 57

Note also that Sales and Marketing are also quite low which links back to the fact that most smaller businesses cite generating a consistent stream of quality leads as a key challenge – perhaps not enough emphasis is being placed on it!

Leading and lagging measures/KPIs

There are two types of performance indicators you need to think about – leading and lagging. Our research found that business leaders do not focus enough on measuring the behaviours that will lead to the results we want. The majority (89%) of reported indicators turned out to be 'lagging' KPIs – in other words looking at the result after the 'event' rather than 'leading' indicators looking at the actions/behaviours that should lead to the desired results. Running your business by solely focusing on lagging indicators has been likened to driving your car forward by looking behind you through the rear-view mirror!

Lagging KPIs are results you measure looking back over the previous period, for example your annual accounts or monthly sales figures. They have already happened and we use them for reporting and analysing to make sure we are in control and things don't slip. However, it is an indicator of past performance and it is too late to change it.

Leading KPIs are more about behavioural indicators that we hope or know will lead to the results we want to see – they will effectively lead to our lagging KPIs. Leading KPIs are indicators of performance (actions and behaviours, typically) that might predict future success.

So if we are driving a car around a race track trying to get faster and faster, the lagging KPIs might be our overall lap times, sector times, corner speeds etc. Leading KPIs might be how late we brake, how fast we turn in/where we apex and exit the corner, how soon we are able to get back on the power (these are all things we can change). We can compare sector times (lagging) over several laps to identify where we might be losing/gaining the most time, and then check the leading indicators to help us work out why (perhaps we are  braking too early). We can then change our behaviour (brake later) and monitor the effect on our lagging indicators/sector times.

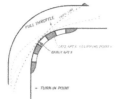 So there are a few lessons here that we can apply back to business:

What's our overall objective? In this case to improve our lap time/go faster. We might set ourself a specific time – or aim to knock a certain amount off our time this season.

What are the key lagging KPIs to check our results? In this case overall lap time, sector times and individual corner times (perhaps apex speed and exit speed). Note we are not measuring everything – we have picked a handful of things.

What is our priority focus for the next period aligned with the overall objective? So what is our focus for the next session in this case? We choose a particular corner where we think we can have the most impact and we work on this corner until we get it right (think Smart90 priorities and rocks).

What are the few leading KPIs that we think will have the most impact on this corner? We might choose braking point and turning-in point to clip the apex at the right point (think Smart90 critical numbers).

We give ourself reference points – or benchmarks if you like. Something to aim for in terms of braking point and turning-in point – that we can check to see if we did it right or better than before.

And we then check back to the lagging KPIs (the sector/lap times etc) to check whether our behaviours have led to the desired results.

So what do we measure and how do we go about it? Well we have already introduced the idea of 'critical numbers' in the section on 90-day planning – identifying the one (or maybe two) critical number(s) that we must achieve this quarter that support our theme and our priorities. We also highlighted the need to be SMART about our priorities and rocks – which includes being specific and including a measure of how we will know when it is achieved.

So this in itself helps us to define some Key Performance Indicators, but to supplement that and to address some of the findings from the research, we will look at the idea of the Balanced Scorecard.

Balanced/Smart Scorecard

The Balanced Scorecard was originally developed by Dr. Robert Kaplan of Harvard University and Dr. David Norton, founder and director of The Palladium Group[88], as a framework for measuring organisational performance using a more balanced set of performance measures. Traditionally companies used only short-term financial performance as the measure of success. The 'Balanced Scorecard' added additional non-financial strategic measures to the mix in order to better focus on long-term success.

We have developed and evolved our own version of the Balanced Scorecard to address some of the findings from our research and through working with leaders of small and medium-sized businesses looking to scale.

The basic idea is for you to determine a handful (ideally 3–5) indicators for nine core areas that together give a 'balanced' view and approach to managing and scaling the business. In addition, these indicators should be a mix of leading and lagging measures so that we are 'balanced' in this respect also.

The nine areas we consider in the Smart Scorecard are:

1. Financial performance
2. Team/People/Internal communications
3. Marketing/Lead generation
4. Operations/Production
5. Sales
6. Stability and value growth
7. Business admin
8. Continual improvement
9. Customers

No more than a handful of measures for each (3–5 max) should be set in light of the 1-year Critical Paths and our Core Purpose.

The easiest way to think of appropriate measures is to ask yourself for each of the nine areas: 'How do we know if we are where we want to be for this area?' Essentially again it is 'What does good look like and how do we know if we are doing well?'

So we need to have in our mind where we are headed (otherwise we are just coming up with numbers/measures from someone else's list) and then we need to ask those questions.

The 'framework' may look something like this:

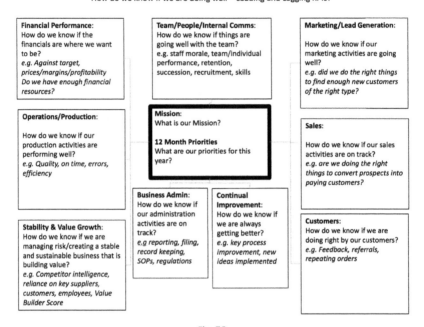

Fig. 58

Note the Mission and 12-month priorities in the centre and then the 9 areas around them so that we ensure we always considering our direction and medium-term goals.

For each measure we need to ensure that we identify the person that is accountable for it, whether it is a leading or lagging indicator (to ensure 'balance' of backward and forward view). We also need to put a number we are aiming for to it and be able to track actual against that number.

So financial performance measures may include debtor days if we are focusing on improving cashflow, profitability of particular service lines, and maybe the proportion of recurring revenue of total revenue. These are all lagging measures (although recurring revenue could be argued to be a leading indicator of the value and stability of the business).

For team/people we might think about team huddles held per month, team events, company updates, employee turnover rate, employee Net Promoter Score, retention interviews held, succession plans in place etc.

Once you have this, it then becomes part of your Smart30, Smart90 and Smart365 rhythm meetings to track progress and to address/adjust course as necessary. Each measure should have an 'owner', someone that is accountable for monitoring and reporting on it.

Note that this is a standalone scorecard from any 'systems' you may have. We don't integrate the Smart Scorecard in the Smart90 software to any accounting or operations systems – or CRMs for example. Neither is it intended to replace those things. The idea is that we **think about** the top few measures to support our strategic priorities, and track those. The danger of pulling in data is we don't think about it so much – we are tempted to go 'the system can pull out this information, let's track it and report it' leading to the potential to be drowned in numbers – or aren't able to see the wood for the trees. This is more of a 'helicopter view' rather than being down in the weeds. If you need more information or detail to explain why things are not where they should be, then you can use the other systems to drill down further.

Equally I was tempted to include here a list of possible KPIs for each of the nine areas, but the danger of this is that you would pick from my list as opposed to thinking of your own much more relevant ones based on what you are trying to achieve – as well as the new understanding you will hopefully have as a result of reading this book.

So that concludes the section on 'Measuring What Matters'. To round out the 'Execution Pillar', we need to consider business development...

BUSINESS DEVELOPMENT – BRING IT!

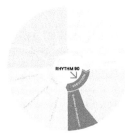

This is essentially around marketing (with a bit of sales thrown in!). This is not a marketing book; there are some great ones out there. The 'go-to' reference is probably *Marketing Management* by Philip Kotler.

However, we need to consider it when we are thinking of the challenges around scaling up and there are some fundamentals that we need to get right that will help our thinking.

Marketing is a fundamental weakness of most businesses trying to scale. 48% of all businesses in our research cited 'Generating sufficient quality leads' as one of the top 5 challenges – particularly in those businesses still looking to prove their business model and those in rapid expansion mode.

Below are the key aspects pulled out from the InFlight Checklist which we will examine in more detail:

	SUBTOTAL
7. Business development activities provide a predictable stream of focus/'on profile' clients	
A value proposition is defined and validated (with customers) for the key service/product offerings	
There are proven processes for lead generation and conversion 'funnels' that are followed and monitored/improved regularly (you know your pipeline and the success/conversion rates at each key step of the funnels)	
Those accountable for marketing and sales have individual 'cookbooks' (activity plans) that are tracked and reviewed	
Budgets are in place and monitored against results for all lead generation activities	

The value proposition

Once you have a really strong idea of your core products or services that are your primary focus (refer back to the 'hedgehog'), we need to build a really strong 'story' for each of them that will form the basis of our marketing and sales activities.

Otherwise all the marketing in the world won't get you very far if you don't get this right – and is often the reason for tactics not seeming to work. So if your website is not delivering what you want, or your email campaigns are not being opened or links clicked on, before you dismiss the tactic, review whether your value proposition is powerful enough. In today's world, it is rarely good enough to be average, you need to have a really powerful offer – or value proposition.

If we refer back to our research, we found that 79% of business owners believe they have a unique selling proposition (essentially a strong value proposition), which translates to a competitive advantage in only 34% of businesses. So really only about a third of business owners have a strong value proposition in the eyes of their customers.

You should develop a value proposition for each of your key products or services as they will be addressing different target audiences and different needs. This is another reason for focus and clarity – keeping the number of different offerings to a minimum.

A good value proposition will synthesise the compelling reasons why someone should buy from you. Done well, it will form the basis of all communications and is also an essential briefing document for use with external agencies.

You should be able to put together a reasonable value proposition from what you know about your customers and your offerings – but it makes sense to test it with a few customers if you can. Sometimes you will find that what you thought was really strong is not actually that important to a customer, and vice versa. So ask one of your best customers if they will help you.

A value proposition consists of seven key elements and we will take each of these in turn:

1. The target audience – Who is it for?
2. Their needs – What are their needs that we are trying to address?
3. The features – What is the service or product and what does it 'contain'?
4. The benefits – Against the needs, what are the benefits we are offering?
5. The primary alternatives – What/who else could they use instead of you?
6. Differentiators – What makes you different from the alternatives?
7. Credibility – What proof can you offer that gives people confidence in your claims?

Now if you think back to your Strategy work and the aligned SWOT, you have already thought about and captured much of this information for your key growth opportunities, so we are pulling it together and firming it up rather than starting from a blank piece of paper.

So first, who is the target audience – who is your product or service for?

The more specific you can be here the better. We are looking to define a 'cohesive' group or segment that we can market to. Essentially who is our product or service for?

This means that the segment should:

- Share similar needs/characteristics
- Be of a size worth going after
- Be identifiable and reachable – it is no good identifying a segment that there is no way we could reach.

You will have thought about this if you have worked through the chapter on Strategy when you considered your participation and positioning strategies. This is where we take it a little further so we can clearly identify who we are going after and why they should buy from us.

You can describe a target market in many terms and the more detailed the better – as long as the descriptions are relevant so that you can use them to help you identify them so you can market your offer.

Fig. 59

There are several ways to think about defining your target audience, sometimes referred to as a segment. Some will be more appropriate for your business than others, so consider them all and then focus on the ones that are most relevant and enable you to build a strong description (avatar) of your ideal customers. You may have several different avatars depending on whether they have different needs that you can fulfil.

Demographics are simply a particular section of a population. You can segment your target market using demographics such as age, location, gender, marital or family status, occupation, income level, education level, and many more besides.

Psychographics are consumers' psychological attributes, like attitudes, values, interests, lifestyle, and behaviour.

Behavioural is about understanding the buying behaviours, why people buy. For example for occasions or events, or maybe they are looking for the latest technology.

Geographic is reasonably self-explanatory, but at what level of detail is it relevant for you?

Sociographic is around factors such as cultural and social class influence.

Ideally break it down into as much detail as possible.

So for our SmartBoards®, here is our broad outline definition of our target audience:

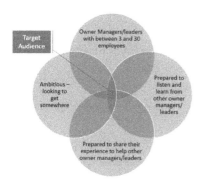

Fig. 60

A selected/chosen group of business owners who have experience to offer other business owners and who are looking to scale their own business and create a valuable business giving them future options should they choose to exit.

The core group will be owners of 'teenage' businesses typically in the £250k to £3m turnover range and therefore typically from 3–30 employees.

What is critical is the desire to be better/get more from their business and the willingness to engage over a period of time. They need to be prepared to change and prepared to share their experiences in a confidential non-competing environment.

So this is reasonably specific. It helps us to be able to 'recognise' a target customer when we see one and enables us to position our service to this group – so you might imagine our qualification process would include questions to be able to help us and the business owner decide if we are right for each other.

Their needs – what are their needs that we are trying to address?

Now we have defined the target audience, the next step is to identify their needs. Some also refer to needs as 'pain points' – the basis being that if they do not have 'pain' then there is little compulsion to find a solution and therefore to buy.

If you identify some strong pain points then you will want to tease these out in any communications with prospects.

So for SmartBoards®:

Want to reach their business potential but not sure how – they know that they could do better/that their business (and they) has/have the potential to do more but are not sure how to unleash it.

- They want to escape the 'owner's trap'/are looking to create the kind of business that is not reliant on them
- Feel 'on their own'/isolated running their business/feel they have to make all the important decisions themselves – sometimes in the dark
- Value peer support/advice from people they rate
- Want guidance, ideas, feedback, tried and tested solutions from people they rate and can come to trust/rely on
- Struggle with accountability/recognise that sometimes important things slip – that they might benefit from being kept accountable to their goals/actions
- Recognise the value of an executive board but can't afford one

So you can see we have pulled out some tangible key pain points and needs that help us to position our messaging.

The features – what is the service or product?

So the next step is to outline what the offering is – and these are basically the features. This is usually pretty straightforward.

In the case of SmartBoards®:

Smart Boards will provide monthly face-to-face and online/virtual challenge-based 'board' meetings and quarterly 90-day priority-based 'board' meetings with typically five other selected credible peers chaired by an experienced business advisor. There are also monthly 1:1 mentoring sessions in between with access to a comprehensive and cohesive set of supporting scaleup materials, software and resources to guide them on their journey through scaling up:

- Monthly 'board' meetings with up to five other selected peers chaired by an experienced business advisor
- Monthly 1:1 mentoring sessions with an experienced business advisor
- Full Flight Academy Access: access to proprietary videos/tutorials, all frameworks in the 4 Pillars, Strategy, People, Execution and Cash
- Work of Leaders Profile DISC®
- Annual Value Builder Score – benchmark
- Flight plan 'manual' and monthly themed printed resources
- Annual planning session to develop and update your rolling 3-year Plan out of which come the 1-year Critical Paths
- Optional financial report (only for Xero accounts)
- Exclusive invitation to our annual event
- BizSmart 'wings' awarded to graduates of VBC & Smart Board members
- Monthly ScaleUp Club membership
- Quarterly Smart90 workshop

But we all know that we should talk benefits rather than features – and that's the next step.

Benefits

An easy way of getting to a benefit from a feature is simply to ask:

'So what...?' or 'What that means is...'

Clearly your features and benefits should link back to the needs/pain points you identified earlier!

So if we take the features of the SmartBoards®:

Monthly Peer Boards with 1:1 support: Which means that you are not on your own and more likely to achieve your goals and go further because you get regular practical support and advice from a diverse range of experienced selected business owners with additional focus and clarity provided by the chair – and also because they will keep you accountable/ not let you off the hook.

Online: Which means that it is time efficient because you do not have to leave your office.

Monthly/regular: Which means that you will build continuity, trust and depth of understanding of each other and their businesses leading to appropriate/useful advice you can trust.

Essentially SmartBoards® enable members to 'Harness the power of structured collaborative working'. Our 'promise' is that you will 'outgrow your competitors by a factor of 3' and our 'catchphrase' capturing the essence of what we are about is taken from an old African proverb – 'If you want to go fast go alone, if you want to go far, go together'.

The primary alternatives

So now we have a pretty good idea of our offer, who it is for and why it is great for them – but we are not doing this in isolation.

We know that the customer does not have to use us – so what else could they do instead, or who else could they turn to? We are not necessarily after names of competitors here (although sometimes that is relevant) but certainly competitor types or groups.

At this point we simply list the alternatives. Try to be complete here and think from the target customer perspective. One option, often overlooked, is to carry on doing what they are already doing or to do it in-house. It is not always a case of looking to a competitor.

Sometimes it may not be a 'direct' competitor but something that isn't the same but could be a 'substitute' – for example for Coca Cola, any flavoured drink or even bottled water would be an indirect competitor. Although it is not a fizzy cola tasting drink, it quenches the thirst. For P&O Ferries, the direct competition would be all the other ferry operators but indirect would include the Channel Tunnel, flights etc.

So try to think about who or what else is competing for your customers' money or budget that they might have in mind for your kind of product or service.

So for SmartBoards®, we would consider the alternatives as follows:

- Continuing as you are
- Trying to run your own advisory board
- Hiring non-executive directors/having an internal board
- Joining a competitor peer-to-peer provider
- Hiring 1:1 support

The differentiators

If we've got ourselves a good set of alternatives, this will help with the next step – which is being clear about what makes us different/what our advantages are.

So for each of the alternatives make a list of your differentiators.

A great question or way to start these is: 'Only we ...'

But try to limit it to what really does make you different/what the customer cares about. If you go back to your aligned SWOT you will have identified strengths and weaknesses, and in your hedgehog you will have identified what you can be the best at – so this will help.

Credibility

The last but critical part of the value proposition is your evidence/proof that what you say is true and not just 'sales speak'.

You should consider all forms of credibility – again putting yourself in the shoes of your target audience. What would they want to know to give them confidence that what you say is true?

For a higher value purchase this is particularly important. Evidence of success, case studies and testimonials clearly is great – but many businesses do this so how can you make yours even more real/believable?

Sometimes for a new service this may be tricky so you might want to think about how your other business activities might give confidence.

For example with SmartBoards:

In the last 5 years alone, we have worked with hundreds of business owners and assisted delivering an average increase in turnover of +29% and a 36% growth in profits within the first 12 months.

In June 2021 we carried out a 'ScaleUp Challenges' survey and the data shows that in the last year (during the pandemic):

- Businesses on SmartBoards® have increased headcount by 31.6% compared with the 'control group' average of +7.5%
- 43% of SmartBoard® members report a greater than doubling of turnover since 3 years ago (control group = 30%)
- 52% showed growth in the last year (despite the pandemic) of more than 20% (control group = 34%)

We also use video case studies featuring different clients using different aspects of our services, highlighting the outcomes they have realised. These are also developed into press releases and social media posts.

So if we recap, a good value proposition will cover seven core elements:

1. The target audience – Who is it for?
2. Their needs – What are their needs that we are trying to address?
3. The features – What is the service or product and what does it 'contain'?
4. The benefits – Against the needs, what are the benefits we are offering?
5. The primary alternatives – What/who else could they use instead of you?
6. Differentiators – What makes you different from the alternatives?
7. Credibility – What proof can you offer that gives people confidence in your claims?

If you use the sentence headings For, Who, Our service will, Which means that... etc. then it will read as a story rather than a list – and can also be used as a two-minute summary for an elevator pitch or similar.

Done well, it will form the basis of all communications and is an essential briefing document for use with external agencies.

Your key messages on any of your communications should flow from the value proposition which will help with consistency of message, further reinforcing the key positioning.

Then we need to use the value proposition to help us generate a predictable and consistent stream of on-profile leads.

Lead generation

Generating a reliable stream of quality leads is cited as one of the key challenges in scaling up – cited by 48% percent of business in general as being one of the top 5 challenges, and by 58% of businesses under £500k turnover.

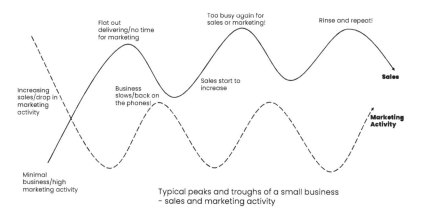

Fig. 61

If you are serious about scaling your business – or even just ensuring that you iron out some of the peaks and troughs – you need to have and execute solid lead generation processes. 40% of new business fail within five years, and of those that survive 96% remain as micro-businesses with little stability. A repeatable and reliable way of generating leads is one key requirement of a sustainable business – it is worth your time and focus!

Typically as we get busy we shift our focus from marketing to delivery.

As there is little or no marketing going on, new business starts to slow down – so we step up our marketing again, but because there is a lag our sales continue to slide whilst we increase our marketing... until things turn around (hopefully) and we get busy again.

Now we are busy we take the foot off the marketing gas to focus on delivery and the whole cycle repeats.

This predictability is what most of us have a challenge with – and there are two key reasons why most don't manage it:

1. Not focusing on a small number of lead generation activities
2. Not doing any of them 'really well'

You will have heard many people, possibly us too, saying you have to know your numbers so that you can focus on improving them – but you don't stand a chance of knowing your numbers if you don't have a system or process you follow.

And the key here is this: if you spread yourself thinly you will simply be poor or at best average at them all – and we all know that means we won't stand out and therefore run the risk of being lost in the noise.

You will have heard of the idea of a 'marketing mix'. This is correct in that generally we want to have more than one way of generating leads (we might need to and also we don't really want to have all our 'eggs in one basket') but it can lead to the idea that we need lots of different tactics. This can be a route to not doing anything very well.

So let's keep it really simple. We are going to develop an idea by Aaron Ross[89] and combine it with a 'Lead Generation Matrix' approach. This will help you to develop three main types of lead/business generation activities, for people you already know and have a relationship with (existing and lapsed customers) and for people you don't.

Seeds, nets and spears

According to Ross, there are three types of leads: seeds, nets and spears.[90] Seeds are leads from word-of-mouth referral type activities, nets are from our marketing programmes that provide inbound leads, and spears result from our targeted activities or outbound sales/lead generation activities.

This is a variation on the idea of direct and indirect, or hunting and farming activities you may have heard of. There a few key points worth mentioning before we progress:

The different lead types have different characteristics and 'value'; seeds based on referrals tend to be low volume but have the highest conversion potential as they are pre-qualified and come with some kind of implicit 'recommendation'. However, they are hard to scale up beyond a certain point. The nets, or inbound leads generated by marketing programmes, are likely to generate higher volumes, are scalable once you find the right activities (often largely automated), but will have lower conversion rates as they include a higher proportion of unqualified/off-target enquiries. The outbound sales tend to be more people intensive, involving sales calls or similar activities.

So we need to think about these three broad types of activities and work out some effective tactics.

One good way to help to do that is the following 'Lead Generation Matrix'.

Audience/Who for?		
	Known/Existing Relationships	Unknown/New
Seeds	1	2
Nets	3	4
Spears	5	6

(Left axis label: Type of Activity)

Fig. 62

Looking along the top we have our audience, split into existing (including lapsed) customers and new customers. It is generally easier to get more business from existing customers than it is to go out looking for new people to do business with – yet so many of us forget this and focus all our efforts on trying to get new customers.

Looking along the side, it is divided into the seeds, nets and spears we discussed earlier.

So we can use this to brainstorm and identify a number of potential activities in each 'box'. There may be things we are doing already that are working, and there may be other ideas we think of. The first thing is to get all the ideas out.

So if we think about box 5, we want to ask ourselves questions like:

- What can we do to ensure we retain our clients (if you have a 'subscription' model this is key)?
- What can we do to sell more/get repeat business?
- How can we generate referrals/build referrals into our activities?

For example we may think that building in an end-of-project review and an annual review (or more frequent) would be the best way of generating referrals – so this would go in here.

And similarly we can identify potential tactics for each of the six boxes.

So by now you will have a number of potential activities in each box, probably more than you can realistically handle given everything else you have to do to keep your business running. Therefore we need to focus – we don't want to spread ourselves too thin.

Ask yourself for each box, 'What one thing if we did it really well would make the most impact?' Also think about coordinating between boxes – perhaps creating an e-book or case studies that could be sent to existing customers/prospects (box 3) and followed up with direct calls (box 5), or downloaded from the website (box 6) by giving their email that enables targeted follow-up (box 4).

Once you've done that, and you have one key thing within each box, be realistic about what other supporting activities you can also do well. You may be able to handle more than one type of net activity but probably not with the seeds and spears – certainly in the early days.

Depending on the stage of our business, we may decide that some of these deserve more focus than others. Often to start with we grow by referrals; we can get out and meet people and form strong personal relationships. We are less likely perhaps to have the money to spend on marketing programmes, certainly not before we are confident that we will get a return. As we grow, however, we are likely to find that there will come a point where seeds/referrals do not provide sufficient volume and in order to scale we need to bring in the other activities – probably particularly the 'nets'.

Funnels/processes

So we have identified the activities that we think have the most chance of making an impact or delivering what we want, if we did them really well. But then we need to ask ourselves – what would it look like if we did that activity really well?

The Purchase Funnel

Fig. 63

So if we think referral marketing is a key focus for us, how do we go about doing that really well rather than just turning up at a few networking events and handing out our business cards?

The way to do this is to take each key activity and map out the steps that need to be done to move prospects through from not knowing about the service or product, to deciding to buy.

You may find you have three steps, or you may have many more. We have a seven-step process for using LinkedIn to attract interest to and ultimately convert from an online 'engagement event'. For each step we capture:

- Why we are doing it
- How to do it/what to do
- When it needs to be done
- Who is responsible for doing it
- How many of them (for example how many connection requests)
- What does good look like – or outcome/success measures

The framework looks a little like this, and it can be adapted for any lead generation/sales activity.

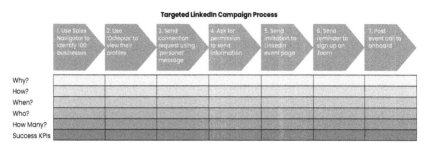

Fig. 64

So we have a seven-step process for which we can define each step in terms of Why, How, When, Who does it, How many and the success indicators – which we can then track and work out how to improve – so if we lose a lot of people from step 5 to 6 we can decide what we might do about it.

You can extend the idea into building a forward look of your sales pipeline from when a qualified lead becomes a sales prospect.

Most CRMs have this functionality built into them (but you still need to have mapped your process first) and then you can measure return on investment.

If you want to scale your business, you will have to get to the point where you know your lead generation numbers in this way. You can then work to improve it – you may generate a lot of registered interest in an event, for example, but then have a lot of no-shows. If you identify this then you can work on understanding why and ways to reduce the no-shows. Equally you may have a lot of people on the event, but not many convert to the offer. You can then review why.

If you do this in a CRM with a pipeline tracker facility, you will also then have forward visibility of likely sales income based on the number of leads/prospects at the different stages and the probability of converting through to a sale of a particular value – which leads to increased predictability and confidence that the sales will be coming in, meaning we might have more confidence in making investments in the business.

The 'cookbook'

A quick recap to set the scene.

We've already covered the value proposition and our three-year planning which is the more strategic end of the marketing plan. Now we're looking at implementing it – the tactics.

We've looked at a framework (seeds, nets and spears) to help develop some activities that we think will consistently deliver the number and quality of leads we need. We then looked at developing a funnel or to make it something that you (and your team) can follow time after time so that it becomes a habit.

This time we are going to take that framework and the process and capture the key behaviours we need to adopt each month – the key things we need to do – in order to consistently generate the leads we want. It's all very well having goals and targets, but they are not going to happen on their own! This is a bit like a recipe, or cookbook of recipes, that we can follow to make sure it turns out perfectly every time.

Businesses that manage to scale successfully execute their plans consistently and effectively – including lead generation. Originally conceived with sales roles in mind, the cookbook concept can equally well be applied to any role. Essentially the idea is to map out the behaviours/actions that need to be undertaken in a given role to achieve the results we are looking for. We use marketing/sales as the example to illustrate the idea.

So at its simplest, we are identifying the key activities that need to be done for a given role (the 'whats'), providing a way to track them whilst linking them to the processes (the 'hows'). If you do this well for each role then you will essentially have developed an operations manual for the business.

Below are a couple of screen grabs illustrating what I mean. The first shows the 'leading activities' or behaviours (the actions that we need to do to generate leads) and the second shows the 'lagging activities' or results-type activities in terms of delivery. Each 'category' such as 'ScaleUp Club Engagement' is hyperlinked to the relevant tab that contains the process flow/the how to do it.

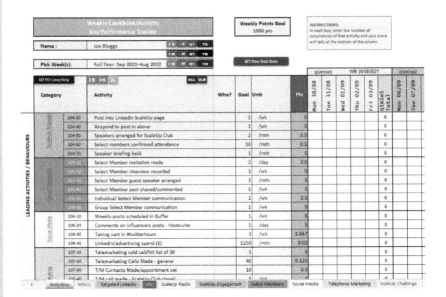

Fig. 65

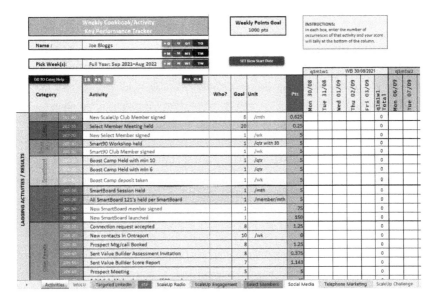

Fig. 66

We've assigned goals to each activity (daily, weekly, monthly or quarterly) and the actuals can be tracked daily. In this example we have also assigned points to each activity and set a weekly 'points' goal so that we can determine whether we have done the right number of activities that week. This means that if we don't get the results we would hope for, we can review whether we are doing sufficient activity. If we are doing sufficient activity, then we know that we need to look at how that activity is being done to look for ways to improve it – or to decide that it is not an activity worth doing.

Even if you don't develop it this far, think about getting each of your team members to develop a simple 'cookbook' of the key activities they need to be doing on a daily, weekly, monthly and quarterly basis. It could be printed out on a piece of paper even; it does not really matter. The important thing is that the key activities are identified along with the target numbers (e.g. 10 phone calls per day) – and that the actuals are recorded. Start with marketing and sales as this is generally both the most straightforward and the likely greatest immediate impact on the business as it should improve the number of leads generated.

Default diary

Linked with the 'cookbook' is another simple concept – simple in concept but not easy to implement! This is something called the 'default' or 'ideal' diary. I could easily have included this in the leadership section or the 90-day planning section. It's about making time for the important things. Remember the idea of 'rocks, pebbles and sand'? If the strategic priorities for our role are our rocks, then the cookbook activities are our pebbles. They need to be done and we need to make time for them, and not have them buried in sand!

So the default diary concept is simply taking all the important things from our cookbook (and our rocks) and deciding when we will do them – and putting them in our diary. So we reserve or 'ring-fence' time for the activities we need to carry out and then anything else is fitted in around those, rather than the other way around (which is what normally happens). So we review the daily, weekly, monthly and quarterly activities and put them in our diaries. Some things like our Smart90-day planning only happen once every three months and some things like our Smart30 sessions once a month – so not every week is identical.

This is really easy to do if you don't have anything in your diary already – which applies to precisely none of us I should think. So we have to initially overlay the default or ideal diary on top of our current busy schedule and then try to make sure that we don't add anything else on top of the rocks and pebbles.

Thus your sales team might decide that the best time to do cold calling is Tuesday through to Friday between 9 and 11am. Maybe proposal writing and quoting is best done on the same days between 3 and 4pm etc etc.

This requires real discipline – to get it started but then in particular to follow it through. But imagine how much simpler yours (and your employees') lives will be if you make this work and how much more of the right things everyone will get done. Of course there will be times when it is not possible to stick to it, but at least you will know that you have missed a session on cold calling, for example, and can then look to find another time to make it up.

Marketing budget

7. Business development activities provide a predictable stream of focus/'on profile' clients	SUBTOTAL
A value proposition is defined and validated (with customers) for the key service/product offerings	
There are proven processes for lead generation and conversion 'funnels' that are followed and monitored/improved regularly (you know your pipeline and the success/conversion rates at each key step of the funnels)	
Those accountable for marketing and sales have individual 'cookbooks' (activity plans) that are tracked and reviewed	
Budgets are in place and monitored against results for all lead generation activities	

The last part of what we need to consider in terms of our business development or lead generation activities is the budget. I'm going to take you through a very simple way to develop and track your own marketing budget/forecast and to track actuals, return and variance. There are software tools out there and your accountant or bookkeeper may be able to help you, but it is generally a good idea to develop the basics yourself before investing in something that may not be what you need, or that you are not able to fully utilise because you haven't developed the basics.

Why bother?

Well for one thing to make sure you have enough cash! How do you know whether your marketing – or what bits of it – are providing a return on your investment?

No marketing plan is complete without a budget – none of us have unlimited time or money to spend on things that don't work – so we need to commit to a plan that we can afford/deliver on and that we can review to see if it is working.

Keeping a close eye on the cash is one of the four essential areas to get right in scaling up a business – and if you don't have a scalable marketing plan with budget that can be monitored and adjusted then you are unlikely to scale successfully.

When we look more at managing the cash we are going to want to include our marketing costs within our cashflow forecast – so we'll need them for that also.

A marketing budget does not have to be complicated. We've done a lot of the work already in thinking about our lead generation activities and behaviours.

At its simplest, all we need to do is take each of the activities with their behaviours and list any costs associated with them.

Remember that your time (or your staff's time) is also a cost – not just things you have to buy – so estimate the time involved with the tasks and an appropriate hourly rate depending on who is doing it. We need to include our staff costs allocated to marketing and sales if we are going to be able to accurately monitor our return on investment.

Most of these costs will happen every month and you can therefore repeat them across the year – a simple spreadsheet with tasks down the left and months across the top would do.

We can then add any one-off costs such as annual subscriptions or events in the appropriate month.

This is OK as far as it goes – but it could be better and I'm going to share with you a template that is simple enough but also detailed enough to enable it to be useful.

Ideally we want to be able to use it to keep track of progress as we go along as well as identifying the costs in advance.

We've just been through the lead generation and framework and cookbook exercise so why not start here?

We can list down the left according to the audience (whether the activity is aimed at existing or new clients) and then whether seeds, nets or spears.

Then we can list the behaviours or tasks and input the relevant costs – things we have to pay extra for and things we use internal resources for based on our marketing cookbook.

This gives us the monthly totals for external and internal costs that we can use to input into our months as we go across the year.

You may ask why split out external and internal – two reasons. First, often we forget the internal costs because we don't tend to get an extra bill for them, but it is a cost nonetheless as you or the team member could be doing something different with that time – so there is an 'opportunity' cost of that activity.

Second, we want to be able to keep the external costs separate so that we can input these into our cashflow forecast because they represent an additional cost to the business over and above regular costs that are accounted for, e.g. salaries.

So we can map out our expected costs over the year and this becomes our budget; we can total up each activity as well as by type (Seeds, Nets, Spears) and by target audience (existing or new) and also as the overall total.

So that's pretty much that: add a few totals in at the end and at the bottom and you can calculate cost per lead, for example by activity and overall.

And if you add your sales projections you can also calculate cost of marketing as a percentage of predicted sales.

Although this may sound complicated, it is actually very simple and logical to put together. You may have a few extra subtleties to include when you do yours depending on your activities, but broadly speaking this structure will work for all businesses and does not take much time to put together.

I mentioned tracking over time. At the moment this is a budget forecast.

To turn it into a tracking tool all you need to do – once you have this sheet completed – is to copy the sheet twice and name the sheets Budget, Actual, Variance (or similar).

Then in the Actual, delete all the cells in the months leaving the calculations/totals and subtotals.

In the Variance sheet, input a formula into these cells that subtracts budget from actual and you then have a way of tracking and comparing with your original budget forecast.

Execution summary

Remember we are not suggesting you do everything all at once, rather that you identify the next thing to work on that you think will bring the most improvement to your business, plan it, implement it, review and adjust as required over the next 90 days whilst then identifying the next thing to work on for the following 90 days.

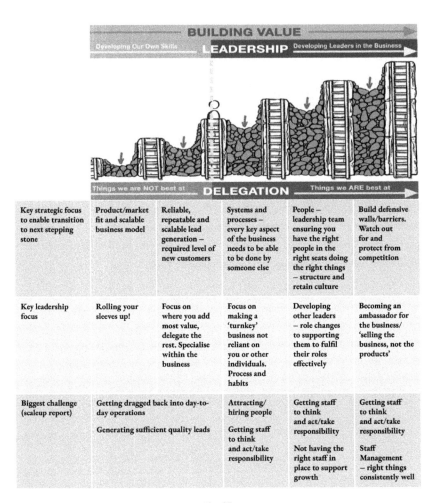

	Product/market fit and scalable business model	Reliable, repeatable and scalable lead generation – required level of new customers	Systems and processes – every key aspect of the business needs to be able to be done by someone else	People – leadership team ensuring you have the right people in the right seats doing the right things – structure and retain culture	Build defensive walls/barriers. Watch out for and protect from competition
Key strategic focus to enable transition to next stepping stone					
Key leadership focus	Rolling your sleeves up!	Focus on where you add most value, delegate the rest. Specialise within the business	Focus on making a 'turnkey' business not reliant on you or other individuals. Process and habits	Developing other leaders – role changes to supporting them to fulfil their roles effectively	Becoming an ambassador for the business/ 'selling the business, not the products'
Biggest challenge (scaleup report)	Getting dragged back into day-to-day operations. Generating sufficient quality leads		Attracting/hiring people. Getting staff to think and act/take responsibility	Getting staff to think and act/take responsibility. Not having the right staff in place to support growth	Getting staff to think and act/take responsibility. Staff Management – right things consistently well

Fig. 67

That now completes the main elements of Execution around scaling up. You should now be able to see how you can work towards being strong at the habits and questions from the InFlight Checks.

Now that you understand a little more behind each of these, take a moment to re-rate yourself/your business on each of the key questions on a 5-point scale where 1=Very weak/'We don't do this', 2='We sort of do this a bit', 3='We're OK but not great at this', 4='We're quite good at this but not perfect', 5='We've got this nailed'

Now take a look at where you think you are weak and prioritise one or two of them that you think would make the most impact on your business if you were to improve them.

EXECUTION		
4. 90-Day Planning is a strong habit within business	SUBTOTAL	
The Leadership Team (or you if you are on your own!) meet quarterly (offsite) to work on and set robust/well considered 90-day priorities working to a structured agenda		
The critical number is identified along with 3-7 supporting SMART priorities		
The above are rolled out to the rest of the team, tracked and visible to all along with an overarching 'theme' for the quarter		
All staff (or you if on your own) identify their own supporting critical number and 3-5 'Rocks' that include personal and development priorities		
5. Everyone in the business is clear about what good looks like – daily, weekly, monthly, collectively and individually	SUBTOTAL	
A Balanced Scorecard is in place and visible along with KPI dashboards for tracking daily and weekly metrics		
All staff have developed supporting actions for their 'Rocks'		
All staff can state their goals for the week and for the day towards achieving their individual and team 'Rocks' (they can state 'what good looks like' for the end of the day/week)		
Each team celebrate successes and the business celebrates achieving the quarterly theme		
6. There is a well-functioning Business Rhythm supporting the 90-day habit	SUBTOTAL	
All teams (including the Leadership Team) have a weekly meeting that includes progress against 'Rocks' (or you if you are on your own!)		
All staff are in a short (less than 15 minute) daily huddle/standup		
The Leadership Team meet monthly for at least half a day to include progress against the 90-day plan and work on an improvement initiative		
The Leadership Team meet annually to reset against the 3-yr plan and work on the 4 Pillars (Strategy, People, Execution and Cash)		
7. Business development activities provide a predictable stream of focus/'on profile' clients	SUBTOTAL	
A value proposition is defined and validated (with customers) for the key service/product offerings		
There are proven processes for lead generation and conversion 'funnels' that are followed and monitored/improved regularly (you know your pipeline and the success/conversion rates at each key step of the funnels)		
Those accountable for marketing and sales have individual 'cookbooks' (activity plans) that are tracked and reviewed		
Budgets are in place and monitored against results for all lead generation activities		
Execution Pillar – add all the green subtotals above	SECTION TOTAL	

CHAPTER 7:

CASH

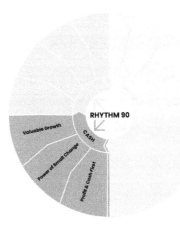

RHYTHM 90

Setting the scene for Cash

When it comes to managing a scaling business there is little more important than managing the cash in the business. Below are the relevant sections from the InFlight Checklist.

13. Budgeting and financial reporting are strengths of the business		SUBTOTAL
We have budgets and cashflow forecasts for the overall business and for key profit and cost centres		
We have a management Profit and Loss statement free from distortion that is used for decision making		
We have a set of financial Key Performance Indicators and ratios that are reviewed monthly		
We have at least 6 months' worth of operational expenditure in the reserves (over and above any tax payments such as VAT)		
14. We are focused on continually improving our cash position		SUBTOTAL
The 7 Financial Levers are understood by all senior managers – as are basic financial statements, the Cash Conversion Cycle and 8 Wastes		
Financial statements have a person assigned to each significant line item		
Changes in cash position are monitored frequently (at least weekly) and explained		
At least one cash improvement initiative is undertaken quarterly/included in each Smart90 90-day plan		
15. We are focused on Valuable Growth		SUBTOTAL
We manage our growth cycles between a 10–15% net profit band (score 5 if genuine free from distortions net profit is 15% or more)		
We understand, track and improve our Lifetime Value (LTV) to Customer Acquisition Cost (CAC) ratio		
We have contracts in place for all our customers		
A significant proportion of our turnover is from genuine recurring (not just repeat) revenue (score 5 if >75%)		
Cash Pillar – add all the light blue subtotals above		SECTION TOTAL

In our Scaleup Challenges research, we reported a number of interesting cash related findings:

- In early stage businesses (£100k to £500k turnover), financial planning (knowing how to use the numbers to make decisions) and unstable cashflow were ranked 3 and 4 out of the top challenges preventing growth
- As we scale to over £1m then the challenge of accessing funding becomes a greater challenge, with 60% of £3m–£5m turnover businesses reporting it as a top 5 challenge preventing growth – although this percentage dropped in those businesses that felt they had established their model and were in rapid expansion mode (perhaps because the business was generating sufficient cashflow to fund expansion)
- There is a level of disconnect between what business owners thought they were achieving when compared to the reality – particularly in terms of net profit

Expanding on this last point, 37% of business owners in our research reported net profit levels greater than 20%, yet when asked to take into account paying themselves (and fellow directors) a market rate salary, this figure dropped to 17%. What is more, 32% of businesses would actually report a loss or sub 5% net profit if the company director was paid a market rate salary via the P&L rather than via dividends in the balance sheet. This means that many business owners are mistakenly believing they have a profitable business model, when in reality they do not, which in turn means that they will not be able to scale.

So there is an important element around understanding 'true profitability' that we need to explore.

This chapter on managing the Cash is split into three main sections within ESUS. The first is about cash acceleration strategies (**Profit and Cash First**), the second is about the **Power of Small Change** and thirdly we look at **Valuable Growth**, including the idea of understanding the Lifetime Value of your customers and the cost of acquiring them – something that is particularly relevant with creating recurring revenue streams.

We are going to assume a certain amount of knowledge here. The intention of this section is not to cover the basics of financial statements, nor to turn you into an accountant! We start from the point that you know what a Profit and Loss statement is as well as a balance sheet and a cashflow forecast. If you don't then you need to make an effort to get up to speed. Talk to your accountant or bookkeeper and/or take a look online – perhaps seek out some online training.

In the 'Strategy' chapter we covered the need to plan for the next three years and out of that we created a summary three-year Profit and Loss forecast – and discussed the need to do a little bit of sensitivity analysis to identify the key variables or drivers so that you can then pick these out as Key Performance Indicators and monitor/work on them regularly. We discussed financial Key Performance Indicators in the 'Execution' chapter and the importance of keeping on top of your numbers.

We covered the idea of setting budgets in the 'Execution' chapter when we looked at creating a marketing plan of which the final step was the marketing budget. We are going to take a short look at the 'profit first' approach to budget setting proposed by Mike Michalowicz.[91]

In the section on cash acceleration strategies we will look at something called the Cash Conversion Cycle and propose a framework for reducing the time to get your money into the business, and we'll look at the seven key financial levers you can pull to increase the cash in your business and a brief look at something called the '8 Wastes'. We'll also look at the power of small change and model the effects of small changes in these levers on the cash in your business – as well as other key financial ratios.

In the section on Valuable Growth we will challenge the traditional Profit and Loss statement and explain why you need to run two versions, and how the Smart P&L can be used to control scaling up by balancing investment with profitability, ensuring we maintain profitable but valuable growth. We will also look at ways to calculate the Lifetime Value of your customers, the cost of acquiring those customers and therefore the ratio between the two – and how to use it to ensure your business is scalable.

To frame the section though we will start with a financial mindset that helps us move through the Scaleup Journey and links into each of the three main sections in 'Cash'.

'PROFIT FIRST' (AND CASH!)

You should read Mike Michalowicz's book of the same name for the detail on this approach[92]; we will simply introduce the concept here. We like this approach, partly because it turns the traditional way of looking at your P&L upside down (like we did with the org chart), and partly because it provides a way to ensure that you develop a scalable business model from the outset.

Referring back to the idea of the ScaleUp Journey you will recall that building a successful one-person business is very different from one with a team of 3–5 people, which in turn is different from one with 8–12 etc. You will also recall the 'valleys of death' in between – where we are transitioning between two stepping stones and need to be careful not to get stuck. The Profit First approach helps us to think about that transition by ensuring we focus on the profits, as well as acknowledging that there are differences in how the income and cost structure need to evolve at different stages.

It also encourages good habits (there's that phrase again), linking in with the 90-day rhythm, and it encourages creative and efficient thinking and planning – because it makes us recognise that there are 'constraints' in how we can spend our revenues. So we operate with a 'scarcity' mindset, which for those of you familiar with lean methodologies will recognise.

The other key thing that it does, particularly for early stage businesses, is that it 'gives permission' for the business owner to take a sensible salary from the outset – and this comes out before operating expenses. Therefore the onus of making ends meet is on the business operating expenses, not on the owner (all too often we see business owners drawing minimal take-home pay for years in the hope that it will increase as the business grows).

The starting point is the table below, adapted for the UK from one by Mike Michalowicz[93]. In it Mike provides guideline percentages for the key lines: Profit, Owner's Pay, Tax and Operating Expenses. Note how they evolve as the business scales, how profit and owner's compensation are the first after the 'real revenue' line, and that operating expense is at the bottom – i.e. what is left after the others have been covered.

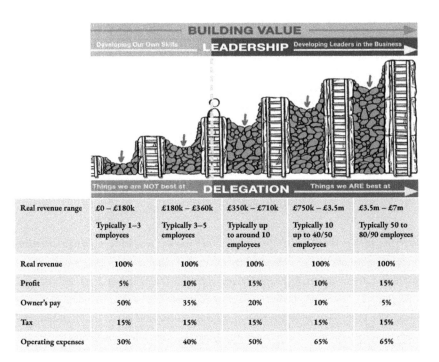

Real revenue range	£0 – £180k	£180k – £360k	£350k – £710k	£750k – £3.5m	£3.5m – £7m
	Typically 1–3 employees	Typically 3–5 employees	Typically up to around 10 employees	Typically 10 up to 40/50 employees	Typically 50 to 80/90 employees
Real revenue	100%	100%	100%	100%	100%
Profit	5%	10%	15%	10%	15%
Owner's pay	50%	35%	20%	10%	5%
Tax	15%	15%	15%	15%	15%
Operating expenses	30%	40%	50%	65%	65%

Fig. 68

Another key point is 'Real Revenue'. We will come back to this in the next section but essentially this is our Gross Margin which is Sales (revenues or turnover) minus Cost of Sales. So if we sell something for £10 and the materials cost £4 then our Gross Margin or 'real revenue' is £6. All the percentages are then based off this. The reason Mike calls it real revenue is because that is what it is! All too often we focus on our sales line which is simply vanity. In some businesses you would immediately agree, for example an estate agent that reports turnover as the total value of the houses sold would seem ludicrous when their commission is typically less than 3%. They only have the 3% to spend on salaries and other overheads. It is no different in principle with any business; just the proportions change. So focus on Gross Margin as your 'real revenue'.

Then you use this firstly to see what your current proportions are (simply analyse your latest P&L and calculate the actual percentages), identify the gap to the above, and then you manage your future cash to transition from where you are now to the desired percentages above. Build this into your 90-day priorities and set targets and actions to get there over time.

To make it happen in the early days, set up different bank accounts and start putting the relevant proportions aside regularly (ideally twice a month) so that you are not tempted to spend money you don't really have – or spend it without realising it was needed elsewhere.

You may have noticed that if you do this, you are now using your understanding of your numbers to make forward thinking decisions on how you scale your business, including where you spend the business's money. Immediately you become a rarity – the majority of us get our financial figures from the last full year and look backwards, essentially.

For more detail on this approach you should read Mike's book, *Profit First: Transform Your Business from a Cash-Eating Monster to a Money-Making Machine*.[94]

Cash acceleration strategies

What's more important – profit or cash?

You can get by with a decent strategy and some hard work – but not without cash. Many 'profitable' businesses (according to the P&L statement) have run out of cash and come to a grinding halt.

And cash becomes even more critical as the business scales up. Growth sucks cash and particularly in the transitions between stepping stones. Ensuring we have enough cash to get us through the transitions and/or to weather storms is of course very important.

Following the Covid-19 pandemic the benefits of a large cash reserve are only too obvious and ideally we should be aiming to have at least six months of operating expenses in reserve.

Whilst this might be a pipe dream for many of us, the principle stands, so how do we manage to get to the point where we are able to hold some cash in reserve? Aiming for two months of operating expenses in cash in the bank is an excellent target.

In this section I'm going to take a look at improving our Cash Conversion Cycle (CCC) – and then the 7 Financial Levers to improve cash and retained profits in the business. We'll also look at a couple of tools to help keep on top of cash.

The Cash Conversion Cycle (CCC)

So let's take a look at the Cash Conversion Cycle.

Most businesses will have some aspect of each of these four cycles:

- Sales
- Make or produce – which includes inventory
- Delivery
- Invoicing and payment

Fig. 69

The 'make or produce' cycle includes inventory even if we are a service businesses.

That may seem a little strange but service businesses have a form of inventory in their staff work in progress; we are paying our staff and if they are not being used productively then it is not dissimilar to stock or inventory sitting on the shelf.

All businesses have a form of this cycle; what might differ between businesses is the sequence and overlapping of these elements.

What is important to consider is that during this cycle cash is basically tied up in your business. If you want to be able to scale then you are going to need to minimise the amount of time cash is tied up, as well as free it up to enable you to draw your owner's compensation as described in the 'profit first' approach.

At this point you are probably nodding and thinking 'Yes – I get that' but think about it again. It is vitally important and something that, when you fully realise its impact on growth, you will want to focus on really closely.

It's a good idea to look at your cash daily – at the very least weekly! Particularly in times of change, for example when you are growing rapidly or at times of crisis such as the recent pandemic.

You need to see the change in cashflow but you may want to consider tasking someone else to report on it to you with a short explanation of why it has changed. Cross-check with your accounts receivable and payable also.

Growing businesses should set time aside each month – ideally in the monthly management meeting/board meeting – to brainstorm ways to improve each of these components. Even if you are the only person in your business it is still worth doing the exercise. You should also identify a cash improvement focus to include as a priority every 90 days in your quarterly planning.

Most of the ways you can make improvements fall into three general areas:

- Speed things up/shorten cycle times
- Reduce errors
- Change the model

You can use this idea in your quarterly planning to look at each of the four cycles and brainstorm ways to shorten the cycle, reduce errors or to change how you do it completely (for the better of course!).

In other words, think through the steps that make up each of these elements for your business and brainstorm ways to improve them. Identify a focus for the quarter and assign ownership in the way described in the 'Execution' chapter.

When you do this, try to keep your mind open and not be trapped by 'Can't change that – it's just the way things work in our market or industry'. Ask exploratory questions like 'What if ...?'

Normally when we challenge a business owner to look at their Cash Conversion Cycle for improvements, they immediately focus on the billing and payment cycle. But this is only one part of it and whilst improvements can generally be found, we are limiting our thinking. You might have a long sales cycle for example with many steps, hoops and hurdles before a customer signs the order. Reviewing this and challenging the current approach can make a huge difference – are you wasting time on the wrong type of prospects, for example? Are you wasting time on preparing proposals that are unlikely to convert?

Essentially what we are doing here is continually looking for ways to improve our efficiency across the Cash Conversion Cycle – although we are in the 'Cash' chapter, this approach should become a way of thinking throughout the business. We want every individual to be on the lookout for ways to do things better – all the time, in everything they do – and then to make sure that the habit/process is documented and kept updated. This ties back to some concepts within 'lean' thinking and the questioning approach that we want people to have. You may think of yourself as an optimist, a glass half full kind of person, and maybe some others as pessimists, or a glass half empty person. Well lean thinking would ask, 'Why is the glass twice as big as it needs to be?!'

Waste thinking

Whilst it is not the intention of this book to make us all 'lean experts', there's a great approach and thinking around 'waste' that helps lean thinking and can work well with the Cash Conversion Cycle.

Every time we or anyone else carries out work in our business, no matter what we do, we consume time. This time we can break down into three categories:

- Value added work time
- Non-value added work time
- Wasted work time

Fig. 70

Value added work is the time when we are changing our service or product to get closer to what the customer wants and is directly impacting the customer – so the customer would perceive it as added value to them. If you are in doubt, ask yourself whether the customer 'cares' about the fact you just spent time on it. Examples: when we press 'send' on the email proposal to the customer; the customer signs the contract; when we release the code live; when the product is machined; when the box is sealed; when the payment is in your bank account.

Non-valued added work time is the time we need to spend to make the value added happen but does not add value. Examples: altering the proposal depending on the customer needs; getting the contract set up for signature; testing the code before go-live; loading the part into the machine; making the box and loading it; chasing the outstanding payment.

Wasted work is all the other time we use up to get our work done. Examples: can't find the proposal I started yesterday; the contract has errors in it so can't be signed; the code requirements don't make sense so we have to guess or chase; the product is in a large batch so they spend a lot of time idle on the shop floor; the box is the wrong size and we have to cut it down; it takes 20 clicks on the computer to find and chase who has not paid.

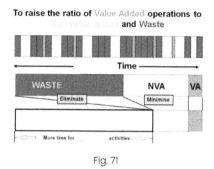

To raise the ratio of Value Added **operations to** Non-value added **and Waste**

Fig. 71

Throughout our day we do all three types of work, mixed up. If we were to map the day and then pull all the three types of work together we get to see the real amount of time we spend on each type of work.

The reality is that value added work is always less than 5% of the time spent working. Non-value added is 25%, and waste is the remaining 70%. Yes, value added time is so small, and often is even smaller at less than 0.1%.

So when we start to think about improving, mostly people look at the value added, i.e. we buy faster broadband; we build search systems; we write bigger requirement documents; we buy faster machines; we buy auto packing machines; we buy the next computerised account package. It's spend spend spend.

Lean thinking tackles the other end. It focuses on eliminating waste, and reducing the non-value added time. But the problem for most of us is that 'This is just the work we do'. Like fish, we don't see the water we swim in. So to help us see the waste, the categories of the 8 Wastes were created. They help us see the waste, then think about it. Why is it here, and what can we experiment with right now to try and remove it? It may take time, but it can always be done.

You may like to include a discussion on the 8 Wastes when you are brainstorming improvement initiatives.

8 Wastes for the office:

Fig. 72

8 Wastes for operations:

Fig. 73

Waste can also be spotted by noticing:

- When work piles up and is not flowing – email inboxes, boxes of stuff.
- The mess we have around us – can't find things quickly or not to hand.
- What frustrates you! – fix what bugs you.

If you back up the brainstorming by picking one cash improvement strategy as a quarterly/90-day focus then you will be well on the way to building a business with good cashflow management and capable of scaling and reducing waste.

Combining the Cash Conversion Cycle approach with the 8 Wastes and the 7 Financial Levers below should help to identify some great initiatives every time – and the beauty is that you do not need to be a financial wizard or a 'lean' expert to contribute! Everyone can understand them and can contribute ways that they can be improved within the business.

The 7 Financial Levers

Don't forget that improving margins will also improve your cashflow, so we also need to consider some key financial levers alongside the Cash Conversion Cycle and 8 Wastes. They are:

1. Price (average transaction value)
2. Volume (not just the number of customers but also the frequency of purchase/ repurchase)
3. Cost of goods/Cost of sales (the direct costs with each sale)
4. Operating expenses (overheads)
5. Accounts receivable (money owed to you)
6. Accounts payable (money you owe to others)
7. Inventory/Work in progress (sometimes called 'lock up')

A focus on these combined with the cash strategies earlier will pay dividends in both short and longer term cashflow. And don't think you necessarily need to make huge changes – a small percentage change in each will make a major change in profitability and cash when combined.

Again, building time to brainstorm these levers will yield some powerful results. Try to think beyond the obvious, for example price is not just about increasing your headline rate. It might be about upselling or bundling to increase your average order value.

Volume is about lead generation to find new customers, yes, but again think beyond the obvious. What about frequency of purchase: what can you do with existing customers to get them to buy again, and again?

For example, how can you increase average spend?

- Add-on sales and upgrades
- Use sales scripts – e.g. McDonald's
- Upskill/train your salespeople
- Focus on key products and services – on the 80% of the 80/20 rule
- Use sales checklists
- Build a retainer model
- Increase your prices
    - e.g. introduce a premium product/service

THE POWER OF SMALL CHANGE

A note on increasing prices seems appropriate here. Many of us are anxious about losing customers if we do. Price is rarely the reason why customers leave – as evidenced by research carried out by the Rockefeller Corporation[95] showing that the vast majority of reasons are around customer service and feeling valued. A customer being persuaded to go to a competitor (in which price may be a factor) accounts for a mere 9% of reasons.

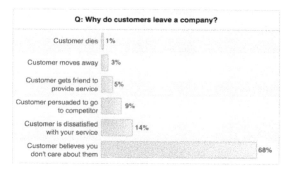

Q: Why do customers leave a company?

Customer dies	1%
Customer moves away	3%
Customer gets friend to provide service	5%
Customer persuaded to go to competitor	9%
Customer is dissatisfied with your service	14%
Customer believes you don't care about them	68%

Fig. 74

So this links straight back to the importance of the Value Drivers, customer experience (how loyal are your customers?) and monopoly control (how differentiated do they perceive your offer to be?). If we truly create a great customer experience, then pricing is unlikely to be an issue.

If you're still not convinced, then maybe this will help:

How many customers could you afford to lose if you raised your prices by 10%? Do you know?

Well the answer will depend on your margins but let's take an example:

In this business we are selling something for £10 that costs us £7 to make.

If we make and sell 10 of them then we make £100 sales, but it costs us £70 so our Gross Profit (or 'Real Revenue') is £30.

If the rest of our costs are £20 then we make a 10% net margin or £10.

Unit Price	£10
Unit Cost	£7
Volume	10
Sales	£100
COGS	£70
GP	£30
Fixed Costs	£20
Net Profit	£10

Fig. 75

So what is the effect of increasing our price by 10%?

Assuming no lost customers – how much more profit would we make?

Well in this example the answer would be £20 additional profit – or put another way we would triple our profits from a 20% price increase!

Unit Price	£10	£12
Unit Cost	£7	£7
Volume	10	10
Sales	£100	£120
COGS	£70	£70
GP	£30	£50
Fixed Costs	£20	£20
Net Profit	£10	£30

Fig. 76

And that is because any price increase flows straight to the bottom line profit – we aren't making or selling any more than we were in terms of volume and we aren't adding any overheads, so the costs stay the same but the revenue and profit increases by £20.

Note our sales turnover increase by 10%, our Gross Profit or Real Revenue increases by 67% and our net profit by 200%!

But you say we might lose some customers if we put the price up.

Well we might – although price in most businesses is not the key reason people do business with you and is not the key reason customers leave as we saw earlier.

However, how many customers could we lose and make the same profit?

Well in this example business we could lose 40% of our customers and still make the £10 profit we were making before – even though our sales drop from £100 to £72.

This is because our cost of goods also drops and we are now making a 42% Gross Margin instead of 30%.

Unit Price	£10	£12	£12
Unit Cost	£7	£7	£7
Volume	10	10	6
Sales	£100	£120	£72
COGS	£70	£70	£42
GP	£30	£50	£30
Fixed Costs	£20	£20	£20
Net Profit	£10	£30	£10

Fig. 77

So think about price very carefully – work this through for your business margins and see what the impact might be. Note how sensitive the net profit is to the Gross Margin – any improvement you can make in price or in reduction of cost of goods/cost of sales will flow directly to the bottom line.

One last question: If we dropped our price by 10%, how many more customers would we need to make the same profit?

If you work the numbers through we would need to sell 15 to make a £10 profit – or in other words we would need a 50% increase in volume to cover a 10% price decrease. So beware of discounting your products or services!

So just like we looked at some examples of how you can increase average spend, you can do the same for each of the 7 Financial Levers.

When you think of volume – think outside the box again and not just selling to more customers – start with how you can increase the repeat purchase rate, the frequency with which they come back. It is normally much easier and often overlooked. Acquiring a new customer is five times as expensive as retaining an existing customer and the success rate of selling more to a customer you already have is 60–70%, while the success rate of converting a new customer is 5–20% depending on industries.

Imagine in your business making a small percentage gain in your financial levers every 90 days. You will always be able to find an improvement – most often it will be small (although every now and then you might be able to make a step change). This is referred to under many different names – we use the Power of Small Change, but you may have heard it referred to as the Theory of Marginal Gains, or the Power of 1 (as in 1% improvements). This is not just about the individual marginal gain but the cumulative effect of multiple small gains.

Mazda used this idea in their production processes where they challenged themselves on making a 1% improvement in each step – for example in their Gram Strategy[96] weight reduction programme for the new MX5 where every component of the car did this – and overall they saved 100kg or something in the order of 8% of the total weight.

The British Cycling team under Sir Dave Brailsford[97] applied the theory of marginal gains to go from almost no record of success to 7 out of 10 gold medals available in one Olympic 'cycle'.

So what we are looking for is a continuous focus on improving the 7 Financial Levers combined with the Cash Conversion Cycle.

This example shows a way of modelling the effect of improvements.

With this business, although it is profitable with an EBIT (Earnings Before Interest and Tax) of £38k, because of the high working capital requirement its net cash requirement was minus £20k.

So this shows the effect on a business with a £306k turnover improving all of the key levers by 10%. Now I grant you that that is unlikely in any one year but the effect is to improve the EBIT from £38k to £115k and the net cash position from minus £20k to plus £50k.

Often with scaling businesses, there is significant cash to be found within the business before needing to look for external help – either debt or equity financing. An approach like this can free up significant cash that can be used to fund investment and support scaling. If you combine it with the 'profit first' approach then you will ensure that you manage the cash in the business appropriately, increasing the focus on being 'lean' with operating expenses and enabling you to draw a sensible compensation for your blood, sweat and tears!

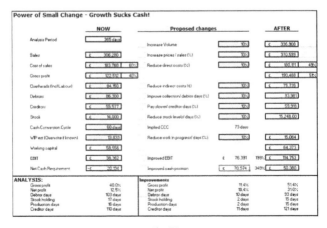

Fig. 78

VALUABLE GROWTH

Smart P&L

We probably all have a basic understanding of a Profit and Loss (P&L) statement.

However, are we able and do we know how to use it to drive profitability in our businesses on a monthly basis?

We've touched on a couple of these ideas in the section on profit first and here we will look at why you need two sets of books (!) and why Gross Margin doesn't get enough respect! I'll propose a 'Smart' P&L that will help you to drive profitability and value in your business as you scale up.

If you are not a 'numbers' person then this is going to be a little harder to get your head around than some of the other sections.

In line with our whole approach, we are trying to sift out theory for theory's sake and focus on things that really matter and are relevant to us as owner-managers of small and medium-sized businesses trying to scale. This section is no exception.

We are however going to be talking accounting and numbers and even if you struggle I urge you to take it in steps, go back over it and try to apply it to your thinking. It would be great to talk it through with your bookkeeper and accountant.

It will be less relevant if you are running a lifestyle business and have no intention of scaling up the business beyond you. If you are turning over £200k or more though and growing then you should review carefully!

The main weakness of firms looking to scale is marketing – the second is accounting.

Most of us see accounting as a necessary evil and something to keep the tax man away – and most of us do little more than glance at our P&L.

We tend to see paying for accounts and bookkeeping as an expense to be avoided and would rather spend money on making/delivering or selling stuff.

However, the returns in terms of profits and cash of investing a little more time (whether internal or outsourced) and attention on accounting can be significant – and for a business trying to fund growth and give the owner a decent pay packet it's essential.

So let's take a look at the P&L – the Profit and Loss statement.

We're all I hope familiar with a basic P&L, and as a minimum will have been shown ours by our accountant at the end of the tax year. Some of us will be producing a monthly P&L and keeping an eye on the top and bottom lines – and maybe one or two items in between.

But a P&L can look quite different between two identical businesses, depending on how you treat different items of expenditure. And a P&L produced by most accountants is aimed generally at meeting the HMRC requirements or equivalent tax authorities – and potentially to minimise tax or to meet some other agenda.

But the point is the P&L may not have been put together with the aim of helping us to make business decisions; it is likely to have been put together to meet reporting requirements. This means it can be distorted – or have distortions in it.

There are two key distortions in a typical owner-manager P&L:

1.   The way the owners treat their income
2.   The way Gross Margin is calculated

So the first thing we need to do if we want to be able to make business decisions is to clear the distortions.

That is why we need two sets of books – for the right reasons! Not to hide anything, in fact quite the opposite. We want to reveal what is hidden in the numbers.

Take owner's compensation first. Most of us take a mix of salary and dividends and in addition most of us don't pay ourselves at full market rate. Both of these things can distort the P&L – leading to an incorrect picture of the true profitability. We may kid ourselves that we have made a 20% profit but in reality if we had to pay someone else the market rate to do our job then we may have made a much lower profit. If you recall, there were statistics at the beginning of this chapter on the disconnect between what profits many of us think we are making and the true profit.

If we really want to build a business that will scale, we have to see the true profitability of the business. If we kid ourselves we are making a 20% profit we probably won't make as much effort to improve the profitability as if we see that in reality we are only making 3%.

What is more, if you ever think about valuing your business or selling it, then you would get a misleading valuation if you didn't do this. You may have heard a business might be worth typically 3–4 times EBITDA (Earnings Before Interest, Tax, Depreciation and Amortisation). Well EBITDA needs to be corrected to allow for market rate salaries of owners; after all a buyer will need to think about paying someone to replace you.

So the first thing is to restate the P&L using market rate wages for the owners – and then asking ourselves the hard questions about how we get the profit to where we want it to be whilst being able to pay ourself a market rate salary! Here is the first link back to profit first.

The second distortion is around Gross Margin.

Nearly every business owner I know talks about revenue. They know the saying that revenue is vanity – but we still focus on it nevertheless. It sounds great to say we have a big number turnover rather than a small Gross Margin.

I used a property agent as the example earlier, but a distributor turning over £4m of product and making a 5% commission is clearly very different from a service firm turning over £4m – which in turn may be very different from a manufacturer turning over £4m.

Instead of focusing on revenue we should be focusing on a redefined version of Gross Margin – and why redefined?

Because again we can have very different stated Gross Margins depending on how we define it. For external discussions then fine – talk about revenue if you like – but for internal discussions and decisions always talk about Gross Margin – or 'Real Revenue'.

Gross Margin (GM) is typically sales/revenue minus variable or direct costs (Costs of Goods Sold or COGS) – any costs that vary for every £ of sale you make. So if you buy a widget for £5 and customise it by working on it and incur £2 of labour per widget in doing so and sell it for £20, then your COGS are £7 and your GM is 13/20 or 65%.

The trouble here is we have mixed Cost of Goods Sold and labour – so we can't measure and work on the efficiency of our labour.

So here's how you should redefine Gross Margin (Real Revenue):

Revenue minus all non-labour direct costs. If you are a service company and you subcontract some of your direct labour then this is effectively a cost of goods sold (COGS) and should also be taken off the revenue to give your GM. (So if I'm an accountant and I subcontract the bookkeeping for my clients, this should be treated as a cost of goods sold, but only for subcontracted costs of work that are linked directly or 'vary' according to the sales/ work done with clients. Clearly if I subcontract general admin then this is a fixed cost not a variable cost and would not be included here.)

So now we have a measure of GM free of distortions and we have removed the distortion of owner salaries – so we have a true measure of profit and can start thinking about setting our profit targets. We should focus on Gross Margin and net profit rather than sales. We also need to decide whether to calculate our profit as a percentage of revenue or of Gross Profit.

This may sound strange and most of us will have always thought of profit as a percentage of sales. However, as we've already seen there are some industries where revenue doesn't represent the true income to the business. In these cases it makes much more sense to calculate profit as a percentage of Gross Profit. Typically if your Gross Margin is below 40% then you should relate profit to Gross Margin. The profit first methodology requires all businesses to report it as a percentage of 'Real Revenue'.

Why does this matter?

Well here's what has been found (by Crabtree in 'Simple Numbers'[98]) across businesses if you calculate profit in this way:

- 5% or less pre-tax profit then your business is on life support!
- 10% the business is doing well but has some untapped potential
- 15% the business is in great shape
- Over 15% indicates you should make hay whilst the sun shines – it will not last as the market will figure it out and you will see increased competition

Effectively Crabtree is saying that '10% is the new break-even'!

So this gives us a framework to manage our scaling up. If we are not at 15% profitability then scaling up is risky – certainly taking on more staff. The focus should be to prove that we can get to 15% with what we have, and then we can add staff which will drop our profit margin back to 10% or so, so we focus on getting back to 15% and then repeat.

So here is what we should be looking at as a summary P&L:

Note the Gross Margin and the Contribution Margin both before fixed costs.

Then that we have split out different internal labour costs before other fixed costs – of course in a full P&L we would include the key fixed costs lines but for simplicity here we have shown them summed up as other fixed costs.

Smart P&L

Revenue/ Sales
Direct Costs (Materials & Outsourced Direct Labour)
Gross Margin £
Gross Margin %
Direct Labour Costs (Internal)

Contribution Margin £
Management Labour Costs £
Sales Labour Costs £
Other Fixed Costs/ Operating Costs
Pre-tax Profit £
Pre-tax Profit % (Sales or GM)

Fig. 79

The pre-tax profit margin we are calculating either as a percentage of sales or GM as discussed earlier.

Labour Efficiency Ratios

Direct Labour – GM/ DLC
Sales Labour – CM/ SLC
Management Labour CM/ MLC

Fig. 80

Note also the ratios at the bottom.

So this gets us to the number one driver of profitability – labour efficiency – or in other words how much do we get back for every £ we spend on labour? This is a ratio, not simply how much we spend on staff costs. Without redefining Gross Margin you can't get at this ratio.

You can see that we have split out direct labour, sales and management labour – and the ratio calculations are shown here where GM is Gross Margin, CM Contribution Margin, DLC is Direct Labour Costs, SLC is Sales Labour Costs and MLC is Management Labour Costs.

The numerator is always larger than the denominator so the ratio will be greater than one (well unless your business is in real trouble!).

Notes:

- CM is the equivalent of most accountants' GM – but the normal GM mixes labour and non-labour costs and masks labour productivity.
- Anyone that spends 50% or more of their time delivering the product or service/doing the doing goes into direct labour. The rest goes into management unless you have a sales team – in which case break them out separately.
- Don't split employees across groups.
- Don't confuse it by including payroll taxes and benefits.

In this example we are turning over £500k and making a 6% net profit. So we are barely off life support according to Crabtree's definitions.

So first we need to get to 10% net profit whilst holding the costs constant – we don't try to spend our way towards 10%. This means a focus on productivity and may mean changing one or two employees if they aren't performing optimally but we don't increase the labour bill – simple in principle but implementing it is hard!

But this is where the work we've talked about before in the module on cash acceleration comes in around finding ways to improve productivity and profitability – remember the 7 Financial Levers, Cash Conversion Cycle and 8 Wastes – and for a business at this stage this is where the focus has to be rather than simply trying to add more at the top end.

In this example we have found some ways to increase the volume by a small percentage although we have kept the Gross Margin the same, but our Contribution Margin is improved slightly because we have kept direct labour constant. All other labour costs and fixed costs have remained constant resulting in that 10% profit margin.

Column1		Now	Step 1	Step 2	Step 3	Step 4
Revenue/ Sales	£	500,000	£532,056	£578,707	£578,707	£627,834
Direct Costs/ Cost of Goods/						
Excluding Internal Labour	£	140,000	£148,976	£162,038	£162,038	£175,794
Cost of materials	£	120,000	£127,693	£138,890	£138,890	£150,680
Outsourced direct labour	£	20,000	£ 21,282	£ 23,148	£ 23,148	£ 25,113
Gross Margin £	**£**	**360,000**	**£383,080**	**£416,669**	**£416,669**	**£452,041**
Gross Margin %		72%	72%	72%	72%	72%
Direct Labour Costs	£	90,000	£ 90,000	£ 90,000	£ 98,000	£ 98,000
Contribution Margin £	**£**	**270,000**	**£293,080**	**£326,669**	**£318,669**	**£354,041**
Management Labour Costs	£	50,000	£ 50,000	£ 50,000	£ 58,000	£ 58,000
Sales Labour Costs	£	25,000	£ 25,000	£ 25,000	£ 37,000	£ 37,000
Other Fixed Costs/ Operating Costs	£	165,000	£165,000	£165,000	£165,000	£165,000
Pretax Profit £	**£**	**30,000**	**£ 53,080**	**£ 86,669**	**£ 58,669**	**£ 94,041**
Pretax Profit Margin % Sales		6%	10%	15%	10.1%	15%
Labour Efficiency Ratios						
Direct Labour (GM/DLC)		4.0	4.3	4.6	4.3	4.6
Sales Labour (CM/SLC)		10.8	11.7	13.1	8.6	9.6
Management Labour (CM/MLC)		5.4	5.9	6.5	5.5	6.1

Fig. 81

When we get to 10% we review our people and see if any are not able to stay with the programme. Reset and keep going until we hit 15%.

Then you can think about adding staff costs where you see stress points; this may be new people or it may be salary increases or bonuses, just keep the same level of productivity. Limit it so that you don't go back below 10% net profit and repeat.

As you do this you will see the Labour Efficiency Ratios change at each level of profitability – and you will begin to develop a real perspective on how your business model operates. You will get to know from the ratios when and where you are overheating and need to add people and likewise when you are running slack and need to make other adjustments.

This and the profit first approach combine to provide a model with which to scale your business profitably whilst creating value (for you and other stakeholders). One of the fundamental things that it does also, though, is it makes us focus on efficiency and productivity – not spending or investing our way out of trouble. We look first to ensure that the profitability is there, we are operating efficiently, before we invest into bridging the next 'valley of death'. This is a very 'lean' way of thinking and provides the financial insights into everything we have proposed through ESUS.

LESSONS LEARNED

- Standard P&Ls have distortions in them making it hard to make sound business decisions, namely:
  - Owner's compensation
  - Gross Margin distortions
- So we need two sets of books – or at least two P&Ls
- We also need to redefine Gross Margin to help us reveal our direct labour efficiency, because otherwise it mixes labour and non-labour costs
- We should get to 15% profitability before taking on more staff costs – and treat 10% as the new break-even!

Lifetime Value and Customer Acquisition Cost (LTV:CAC)

Part of Valuable Growth is ensuring that we 'create value' for the business as we scale. You can define value in many ways but one simple way to look at it is to say that for every amount we spend acquiring customers, they should bring a multiple of that amount back in terms of their Lifetime Value. A rule of thumb ratio increasingly used (particularly with recurring revenue-based businesses) is that the Lifetime Value of the average customer should be at least three times the cost of acquiring them. This ratio is known as the LTV:CAC ratio. Investors will look at this ratio and expect it to be greater than 3 for them to invest (some will have a higher investment threshold).

Obviously if the ratio is less than 1 then the business is destroying value – it is costing more to acquire each customer than is received back over the customer lifetime. Hopefully not a position you are in!

This section may seem a little 'mathematical' but the essence is that we should know and track how much it costs us to acquire a customer (on average), and how much that customer is worth to us – and for us to be confident that we have a scalable business model, the value should outweigh the cost by a factor of 3.

It provides another way to help focus our attention on the right things and gives us confidence to push on and scale, or identifies what we need to fix before we do. It will become clearer as I explain further. For a more detailed look into this 'new maths' I recommend reading *The Automatic Customer* by John Warrillow and the team at The Value Builder System™ – in addition to an in-depth review of the calculations, he also explores a range of nine recurring revenue models to help develop 'automatic customers' within your industry.

I'm going to explain how to calculate it for a recurring revenue business. It is possible to calculate it for non-recurring revenue, it just requires a little more thought particularly into how we arrive at a figure for the Lifetime Value. We can still do it but we would need information on repeat purchase rates over time, for example, whereas with a subscription type service we know this.

So with regards to the ratio we need to know or calculate the following:

- CAC – Customer Acquisition Cost
- MRR – Monthly Recurring Revenue
- CM – Contribution Margin
- CR – Churn Rate
- LTV – Lifetime Value

CAC or Customer Acquisition Cost is defined as: the total expenditure on sales and marketing in the month divided by number of new subscribers won during the month.

CAC=£Total Sales and Marketing Expenses/(#) new customers acquired

MRR or Monthly Recurring Revenue is the average monthly recurring revenue per customer. In other words, the total amount of recurring revenue collected in the period divided by the number of customers.

Your Contribution Margin or CM is as defined earlier. This is not just the Gross Margin but should also include the time cost taken to service your recurring revenue clients – so what proportion of someone's time/salary is spent in account/customer management.

Churn Rate (CR) is the percentage of customers lost in the month. This is defined as: lost MRR in the month divided by the MRR at the start of the month. If you have a Churn Rate of 10% per month then you are effectively having to replace your customer base every 10 months just to stand still.

LTV or Lifetime Value can now be calculated. Take the Monthly Recurring Revenue, multiply by the Contribution Margin % and then divide by the Churn Rate %.

$$LTV = (MRR \times CM)/CR$$

To calculate the ratio, you simply divide the Lifetime Value by the Customer Acquisition Cost.

$$LTV:CAC = LTV/CAC$$

Once you get your head around it, it is quite logical. If monthly is too sporadic (particularly with younger businesses), then try calculating a rolling 3-month and 12-month ratio. This will smooth out any large monthly swings.

This ratio is very sensitive to the Churn Rate because it is the denominator in the calculation of Lifetime Value. If you halve the Churn Rate, you effectively double the average length of time the average customer remains with you and you double the Lifetime Value. So if your ratio needs improving, this is often a good place to start – you might want to analyse where customers typically drop off and look at ways to address it. Often the first three months of any service are the most critical so you may want to look at your onboarding and first 90-day support in particular – including measuring Net Promoter scores at that point.

If you have a business based on recurring revenue then you need to understand your LTV:CAC ratio and monitor it as one of your Key Performance Indicators. Even if you don't, you should still consider how you are going to calculate a 'proxy' for this ratio. You will still be able to calculate a Customer Acquisition Cost and you will have a way to calculate what each customer is worth to you.

That now completes the main elements of 'Cash' around scaling up. You should now be able to see how you can work towards being strong at the habits and questions from the InFlight Checks.

Now that you understand a little more behind each of these, take a moment to re-rate yourself/your business on each of the key questions on a 5-point scale where 1=Very weak/'We don't do this', 2='We sort of do this a bit', 3='We're OK but not great at this', 4='We're quite good at this but not perfect', 5='We've got this nailed'

Now take a look at where you think you are weak and prioritise one or two of them that you think would make the most impact on your business if you were to improve them over the next 90 days.

		SUBTOTAL
	13. Budgeting and financial reporting are strengths of the business	
	We have budgets and cashflow forecasts for the overall business and for key profit and cost centres	
	We have a management Profit and Loss statement free from distortion that is used for decision making	
	We have a set of financial Key Performance Indicators and ratios that are reviewed monthly	
	We have at least 6 months' worth of operational expenditure in the reserves (over and above any tax payments such as VAT)	
	14. We are focused on continually improving our cash position	SUBTOTAL
CASH	The 7 Financial Levers are understood by all senior managers – as are basic financial statements, the Cash Conversion Cycle and 8 Wastes	
	Financial statements have a person assigned to each significant line item	
	Changes in cash position are monitored frequently (at least weekly) and explained	
	At least one cash improvement initiative is undertaken quarterly/included in each Smart90 90-day plan	
	15. We are focused on Valuable Growth	SUBTOTAL
	We manage our growth cycles between a 10–15% net profit band (score 5 if genuine free from distortions net profit is 15% or more)	
	We understand, track and improve our Lifetime Value (LTV) to Customer Acquisition Cost (CAC) ratio	
	We have contracts in place for all our customers	
	A significant proportion of our turnover is from genuine recurring (not just repeat) revenue (score 5 if >75%)	
	Cash Pillar – add all the light blue subtotals above	SECTION TOTAL

SUMMARY AND NEXT STEPS

Overleaf is a summary table showing the key requirements to transition from one stepping stone to the next. It is not an exhaustive list, simply the primary considerations/focus.

Things we are NOT best at DELEGATION Things we ARE best at

Real revenue range	£0 – £180k	£180k – £360k	£350k – £710k	£750k – £3.5m	£3.5m – £7m
	Typically 1–3 employees	Typically 3–5 employees	Typically up to around 10 employees	Typically 10 up to 40/50 employees	Typically 50 to 80/90 employees
Key strategic focus to enable transition to next stepping stone	Product/Market fit and scalable business model	Reliable, repeatable and scalable lead generation – required level of new customers	Systems and processes – every key aspect of the business needs to be able to be done by someone else	People – leadership team ensuring you have the right people in the right seats doing the right things – structure and retain culture	Build defensive walls/barriers. Watch out for and protect from competition
Key leadership focus	Rolling your sleeves up!	Focus on where you add most value, delegate the rest. Specialise within the business	Focus on making a 'turnkey' business not reliant on you or other individuals. Process and habits	Developing other leaders – role changes to supporting them to fulfil their roles effectively	Becoming an ambassador for the business/ 'selling the business, not the products'
Key value focus (Financial cntrl/& Valuation seesaw & Customer score all through)	Monopoly control	Recurring revenue	Hub & spoke	Switzerland structure	Hub & spoke Opportunities for growth
Biggest challenge (scaleup report)	Getting dragged back into day-to-day operations Generating sufficient quality leads		Attracting/ hiring people Getting staff to think and act/take responsibility	Getting staff to think and act/take responsibility Not having the right staff in place to support growth	Getting staff to think and act/take responsibility Staff Management – right things consistently well
Primary DISC/ bird style needed to transition	C – Owl D – Hawk/ Panther	D – Hawk/ Panther I – Cockatoo/ Monkey	C – Owl S – Dove/ Dolphin	S – Dove/ Dolphin I – Cockatoo/ Monkey	I – Cockatoo/ Monkey
E-Myth primary role	Technician	Manager		Entrepreneur	

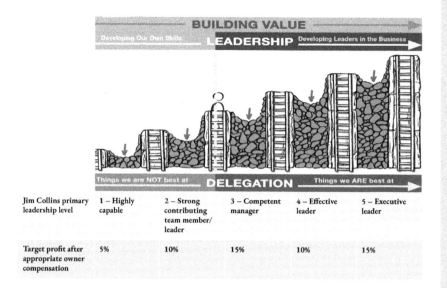

Jim Collins primary leadership level	1 – Highly capable	2 – Strong contributing team member/ leader	3 – Competent manager	4 – Effective leader	5 – Executive leader
Target profit after appropriate owner compensation	5%	10%	15%	10%	15%

NEXT STEPS

Two things to do right now!

Thank you for reading this book. You should now have an overview of the big picture – what is important in order for you to be able to build a scalable business – and the detail of how to go about it over time.

Following the ESUS methodology will give you the structure to overcome the challenges you will undoubtedly face as you scale. It won't give you the answers to every question you will face, or the solution to every challenge, but it will give you the approach to going about finding the answers and solutions in the right way. You could call it a manual, a system, a methodology, a structure – I really don't care as long as you take action and implement it in your business!

If you are itching to apply some of the things contained in this book and want to know where to start, then what a great question! And the answer is really simple. There is arguably only one key next step – but I have added a second for good measure!

1. Implement Smart7 and Smart90 (don't wait 90 days – do it now) and then clarify the remainder of Business Rhythm within the next quarter.

2. Get everyone in the business to read this book!

By doing these two things, you will have ignited the spark that will, over time, enable you to engage full afterburn!

 You can find further help and guidance on implementing ESUS at www.esusgroup.co.uk. Readers of this book can trial our Smart90 software (which includes access to the InFlight Checks) for 90 days at no cost by using the code ESUS90.

InFlight Checks

1='Very weak/'We don't do this', 2='We sort of do this a bit', 3='We're OK but not great at this', 4='We're quite good at this but not perfect', 5='We've got this nailed'	Score 1-5
STRATEGY	
1. Leadership and Vision are strong within the business	SUBTOTAL
The Leadership team understand each other's personality and leadership styles and all team members identify one specific leadership/personal improvement habit each 90 days	
Core Ideology (Values and Purpose) are defined, known and made role-relevant by all employees	
Core Ideology is embedded into all aspects of the 'way we do things' (recruitment, onboarding, reviews, feedback etc.)	
A Core Ideology improvement priority is identified and implemented every 90 days	
2. We have a truly differentiated strategy and scalable business model and all team members can articulate the following components:	SUBTOTAL
The team are aligned with and passionate about the Mission/Stretch Goal (SmartStretch Goal is clearly defined, understood, 'lived' and tracked)	
Our Participation (Markets/Segments) and Positioning (Offer/Cost) Strategies are clear and understood and translate to a demonstrable competitive advantage	
We know where we are on the ScaleUp stepping stones and whether we are in a period of consolidation or striking out for the next stepping stone	
Everyone can give a compelling answer to the question 'What does your company do?'	
3. The Leadership Team can articulate:	SUBTOTAL
The 3-year 'Thrusts' – the focus areas for the 3-year plan – and progress is tracked	
The 4–9 'Critical Paths' for the next 12 months and progress is reviewed quarterly (the critical things that must be achieved in order to be on track for the 3-year goals)	
The 1–2 focus Value Drivers to increase the value of the business over the next 12 months	
The 'theme' and priorities/business 'rocks' for the current quarter	
Strategy Pillar – add all the blue subtotals above	SECTION TOTAL
EXECUTION	
4. 90-Day Planning is a strong habit within business	SUBTOTAL
The Leadership Team (or you if you are on your own!) meet quarterly (offsite) to work on and set robust/well considered 90-day priorities working to a structured agenda	
The critical number is identified along with 3-7 supporting SMART priorities	
The above are rolled out to the rest of the team, tracked and visible to all along with an overarching 'theme' for the quarter	
All staff (or you if on your own) identify their own supporting critical number and 3-5 'Rocks' that include personal and development priorities	
5. Everyone in the business is clear about what good looks like – daily, weekly, monthly, collectively and individually	SUBTOTAL
A Balanced Scorecard is in place and visible along with KPI dashboards for tracking daily and weekly metrics	
All staff have developed supporting actions for their 'Rocks'	
All staff can state their goals for the week and for the day towards achieving their individual and team 'Rocks' (they can state 'what good looks like' for the end of the day/week)	
Each team celebrate successes and the business celebrates achieving the quarterly theme	
6. There is a well-functioning Business Rhythm supporting the 90-day habit	SUBTOTAL
All teams (including the Leadership Team) have a weekly meeting that includes progress against 'Rocks' (or you if you are on your own!)	
All staff are in a short (less than 15 minute) daily huddle/standup	
The Leadership Team meet monthly for at least half a day to include progress against the 90-day plan and work on an improvement initiative	
The Leadership Team meet annually to reset against the 3-yr plan and work on the 4 Pillars (Strategy, People, Execution and Cash)	
7. Business development activities provide a predictable stream of focus/'on profile' clients	SUBTOTAL
A value proposition is defined and validated (with customers) for the key service/product offerings	
There are proven processes for lead generation and conversion 'funnels' that are followed and monitored/improved regularly (you know your pipeline and the success/conversion rates at each key step of the funnels)	
Those accountable for marketing and sales have individual 'cookbooks' (activity plans) that are tracked and reviewed	
Budgets are in place and monitored against results for all lead generation activities	
Execution Pillar - add all the green subtotals above	SECTION TOTAL

		SUBTOTAL
PEOPLE	8. All teams function Cohesively	
	Team members understand each other's styles, differences and priorities	
	Team members trust each other enough to admit mistakes	
	Team members feel able to challenge each other and engage in constructive debate	
	Team members are motivated to and work well to achieve the team goals	
	9. We have a culture of Individual Accountability and Joint Responsibility	SUBTOTAL
	We have the right people in the right roles with clear roles and accountabilities	
	Individuals are empowered to make decisions for their area of responsibility	
	Teams are focused on achieving collective results and we celebrate team success	
	Everyone has visibility of and religiously track progress against 'Rocks' and Critical Numbers	
	10. Our ability to retain and hire good people is a strength of the business	SUBTOTAL
	We have a retention, development and succession/contingency plan for every key employee (score 1 if just you in the business) and hold regular (quarterly) 'retention discussions' with key employees	
	We have a clear view of organisational needs/structure over the next 3 years and whether we are hiring in or developing internally for each role	
	We are clear on our Employee Value Proposition and are able to attract sufficient good candidates (we are able to 'punch above our weight' in recruitment)	
	We have a robust hiring process in place that minimizes the chances of making a bad hire	
	11. We actively listen to our staff and track engagement	SUBTOTAL
	Managers actively seek ongoing feedback from team members – e.g. all managers have a 'Stop, Start, Continue' discussion with at least one employee each week and feedback is shared at weekly leadership meetings (score 1 if just you)	
	A 'Balance Wheel' or equivalent personal and professional 'happiness' discussion is held monthly with all team members (or you if you are on your own)	
	We have a working process for informing staff on actions taken following feedback	
	We track and work to improve employee engagement levels (e.g. NPS, Gallup12, TPS)	
	12. We actively listen to our Customers	SUBTOTAL
	Net Promoter Score or equivalent is tracked as a KPI	
	All managers have a meaningful discussion with a customer each week (How are things going, What's the latest in your industry, What do you hear about our competitors, How are we doing?)	
	Insights from these discussions are shared at the weekly leadership meeting	
	One of the leadership team is accountable for actioning and reporting on customer feedback – positive and negative	

People Pillar – add all the yellow subtotals above | SECTION TOTAL |

		SUBTOTAL
CASH	13. Budgeting and financial reporting are strengths of the business	
	We have budgets and cashflow forecasts for the overall business and for key profit and cost centres	
	We have a management Profit and Loss statement free from distortion that is used for decision making	
	We have a set of financial Key Performance Indicators and ratios that are reviewed monthly	
	We have at least 6 months' worth of operational expenditure in the reserves (over and above any tax payments such as VAT)	
	14. We are focused on continually improving our cash position	SUBTOTAL
	The 7 Financial Levers are understood by all senior managers – as are basic financial statements, the Cash Conversion Cycle and 8 Wastes	
	Financial statements have a person assigned to each significant line item	
	Changes in cash position are monitored frequently (at least weekly) and explained	
	At least one cash improvement initiative is undertaken quarterly/included in each Smart90 90-day plan	
	15. We are focused on Valuable Growth	SUBTOTAL
	We manage our growth cycles between a 10–15% net profit band (score 5 if genuine free from distortions net profit is 15% or more)	
	We understand, track and improve our Lifetime Value (LTV) to Customer Acquisition Cost (CAC) ratio	
	We have contracts in place for all our customers	
	A significant proportion of our turnover is from genuine recurring (not just repeat) revenue (score 5 if >75%)	

Cash Pillar – add all the light blue subtotals above | SECTION TOTAL |

Add up your total score for the 4 'Pillar' totals, multiply by 100 and divide by 300 to give a percentage

Overall Total - add the 4 'Pillars'	TOTAL
Overall Score	TOTAL

If your scoring falls between:

20 and 34%	35 and 49%	50 and 64%	65 and 79%	80 and 100%
Things may be tough now. Focusing on these 14 areas will change your life	You are pretty normal – but wouldn't you prefer to be above average and really get control over your business?	You are above average – but you know you could do better!	You are doing well and on the ScaleUp path	This is where you want to be if you want the kind of business you can retire on!

REFERENCES

Some websites listed below require that you register or pay for access to the full text of articles or resources.

1 As identified by Verne Harnish and his team at Scaling Up, https://scalingup.com/growth-tools/

2 https://docs.aws.amazon.com/whitepapers/latest/introduction-devops-aws/two-pizza-teams.html

3 Based on the experience of ex-McKinsey management consultants advising 200+ companies; *Essentials of Strategic Management: Effective Formulation and Execution of Strategy*, Thomas Wunder, 2016, Schaffer Poeschel, fig 4.1 p273.

4 Verne Harnish and the Gazelles, https://scalingup.com/growth-tools/

5 https://resources.franklincovey.com/the-8th-habit/big-rocks-stephen-r-covey

6 The European Union definition of micro-businesses is that they employ 0–9 people, https://ec.europa.eu/growth/smes/sme-definition_en

7 ScaleUp Institute Annual Review Executive Summary 2021, https://www.scaleupinstitute.org.uk/scaleup-review-2021/executive-summary/

8 https://en.wikipedia.org/wiki/William_Moulton_Marston

9 Defined by: 25% or more of sales based on recurring revenue; low reliance on the business owner (business would either not suffer or suffer only a little if the business owner took 3 months off); would find it fairly or very easy to handle 5 times the volume; have a competitive advantage (cost or offer).

10 Verne Harnish and the Gazelles, https://scalingup.com/growth-tools/

11 Ibid

12 *The E Myth Revisited*, Michael E. Gerber, Harper Collins, 1995, p40.

13 Based on the experience of ex-McKinsey management consultants advising 200+ companies; *Essentials of Strategic Management: Effective Formulation and Execution of Strategy*, Thomas Wunder, 2016, Schaffer Poeschel, fig 4.1 p273.

14 https://www.dominican.edu/sites/default/files/2020-02/gailmatthews-harvard-goals-researchsummary.pdf, page 2

15 https://en.wikipedia.org/wiki/SMART_criteria

16 *Scaling Up*, Verne Harnish and the team at Gazelles Inc, 2014, p90 and 91.

17 The origin of OKR can be traced to Management By Objectives (MBO), https://en.wikipedia.org/wiki/Management_by_objectives, a goal setting framework coined by Peter Drucker, https://en.wikipedia.org/wiki/Peter_Drucker

18 https://scalingup.com/growth-tools/

19 *Beyond Entrepreneurship 2.0*, Jim Collins, Penguin Random House, 2020, p172.

20 Defined by: Low reliance on the business owner, would find it easy to handle 5 times the volume of clients, have 25% or more of sales based on recurring revenue and have a competitive advantage (offer or cost)

21 *Beyond Entrepreneurship 2.0*, Jim Collins and Bill Lazier, Penguin Random House, 2020, p44.

22 https://www.linkedin.com/pulse/liberating-leader-work-self-awareness-dr-tom-nebel/

23 https://www.everythingdisc.co.uk/work-of-leaders

24 *The EMyth*, Michael E. Gerber/The E-Myth Revisited, 2021

25 *Beyond Entrepreneurship 2.0*, Jim Collins and Bill Lazier, Penguin Random House, 2020, p156.

26 L. David Marquet, author of *Turn the Ship Around*, https://www.youtube.com/watch?v=OqmdLcyES_Q; https://davidmarquet.com/

27 L. David Marquet, https://www.youtube.com/watch?v=OqmdLcyES_Q; https://davidmarquet.com/

28 *Beyond Entrepreneurship 2.0*, Jim Collins and Bill Lazier, Penguin Random House, 2020, p44.

29 *The 7 Habits of Highly Effective People*, Stephen Covey, first published in 1989.

30 https://en.wikipedia.org/wiki/The_7_Habits_of_Highly_Effective_People

31 *Beyond Entrepreneurship 2.0*, Jim Collins and Bill Lazier, Penguin Random House, 2020, p156.

32 John Warrillow is the creator of The Value Builder System™. He is also the author of *The Automatic Customer: Creating a Subscription Business in Any Industry* and *Built to Sell: Creating a Business That Can Thrive Without You*.

33 https://en.wiktionary.org/wiki/round_tuit

34 The Value Builder Score, https://valuebuilder.com/get-your-score/

35 https://score.valuebuildersystem.com/bizsmart/kevin-brent

36 Frederick F. Reichheld, December 2003, 'The One Number You Need to Grow', *Harvard Business Review*, https://hbr.org/2003/12/the-one-number-you-need-to-grow

37 *Beyond Entrepreneurship 2.0*, Jim Collins and Bill Lazier, Penguin Random House, 2020, p104.

38 Jim Collins and Jerry Porras, 'Built to Last' and 'Building Your Company's Vision', published by *Harvard Business Review*, Sept–Oct 1996, https://www.cin.ufpe.br/~if275/material/artigos/BuildingYourCompanysVision.pdf

39 https://about.google/philosophy/

40 https://www.uber.com/gb/en/careers/values/

41 https://www.hotjar.com/blog/company-values/

42 https://www.jimcollins.com/tools/vision-framework.pdf

43 https://www.youtube.com/watch?v=u4ZoJKF_VuA

44 https://www.3m.com/3M/en_US/company-us/solving-problems/

45 https://www.jimcollins.com/tools/vision-framework.pdf, p6.

46 Jim Collins and Jerry Porras, 'Built to Last' and 'Building Your Company's Vision', *Harvard Business Review*, Sept–Oct 1996.

47 *Beyond Entrepreneurship 2.0*, Jim Collins and Bill Lazier, Penguin Random House, 2020, p91.

48 http://www.military-info.com/freebies/murphy.htm

49 https://hbr.org/1979/03/how-competitive-forces-shape-strategy

50 https://www.tonyrobbins.com/stories/business-mastery/whats-your-x-factor/

51 *Scaling Up*, Verne Harnish and the team at Gazelles Inc, 2014, p119.

52 Adjusted for typical P&L distortions such as under-salaried directors!

53 Conversations with Isaiah Berlin, Ramin Jahanbegloo, 2000, London, p188.

54 James C. Collins, 2001, 'Hedgehog Concept In the Business Sectors: An Excerpt from Good To Great', available at https://www.jimcollins.com/article_topics/articles/hedgehog-concept-business-sectors.html.

55 Ibid

56 *Built to Sell*, John Warrillow, Penguin Books, 2012, pp116–117.

57 H.I. Ansoff, 1957, 'Strategies for diversification', *Harvard Business Review*, 35(5), 113–124v.

58 Peter Drucker, Austrian-American management consultant

59 Ed Catmull, Creativity, Inc.: Overcoming the Unseen Forces That Stand in the Way of True Inspiration, available at https://slack.com/intl/en-gb/blog/transformation/leadership-lessons-from-ed-catmulls-creativity-inc

60 Bruce Tuckman, 1965, 'Developmental sequence in small groups', *Psychological Bulletin*, **63**(6), 384–399. https://doi.org/10.1037/h0022100

61   Ivan Steiner, 1972, 'Group Process and Productivity', cited in CNN Money via Fortune magazine, June 12, 2006, https://money.cnn.com/magazines/fortune/fortune_archive/2006/06/12/8379238/

62   INSEAD Professor Anil Gaba, Professor of Decision Sciences, stated at a July 2020 webinar attended by the author.

63   *The Five Dysfunctions of a Team: A Leadership Fable*, Patrick M. Lencioni, 2010, John Wiley & Sons, p9.

64   *Five Dysfunctions of a Team*, Patrick Lencioni, first published in 2002, John Wiley and Sons, Inc., pp195–219.

65   https://www.fivebehaviors.com/Home.aspx

66   https://rework.withgoogle.com/blog/five-keys-to-a-successful-google-team/

67   *Overcoming the Five Dysfunctions of a Team, A Field Guide For Leaders, Managers, and Facilitators*, Patrick Lencioni, Jossey-Bass, 2005, p39.

68   Rudyard Kipling, *Just So Stories*, 1902.

69   *Five Dysfunctions of a Team*, Patrick Lencioni, first published in 2002, John Wiley and Sons, p61.

70   https://en.wikipedia.org/wiki/Alan_Mulally

71   https://newageleadership.com/organizational-culture-change/#The_call_for_help_from_Bill_Ford_to_Alan_Mulally_for_organizational_culture_change_and_to_save_Ford

72   Condensed version of Charles Osgood's 'A Poem About Responsibility'

73   *Beyond Entrepreneurship 2.0*, Jim Collins, Bill Lazier, Penguin Random House, 2020, p157.

74   https://www.bni.com/leaders/dr-ivan-misner

75   https://ivanmisner.com/working-flame-vs-wax/

76   *Topgrading*, Brad and Geoff Smart, 2005, Pritchett, p60.

77   *The E Myth Revisited: Why Most Small Business Don't Work and What to Do About It*, Michael E. Gerber, Harper Collins, 1995, p174.

78   *Scaling Up*, Verne Harnish and the Gazelles, 2014, p38, https://scalingup.com/growth-tools/

79   https://www.rec.uk.com/our-view/research/industry-analysis/recruitment-and-recovery

80   *Topgrading*, Brad and Geoff Smart, 2005, Pritchett, p60.

81   Gallup US Employee Engagement Trends 2020, available at https://www.gallup.com/access/239210/gallup-q12-employee-engagement-survey.aspx

82   https://www.recruiter.com/i/3-types-of-employees-how-to-spot-the-silent-killer/

83   https://www.gallup.com/access/239210/gallup-q12-employee-engagement-survey.aspx

84   Gallup, 2013, State of the American Workplace Report, p19.

85   Gallup Access Q12 survey, available at https://www.gallup.com/access/239210/gallup-q12-employee-engagement-survey.aspx

86   George Blakeway and Stu Preston, Team Performance Scan, www.team-performance-scan.com

87 Management By Walking Around

88 Robert S. Kaplan and David P. Norton, 'The Balanced Scorecard – Measures that Drive Performance', *Harvard Business Review*, January-February 1992, https://hbr.org/1992/01/the-balanced-scorecard-measures-that-drive-performance-2

89 Aaron Ross is the former director of sales at Salesforce.com and author of several books including *Predictable Revenue: Turn Your Business Into a Sales Machine.*

90 Aaron Ross, 'Lead Types: Seeds, Nets & Spears', https://www.youtube.com/watch?v=YfhUdgBeV4s

91 https://mikemichalowicz.com/profit-first/

92 *Profit First: Transform Your Business from a Cash-Eating Monster to a Money-Making Machine*, Mike Michalowicz, Penguin Random House LLC, 2014.

93 Mike Michalowicz, https://s3.amazonaws.com/ProfitFirst/Graphics+%26+Charts+From+Profit+First.pdf, p2, figure 4

94 *Profit First: Transform Your Business from a Cash-Eating Monster to a Money-Making Machine*, Mike Michalowicz.

95 Rockefeller Corp. study quoted in https://www.smashingmagazine.com/2011/08/taking-a-customer-from-like-to-love-the-ux-of-long-term-relationships/

96 https://www.insidemazda.co.uk/2016/03/24/the-gram-strategy-how-saving-weight-makes-mazdas-better-to-drive/

97 https://en.wikipedia.org/wiki/Dave_Brailsford

98 Greg Crabtree, The Melting Pot Webinar: Simple Numbers with Greg Crabtree, https://www.monkhouseandcompany.com/podcast/the-melting-pot-webinar-simple-numbers-with-greg-crabtree/

KEVIN BRENT

RECOMMENDED READING

Scaling Up: How a Few Companies Make It...and Why the Rest Don't (Rockefeller Habits 2.0) by Verne Harnish

Beyond Entrepreneurship 2.0 by Jim Collins

The E-Myth Revisited: Why Most Small Businesses Don't Work and What to Do About It by Michael E. Gerber

Built to Sell: Creating a Business That Can Thrive Without You by John Warrillow

The Automatic Customer: Creating a Subscription Business in Any Industry by John Warrillow

7 Habits of Highly Effective People by Stephen R. Covey

The Five Dysfunctions of a Team: A Leadership Fable (J–B Lencioni Series) by Patrick M. Lencioni

Profit First: Transform Your Business from a Cash-Eating Monster to a Money-Making Machine by Mike Michalowicz

Topgrading (Revised Php Ed): How Leading Companies Win by Hiring, Coaching and Keeping the Best People by Bradford D. Smart

Simple Numbers, Straight Talk, Big Profits! by Greg Crabtree

RECOMMENDED ONLINE RESOURCES

Scaling Up https://scalingup.com/growth-tools/

The Value Builder System™ https://valuebuilder.com/

Team Performance Scan™ https://www.team-performance-scan.com/

Everything DiSC® https://www.everythingdisc.co.uk/

Profit First https://mikemichalowicz.com/profit-first/

Built to Sell Radio podcast with John Warrillow https://builttosell.com/radio/

ScaleUp Radio podcast scaleupradio.com

KEVIN BRENT

ABOUT THE AUTHOR

Kevin Brent founded BizSmart® in 2012 with the aim of supporting business owners to build scalable, sustainable and ultimately valuable businesses. Over that time, Kevin and his team at BizSmart have worked with hundreds of business owner-managers and have developed their scaleup programmes to the point where their flagship SmartBoard® service incorporating ESUS has gained full endorsement from the ScaleUp Institute.

Following gaining his private pilot licence at 17 and jet training in the RAF, Kevin has had an extensive and wide-ranging business career spanning three decades. He gained an International Masters in Business at world-leading business school INSEAD in France, has combined senior level corporate experience in the pharmaceutical industry with high-level strategy consulting at a top tier management consulting firm, and has set up four of his own businesses including BizSmart.

He built his own eco-friendly home and earned his Association of Racing Drivers Schools UK motorsport licence, competing in the BRSCC Mazda Super Cup.

KEVIN BRENT